Democratic Respect

Commentators often interpret the resentment of supporters of populism as blindly emotional and unconnected to facts and principles. *Democratic Respect* argues instead that we should approach the populist politics of resentment as a struggle for recognition based on moral experiences that are intimately connected to people's factual and moral beliefs. By associating populist resentment with alleged violations of democratic principles, we can discuss what citizens and governments owe one another in terms of recognition and respect. Populism advances a unique interpretation of democracy and recognition, which Rostbøll confronts with the notion of democratic respect. How democracy should recognize the people is shown to be connected to debates over the meaning and value of democratic procedures, rights, majority rule, compromise, and public deliberation. The book builds a bridge between empirical research and philosophical analysis, while providing insights relevant to a public grappling with the challenges many democracies face today.

Christian F. Rostbøll is Professor of Political Theory at University of Copenhagen, and he holds a PhD from Columbia University. He is author of *Deliberative Freedom* (2008) and numerous articles on political and democratic theory, as well as co-editor of *Compromise and Disagreement in Contemporary Political Theory* (2018).

T0384767

Democratic Respect

Populism, Resentment, and the Struggle for Recognition

Christian F. Rostbøll

University of Copenhagen

CAMBRIDGE
UNIVERSITY PRESS

Shaftesbury Road, Cambridge CB2 8EA, United Kingdom

One Liberty Plaza, 20th Floor, New York, NY 10006, USA

477 Williamstown Road, Port Melbourne, VIC 3207, Australia

314–321, 3rd Floor, Plot 3, Splendor Forum, Jasola District Centre,
New Delhi – 110025, India

103 Penang Road, #05–06/07, Visioncrest Commercial, Singapore 238467

Cambridge University Press is part of Cambridge University Press & Assessment,
a department of the University of Cambridge.

We share the University's mission to contribute to society through the pursuit of
education, learning and research at the highest international levels of excellence.

www.cambridge.org
Information on this title: www.cambridge.org/9781009340908

DOI: 10.1017/9781009340854

© Christian F. Rostbøll 2023

This publication is in copyright. Subject to statutory exception and to the provisions
of relevant collective licensing agreements, no reproduction of any part may take
place without the written permission of Cambridge University Press & Assessment.

First published 2023

A catalogue record for this publication is available from the British Library

Library of Congress Cataloging-in-Publication Data
Names: Rostbøll, Christian F., author.
Title: Democratic respect : populism, resentment, and the struggle for recognition /
Christian F. Rostbøll.
Description: Cambridge, UK ; New York, NY : Cambridge University Press, 2023. |
Includes bibliographical references and index.
Identifiers: LCCN 2022043183 | ISBN 9781009340908 (hardback) |
ISBN 9781009340854 (ebook)
Subjects: LCSH: Populism. | Democracy. | Political participaton.
Classification: LCC JC423 .R6178 2023 | DDC 320.56/62–dc23/eng/20221108
LC record available at https://lccn.loc.gov/2022043183

ISBN 978-1-009-34090-8 Hardback
ISBN 978-1-009-34087-8 Paperback

Cambridge University Press & Assessment has no responsibility for the persistence
or accuracy of URLs for external or third-party internet websites referred to in this
publication and does not guarantee that any content on such websites is, or will
remain, accurate or appropriate.

To the memory of my mother

Contents

Acknowledgments

As many others, I started thinking seriously about populism in 2016 after the election of Donald Trump and the Brexit referendum. For a political theorist who has written on democratic theory as well as the concept of respect, populism raises some pressing questions. The rise of populism seems closely connected to widespread feelings of disrespect and at the same time (and relatedly) it presents a competing view of what democracy is and should be. Thus, I became interested in the question of how democracy should, and perhaps should not, recognize the people. The following pages are a result of my reflections on that question.

Many colleagues, friends, and family members have helped me along the way. A large part of the book was written during the Covid-19 pandemic, which meant both more time for solitary writing and new forms of academic exchange with colleagues. We have learned to share ideas online, which is sometimes less personal and less fun but at least the impact on the climate is smaller than flying across and between continents. I thank all the people who have provided comments and feedback both online and in person.

I would like to start by thanking my colleagues in and visitors to the political theory group in the Department of Political Science at University of Copenhagen for commenting on several parts of the manuscript: Anders Berg-Sørensen, Lars Tønder, Noel Parker, Andy Poe, Lasse Thomassen, Mads Ejsing, Anne-Sofie Dichman, Ingrid Helene Brandt Jensen, Derek Denman, Jonas Hultin Rosenberg, Malte Frøslee Ibsen, and Rune Møller Stahl. I would also like to extend a warm thanks to the students who took my courses on populism, recognition, and democratic theory in 2018, 2019, and 2022. I learned a lot from our discussions.

A one-year research stay at Columbia University in 2019–2020 provided invaluable time and a stimulating environment for research and writing. I am grateful to members of the political theory group at Columbia for their hospitality, discussions, and comments on my work: Jean Cohen, Nadia Urbinati, Jon Elster, Turkuler Isiksel, David Johnston, and Joshua Simon. I owe a special thank you to Jean and Nadia for their support, encouragement, and intellectual inspiration. For their participation in two manuscript workshops on central chapters of the book, I am grateful to Simone Chambers, Stefan Rummens, Michael Frazer, and Cillian McBride. The workshops were extremely helpful for my work on the manuscript.

Papers related to the manuscript were presented (in person or online) at workshops at The Arctic University of Norway, Columbia University, The New School University, Roskilde University, Queen's University Belfast, University of Copenhagen, University of Milan, University of Vienna, and Vrije University Amsterdam, as well as at the Annual Meeting of the American Political Science Association, the Annual Meeting of the Danish Political Science Association, the Annual Conference of the Association for Social and Political Philosophy, the "Philosophy and Social Science" conference in Prague, and in the ECPR Standing Group on Political Theory Seminar Series. I would like to thank the organizers of and participants at these events, including Jonas Jakobsen, Andreas Kalyvas, Patrick Overeem, Enrico Biale, Anna Elisabetta Galeotti, Federica Liveriero, Angela Bourne, Allan Dreyer Hansen, Torben Bech Dyrberg, Simon Laumann Jørgensen, Keith Breen, Christopher Zurn, Manon Westphal, Benjamin L. McKean, Rebecca Marwege, Pablo Gilabert, and Uğur Aytac.

I owe a deep thanks to my friend and colleague since our early student days Tore Vincents Olsen. Tore has read and provided very helpful comments on most of the manuscript. Our friendship and intellectual exchanges are irreplaceable. For diligent copy-editing, I am grateful to Merl Storr. At Cambridge University Press, I would like to thank John Haslam, Tobias Ginsberg, and Claire Sissen.

My immediate family, Kathrin, Leo, and Siri, are always with me. During the writing of this book, my children grew so big that they actually understand at least some of what I am writing about. It is a delight to be with them and they prevent me from becoming too serious and boring. I am grateful to Kathrin for all her ideas, which make our life together so rich and wonderful.

My mother, Grethe F. Rostbøll, passed away during my writing of the manuscript. She had an unsurpassed curiosity regarding the world of politics, philosophy, art, and literature, and she was a great source of inspiration and encouragement during my whole life. Until she got too ill, we would always discuss each other's work. I miss her dearly and I dedicate this book to her.

Chapter 6 draws on my article "Populism, Democracy, and the Publicity Requirement," *Constellations* (2022): 1–14 (e-publication ahead of print). At different points, I have also used ideas from my article "Second-Order Political Thinking: Compromise versus Populism," *Political Studies* 69.3 (2021): 559–576.

Introduction
Recognition of the People

This book is about how democracy should – and, just as importantly, should not – recognize the people. The debate over the meaning and value of populism is essentially a debate over this question. Around the world, voters turn to populism because of the way in which it promises to respect the people.[1] Supporters of populism feel resentment at the alleged disrespect displayed by the political and cultural "elite." They claim that their society does not properly recognize their standing as "the people." Populism provides the recognition that many people feel they have lost or never attained. In short, populism is about recognition of the people.

Since democracy is supposed to be a form of society in which citizens mutually respect one another as equal participants, we should not be surprised – nor necessarily regret – that people feel resentment when society shows contempt or disregard for their identity, way of life, and political opinions. Still, in the face of the rise of populism, we must acknowledge that not all struggles for recognition promote what I call democratic respect.

While struggles for recognition have been central to the progress of modern democracy, to broader inclusion and more equality, current conflicts over recognition and respect often threaten rather than deepen or widen democracy. Populism, with its demand for the recognition of the people, often seems to come into conflict with democratic norms. Why is that so? To answer this question, *Democratic Respect* analyzes the meaning and validity of different kinds of demand for recognition, as well as their connection to democratic ideals. "Recognition of the people" can mean many different things, and these different meanings connect to different interpretations of democracy. Thus, the debate over the meaning and value of populism is a debate both over how best to understand democracy and over what kind of recognition democratic citizens owe one another.

---

[1] As we proceed, I will distinguish more clearly between recognition and respect, as well as other related terms.

Political scientists and sociologists typically understand the resentment of supporters of populism as purely emotional and unconnected to facts and principles. This book argues instead that we should approach populist resentment as part of a struggle for recognition based on distinctively moral experiences that depend on factual beliefs and normative judgments. When people feel disrespected, it is because they believe certain principles regarding how they ought to be treated have been violated. Thus, their feelings are what I call principle-dependent and can be objects of moral evaluation. This approach entails that we take people's resentments seriously as demands for recognition that we should assess on their merits. Are they demands that we should heed in a democracy understood as a society of free and equal participants? Not all demands for recognition raised in contemporary politics are rooted in democratic norms, and this book examines their important moral and democratic differences. In particular, it promotes a notion of democratic respect that helps us to answer questions concerning what citizens owe to each other and what constitutes unreasonable demands for recognition in a democracy.

People can achieve recognition in different settings, but today the struggle for respect and esteem seems to have turned to politics as its primary arena in many countries around the world. Complex social, cultural, and economic developments connected to globalization, migration, the dismantling of manufacturing, growing automation, financial capitalism, increased economic inequality, the weakening of political parties, and changes in cultural values have changed people's roles, obligations, and rights, as well as the distribution of material resources and access to political influence.[2] As a result, many people have lost their formerly secure feelings of identity and status, and they are increasingly turning their frustration at their loss toward the political system by supporting populist parties and leaders. This reaction might seem irrational, and to be a craving for mere symbolic self-affirmation where in fact something more substantial and complex is at stake. However, in the struggle for recognition, material, social, and cultural needs and demands are always intertwined.[3] The problem, this book argues, is not that people engage in struggles for recognition, or that they turn this struggle toward the

---

[2] There is an abundance of sources documenting and discussing these developments in relation to the rise of populism. See, for example, Berman, "Populism Is a Symptom"; Brubaker, "Why Populism," 369 ff.; Cohen, "Populism"; Cramer, *Politics of Resentment*; Gest, Reny, and Mayer, "Roots of the Radical Right"; Gidron and Hall, "Populism as a Problem"; Hochschild, *Strangers in Their Own Land*; Inglehart and Norris, "Trump"; Mair, "Populist Democracy vs Party Democracy."

[3] Cohen, "Populism"; Gidron and Hall, "Populism as a Problem"; Zurn, "Populism, Polarization, and Misrecognition."

political arena. This may in fact be a very democratic way of dealing with these issues. It becomes a problem only when the struggle for recognition takes undemocratic forms. But when is that the case? The question for normative democratic theory is *what kind* of recognition and respect people can demand in political interaction with their fellow citizens and from the government.

As should already be clear, I do not regard struggles for recognition as limited to questions of identity and culture. Thus, in the notion of "struggle for recognition" I include both struggles for the recognition of particular identities and the more universalist politics of respect for dignity. Indeed, the difference between these kinds of recognition will be central to my argument. Moreover, the book's focus on populism as a form of struggle for recognition is not an indication that populism is caused by cultural as opposed to economic factors. Finally, my argument does not assume that recognition is always a good thing, or that all deficits of recognition are bad or wrong.[4] Nor do I assume that struggles for recognition are necessarily struggles for equality. Indeed, my analysis of populist struggles for recognition shows that the latter can protect existing status hierarchies or create new ones.

The question of what kind of recognition populism supplies to the people connects to the question of how populists understand democracy. And the question of which demands for recognition are *democratically* legitimate depends on what we think is the normatively best way to understand democracy. Thus, we need to discuss and assess the populist understanding of democracy and its alternatives. This book regards populism as advocating a distinct conception of democracy, and it assumes that part of the appeal of this conception of democracy lies in how it claims to recognize the people. In addition, I accept the common idea that the norm of equal respect is central to the meaning and justification of democracy. However, while I take it that most of us can agree that recognition is central to democracy – not only to its meaning and justification, but also to its practice and development – we often use this notion in confusing and unclear ways. Thus, the book analyzes and discusses a variety of demands for recognition and distinguishes between associated concepts such as esteem, respect, honor, status, and solidarity.

What is theoretically and philosophically interesting about populism is that in many ways it looks essentially democratic, and that it claims to be committed to core democratic principles such as majority rule and

---

[4] For an argument why it is not always good to be recognized and why struggles for recognition can lead to oppression, see Markell, *Bound by Recognition*. For criticism of what he calls "the recognition deficit model," see McBride, *Recognition*, 6–7, 115–19.

popular sovereignty. The populist conception of democracy is actually close to the understanding of democracy that we find not only among many ordinary people, but also among many political scientists.[5] Moreover, the populist demand for recognition of the people sounds like an essentially democratic demand. Therefore, I think that the rise of populism challenges every democratically minded person to reflect on exactly how we understand our democratic ideals, institutions, and practices. Is not democracy defined by majority rule and responsiveness to the people's preferences? Does this not mean that democracy should recognize the people? And does it not imply that populism has the true and best understanding of democracy? The answers to these questions are by no means easy or straightforward.

This book argues that while equal respect is central to democracy, not all nominal demands for recognition and respect are compatible with democratic equality. Populist politicians, for example, make both valid and invalid demands for recognition and respect on behalf of their supporters, and it is important for our understanding and practice of democracy that we become better at distinguishing between these demands. In particular, the type of respect that democracy requires should not be confused with esteem for one's merits or identity, but must consist in respect for one's status. Moreover, when the demand is for respect for one's status, the democratic requirement is that this claim should be for one's status as a *free and equal participant* in society ("democratic respect"), not as a superior (aristocratic "honor respect").

It is a core idea of the book that democratic respect requires that citizens, as a rule, relate to one another through what I call a "participant attitude," rather than an observer attitude. Participants view one another as free and mutually accountable parts of a shared community, while observers see others as "cases" to be explained and manipulated to achieve desirable consequences. In a democracy, we should consider each other not as cases in need of treatment, but as free, equal, and responsible persons who make mutual claims, which we should consider on their merits rather than as expressions of alien causes. *Democratic Respect* promotes the participant attitude both as an approach in political theory and as central to a democratic ethos among citizens. The book's approach to resentment draws on Peter Strawson's notion of the participant attitude, while the discussion of democratic respect is inspired by Kant's practical philosophy as well as contemporary theories of recognition, respect, and democracy.

---

[5] Sabl, "Two Cultures of Democratic Theory."

This book is written by a political theorist, and political theorists tend to think ideas matter. That is why we write about them and try to counter bad ideas with what we take to be better ideas. As Isaiah Berlin said in his inaugural professorial address at the University of Oxford, it is crucial that "those who have been trained to think critically about ideas" attend to them, because otherwise ideas may "acquire an unchecked momentum and irresistible power over multitudes of men that may grow too violent to be affected by rational criticism."[6] Indeed, this book is motivated by the fear that populism as a set of ideas will acquire unchecked momentum and attain power over millions of people around the world, as well as by the conviction that those of us who are trained to think critically about ideas have an obligation to understand the ideas behind the populist momentum and counter them to the extent we find this justified.

Political ideas shape political culture, and democracy depends on the shape of society's political culture. Ideas about what democracy is and requires of citizens have the power to change the political culture and thereby to transform or even undermine democracy.[7] There are good reasons to think that populism is changing the political culture in many countries around the world in a way that is transforming how we understand and engage in democracy.[8] It is incumbent on everyone, and especially those trained to analyze and assess ideas, to reflect on and discuss the populist ideas that are changing how we understand and hence practice democracy. The point of the kind of normative political theory represented in this book is not to tell people what to do, but to contribute to the common reflection on democratic ideals and how we institutionalize and practice them. In particular, the aim of this book is to consider how best to understand and practice the fundamental attitude of what I call democratic respect.

It is crucial that political theory and philosophy show modesty in an investigation such as this. We should not expect to be able to provide principles, much less some kind of algorithm, from which we can immediately derive determinate answers to actual cases. Kantian theory is sometimes caricatured as if this were its aim, but this is a misunderstanding.[9]

---

[6] Berlin, "Two Concepts of Liberty," 119.

[7] I owe the notion that populism transforms democracy to Urbinati, *Me the People*. On the importance of informal norms for the survival of democracy, see Levitsky and Ziblatt, *How Democracies Die*, 91–117.

[8] Rosanvallon (*Le siècle du populisme*, 78) suggests that beyond strictly populist parties, a "populist atmosphere" that relies on populist ideas and strategies is spreading in many places.

[9] For a rejection of the idea that Kantians aim to provide principles that work like algorithms, see O'Neill, "Abstraction, Idealization and Ideology." See also Rawls (*Theory of Justice*, 319–20) on what we can and cannot expect a theory of justice to provide regarding actual cases.

For Kantians, to treat philosophy as an authority that thinks for others violates the fundamental meaning of enlightenment and would be a form of disrespect for people's capacities to think and decide for themselves. Moreover, for Kant and many neo-Kantians, enlightenment and learning depend on what Kant called "the public use of reason" and what contemporary political theorists refer to as public deliberation.[10] Thus, the purpose of my analysis and discussion is not to substitute for the public deliberation of citizens, but rather to contribute to it. I hope to offer some concepts and distinctions that will help us to see more clearly what the relevant considerations are, and to what we should pay special attention in contemporary cases of demands for recognition of the people. The notion of democratic respect that this book develops should therefore not be understood as a formula that can or should be applied in a dogmatic fashion; it should rather be seen as a basic attitude through which democratic citizens should perceive one another.[11]

In this book, I argue that the notion of democratic respect can show populism and its demand for recognition to be less democratic than they appear. For those who might insist that populism simply has a different conception of democracy, I hope the following chapters will show that in terms of recognition of individual citizens, populism advances a less compelling conception of democracy than one committed to the notion of democratic respect advanced in this book. However, the fact that my critical evaluation of populism and its demands for recognition is mainly negative does not mean that I find contemporary liberal democracies to be flawless – far from it. Nor does it mean that I find all populist demands for recognition to be undemocratic or populism's diagnosis of contemporary democracies to be wrongheaded in all respects. Contemporary democracies do suffer from a misrecognition of and lack of respect for certain members of society. Contemporary democracies do suffer from oligarchic tendencies and elite dominance. Contemporary democracies do need to recognize and be more responsive to the demands of ordinary people. Thus, we can and should learn something from the current rise of populism and listen to its demands for recognition. However, we need to be more discerning regarding exactly what these demands consist in, when they help to deepen democracy, and when they rely on ideas that are inconsistent with equal respect for all citizens.

[10] Kant, "Answer to the Question"; Ellis, *Kant's Politics*, 18; Habermas, *Structural Transformation*, 102–17; O'Neill, "Enlightenment as Autonomy," 195; Rostbøll, *Immanuel Kant*, 21–4.
[11] For a similar reading of Kantian respect, see Hill, *Respect, Pluralism, and Justice*, especially 26, 62. For the idea that respect is an attitude and a way of perceiving and experiencing other people, see Buss, "Respect for Persons."

I.1   Populism as a Set of Claims

Democratic Respect is interested in what makes populism appealing to many people. Populism has been on the rise in many countries around the world in the last few decades, and we need to understand not only the causes of this rise but also the *reasons* people might have for supporting populist parties and politicians. A study of reasons differs from a study of causes in that it focuses not on the factual and explanatory question of what actually makes people think or do something (vote for or support a populist party), but on the arguments and justifications that people give – or could give – for thinking and doing what they think and do. Moreover, while we cannot argue with causes as such, we can evaluate reasons and, when needed, counter them with better reasons.

I should stress that to assume that people have reasons for their beliefs and actions, as my approach does, does not imply that they have *good* reasons. I investigate people's reasons for supporting populism precisely in order to consider their validity. Thus, the aim of this book is to study not only what reasons people may have for supporting populist parties, but also whether they have good, democratic reasons for doing so.

It is important to keep in mind this purpose of the book – assessing the validity of the reasons people may have for supporting populism – when we turn to the question of how best to understand and define populism. How best to define a concept depends on the purpose of the study. Definitions are not true or false, but more or less useful for the purpose at hand.[12] Among political scientists who study the causes and effects of populism, there has been much discussion about the difficulties of pinning down the meaning and definition of populism. While these discussions and attempts to find the best definition of populism inform this study, it is important to emphasize that the most appropriate or useful definition of populism for my study might not be the same as for studies with a different purpose. Moreover, recently there seems to have been some convergence in the academic literature on the key features of populism.

While definitions are not true or false per se, it is important for the relevance of this book that my definition of populism should capture or be applicable to the group of parties and politicians that are commonly referred to as "populist," such as Hugo Chávez, the Five Star Movement, the Law and Justice party, Marine Le Pen, Jean-Luc Mélenchon,

---

[12] Elster, "Some Notes on 'Populism.'"

Podemos, Viktor Orbán, Matteo Salvini, Geert Wilders, and Donald Trump. I am mainly concerned with contemporary populist parties and less with historical cases such as the US People's Party. We can assess whether it is true that these figures or parties are populist, as I define the term, or to what degree they fit the definition. However, it is absolutely crucial to emphasize that the discussion this book aims to raise is not whether this is that characterization truly captures the essence of populism. Rather, the discussion I want to raise concerns the meaning and validity of a number of claims that can be and often are associated with an ideal typical understanding of populism.

The corollary of being interested in people's reasons for supporting populism is to approach populism as making a set of claims. To claim something is to assert the truth or rightness of something (see Chapter 3). Thus, I view populism as asserting the truth and rightness of a set of both empirical and normative propositions. Moreover, I assume that people support populism because they find these propositional claims valid. The reasons people think they have – or that we may reconstruct them as having – for supporting populism correspond to the claims made by populist politicians. It is this nexus of reasons and claims that I analyze and discuss in this book. Understanding populism as making claims and as something people follow for reasons is part of my participant attitude approach. When people view each other through a participant attitude, they see one another as making claims and acting for reasons, rather than looking for causes that operate behind their backs.

Notice that I am neither claiming that supporters of populism always have the reasons I discuss or that these reasons are what cause support for populism. My aim is to understand and assess – from the perspective of democratic principles of freedom, equality, and respect – the kinds of reason people might have for supporting populism and the claims populists make. While the book aims to discuss the claims of populism and the possible reasons or justifications for believing these claims, the issue of causes is by no means irrelevant for our investigation. My discussion of recognition is prompted by and relies on empirical studies that indicate that the desire for recognition is part of the causal explanation for the rise of populism. Indeed, what follows is grounded in a sustained engagement with empirical research on populism and its supporters, and I hope to show how philosophical analysis and empirical research can enrich one another. Nevertheless, the primary question for our discussion is not the factual one regarding whether the desire for recognition actually explains the support for populism, but rather the normative question of whether the kind of recognition that populism supplies gives people good, democratic reasons for supporting it.

Thus, the idea is that if we are interested in people's reasons for supporting populism, we should define populism in terms of the characteristic claims populists make. However, we need to be more precise here
to avoid misunderstanding. It might be said that many people support
populism not because they believe in its claims, but because they are
attracted to its effects. There is nothing wrong about saying that a person
has reason to support or promote a movement or party not because they
agree with the content of its claims, but because they think it will have
good consequences. For example, if you think that politics needs to be
"shaken up" or moved away from the center, this may be a reason to vote
for a radical or extremist party, even if you do not agree with its ideology.
However, this is not the type of reason I am interested in. I am interested
in the types of reason people might have for believing in the content of
what populists claim, and not only in its effects. My reason for this focus
is the conviction that populism spreads a set of distinct ideas or claims
about the very meaning and value of politics and democracy that needs
to be properly understood on its merits and countered if found wanting.

Understanding populism as a set of distinctive claims stands in contrast
to the often-heard proposition that populism has no substantive content
but is a style, a set of rhetorical resources, or a logic of articulation that
can be equally used for all ideological purposes.[13] It also stands in contrast
to the idea that populism's appeal is only emotional. While later chapters
explain why we should see the appeal of populism in terms not only of
emotions but also of principles (or more precisely, why the appeal to emotions is mediated by principles), here I emphasize the idea that populism is
also characterized by a commitment to some principled positions. While it
is true that populists can be found across the political spectrum, from left
to right and even in the center, this does not mean that being populist does
not carry with it some empirical and normative commitments of its own.[14]
Being a populist socialist is not the same ideological position as being a
non-populist socialist, being a populist conservative is not the same as
being a non-populist conservative, and so on with the other traditional
ideologies to which populism can be attached. The adjectival "populist"

---

[13] We find the idea that populism has no substantive content of its own in, for example, Brubaker, "Why Populism?"; Kazin, *Populist Persuasion*, 1–5; Laclau, *On Populist
Reason*; Moffitt, *Global Rise of Populism*; Mouffe, *For a Left Populism*, 10–11.

[14] Here I agree with Müller (*What Is Populism?*, 10), who writes: "Populism is not anything
like a codified doctrine, but it is a set of distinctive claims and has what might be called
an inner logic"; and with Galston (*Anti-Pluralism*, 4), who argues that populism is not
a vacuous category but "a form of politics that reflects distinctive theoretical commitments and generates its own political practice." See also Canovan, "Taking Politics to
the People," 32–3; Urbinati, *Me the People*, 38–9.

brings some additional empirical beliefs and normative commitments to the "host ideology."[15] Moreover, even if the claims and principles of populism are somewhat vague and flexible, they are neither without content nor without effect on how we understand and practice democracy. The language we use to speak about politics and political relations – for example, the way in which we speak of "the people" and political opponents – affects our political culture and transforms political practice.[16]

To view populism as a set of empirical and normative claims falls within an ideational approach and entails regarding populism as a kind of ideology. Understanding populism as an ideology is the most common approach in comparative politics and is mainly associated with the influential definition of populism suggested by Cas Mudde, which sees it as "an ideology that considers society to be ultimately separated into two homogeneous and antagonistic groups, 'the pure people' versus 'the corrupt elite', and which argues that politics should be an expression of the *volonté générale* (general will) of the people."[17] According to Mudde, populism is not a full or thick ideology like liberalism or socialism, but a "thin" or "thin centered" ideology. Whereas a thick ideology speaks to a broad menu of social, economic, and institutional issues, Mudde suggests that the thin ideology of populism includes a narrower and more restricted set of core ideas and concepts.[18]

While I agree that populism shares some of the characteristics of an ideology, I would like to stress two points. First, calling populism an ideology may be misleading. It might make readers assume that it can be placed on a left-right scale, or that it is defined by its policy positions. But to view populism in that way makes it impossible to see what is shared by all populist movements and parties, which can be found across the traditional left-right political spectrum. Second, the idea that populism is a *thin* ideology disregards what I take to be unique about populism, namely that the claims that define populism are not just fewer in number than those made by traditional ideologies; they are also a different *kind* of claim, or their focus is different. The characteristic claims of populism

---

[15] For the idea that populists tend to have a "host" ideology, see Mudde, "Populism," 32.

[16] Laclau (*On Populist Reason*, 10–13) is keenly aware of the fact that language and rhetoric cannot be separated from ideology, but he nevertheless insists that populism as "a logic of articulation" has no specific ideological content. I find his position self-contradictory. It might be connected to the often-made criticism of Laclau that he regards all politics as populist, which makes it impossible to distinguish populist parties from other parties (Arato, "Political Theology and Populism," 157; Mudde, "Populism," 34–6; Müller, "'People Must Be Extracted,'" 484).

[17] Mudde, "Populist Zeitgeist," 543, emphasis altered.

[18] Mudde, "Populism," 30–1. On populism as a thin ideology, see also Abts and Rummens, "Populism versus Democracy," 407–9; Canovan, "Taking Politics to the People," 32.

are about the circumstances and logic of politics, and about the requirements of democratic legitimacy, rather than about policy positions.[19] So the reader should keep these two points in mind when subsequent chapters refer to populism as an ideology.

This book, then, understands populism in terms of the claims it makes, because this will provide us with the opportunity to consider the reasons people might have for supporting populism. Some might respond to this approach by arguing that what matters is not what populists *say* but what they *do*. Moreover, it might be argued that what populists do often contradicts what they say. For example, populists claim that they give all the power to the people, but in fact they delegate it to a leader.[20] This is the basis of Kurt Weyland's political-strategic approach to populism and his criticism of discursive and ideological – or ideational – approaches to populism.[21] However, the focus on populism's claims need not entail an exclusive focus on what populists say. We can also read claims out of what populists do. Moreover, whereas Weyland postulates an opportunistic disconnect between populist politicians' self-depictions and their actions, I want to investigate the possibility of finding a connection between their expressed ideas and their practice. So, whereas Weyland criticizes ideational approaches for emphasizing the idea of popular sovereignty and therefore neglecting the fact that populism is a top-down strategy of personalistic leadership,[22] I ask instead whether the populist conception of popular sovereignty might not entail or in some other way lead to a form of leader-centrism. Thus, I see it as a populist claim that a strong, unconstrained leader is compatible with or even required by the ideal of popular sovereignty.

I do not want to suggest that the actions of populist politicians are always consistent with populist ideas and rhetoric. That would be an outrageous claim. Nevertheless, this book examines how both the rhetoric and the actions of populist actors can be combined in a set of claims that can be seen as defining populism. If we want to consider the reasons people have for supporting populism in the sense explained above, we must consider populism as raising some kind of claim about what is true and false, right and wrong, good and evil. Note here that my approach requires that we try to understand what populism means by "popular sovereignty" and other core ideas, rather than straightaway applying our own understanding of these to the actions of populists. Thus, it might be that personalistic leadership is incompatible with *our* (or Weyland's)

---

[19] Rostbøll, "Second-Order Political Thinking," 562–9.
[20] Weyland, "Populism," 53–5.
[21] Weyland, "Populism"; Weyland, "Populism as a Political Strategy."
[22] Weyland, "Populism," 53–4.

understanding of popular sovereignty and popular empowerment, but this does not mean that it is incompatible with a *populist* interpretation of these ideas. This point in no way entails an uncritical approach to populism, as Weyland fears[23]; rather, it requires a critical engagement not just with the actions of populist politicians, but also with how those actions are connected to and justified by their ideas. Only in this way can our analysis of populism contribute to a discussion of competing interpretations of core democratic principles, rather than merely applying predefined democratic ideals to populist practice.

So what are the distinctive claims of populism? I submit that the claims of populism centrally concern three issues: (1) *the circumstances of politics*, (2) *the logic of politics*, and the (3) *requirements of democratic legitimacy*. In what follows, I explain these three notions and order the claims of populism accordingly.[24]

The circumstances of politics concern the basic elements of society, its divisions and/or unity, as well as the basic motives of political actors, which in combination make politics necessary and possible.[25] The first five claims constitute populism's view of the circumstances of politics.

1. The basic elements of society are "the people" and "the elite" (rather than a plurality of individuals and groups).
2. The two camps are unified and exclusive identity groups (rather than internally divided and overlapping groups).
3. The relationship between the people and the elite is characterized by a fundamental and all-encompassing antagonism.[26]
4. The division between the people and the elite is moral and Manichean, and the people is in the right.[27]

---

[23] Weyland ("Populism as a Political Strategy") argues that only the political-strategic and not the ideational or ideological approach fully understands the threat posed by populism to democracy. Thus, he assumes that focusing on ideas and discourses or the self-depictions of populists will make researchers less critical of populism. By contrast, this book shows that engaging with populist claims can also reveal its threats to democracy.

[24] The following draws on Rostbøll, "Second-Order Political Thinking," 562–9.

[25] I borrow the general idea of the circumstances of politics from Waldron, *Law and Disagreement*, 101–3.

[26] Virtually all contemporary definitions of populism include the idea of conflict between the people and the elite (Laclau, *On Populist Reason*, 74–7; Mansbridge and Macedo, "Populism and Democratic Theory," 60–2; Mudde, "Populist Zeitgeist," 543). I add that this antagonism is seen as all-encompassing in the sense that populists refer to the same opposition for all political purposes. In other words, for populists, the antagonistic division of the people and the elite is stable across different issues. I explain this point further in Chapter 3.

[27] Mansbridge and Macedo, "Populism and Democratic Theory," 60–2; Mudde, "Populism," 29; Müller, *What Is Populism?*, 19–20.

5. Social divisions are products of self-interest, corruption, and group identity (rather than disagreements in good faith).[28]

The logic of politics concerns the core elements, dynamics, and aims of politics. Three claims are central to populism's understanding of the logic of politics:

6. Politics is an all-or-nothing battle with complete losers and complete winners (rather than a matter of accommodation, or a game where victory is always partial).[29]
7. Politics is about will and decision (rather than reason and deliberation).[30]
8. Politics is centrally about the unmediated, noninstitutional mobilization of the people.[31]

Democratic legitimacy concerns what makes the exercise of political power acceptable. The final six claims relate to the populist view of legitimacy:

9. Only a part of the total population is really the people or the demos that should rule.[32]
10. The people have a common will that can be identified independently of political procedures and institutions.[33]
11. The will of the people should be expressed immediately and directly in political decisions, with no accommodation of opponents and no constraints.[34]
12. Democracy should recognize and restore the privileged standing of the people.[35]
13. The people can have only one legitimate representative, and opposition to this representative is suspect and illegitimate.[36]

---

[28] Crick, "Populism, Politics and Democracy," 630; Mudde, "Populism," 29–30.
[29] Krastev, "Majoritarian Futures," 75; Rovira Kaltwasser, "Ambivalence of Populism," 197–8.
[30] Canovan, "Taking Politics to the People," 34.
[31] Arato and Cohen, *Populism and Civil Society*, 68–85; Weyland, "Populism," 50.
[32] According to Müller (*What Is Populism?*, 21), "the core claim of populism [is that] only some of the people are really the people." See also Canovan, *People*, 65–90; Laclau, "Populism," 163. I think this claim is *entailed* by the first claim, and I therefore disagree with Mansbridge and Macedo ("Populism and Democratic Theory," 63–4), who argue that the idea of the exclusive people is not part of the core of populism. If society can be divided into two camps, only one of which is designated "the people," it follows that only some of the people are really the people.
[33] Müller, *What Is Populism?*, 31; Ochoa Espejo, "Power to Whom," 78–83; Wolkenstein, "What Can We Hold."
[34] Rummens, "Populism as a Threat"; Urbinati, "Populism," 579–80.
[35] Canovan, *People*, 81–2; Cohen, "Populism," 13; Mény and Surel, *Par le people*, 181–2.
[36] Müller, *What Is Populism?*, 19–25.

14. The will of the people can be represented by and embodied in a leader who identifies with the people.[37]

I compiled this list of claims from a broad range of empirical, conceptual, and normative literature on populism, and in this way I have ensured that it overlaps and engages with what other researchers call "populism." Next, I settled on these fourteen claims as the most relevant for the normative discussion of democracy and recognition that this book engages in. Thus, I think most scholars will agree that these claims are often made (explicitly or implicitly) by what the academic literature normally designates as populist politicians.

The aim of this book is to consider the meaning, appeal, and validity of these claims (and their elaborations in later chapters), both individually and in combination. Hence, my contention is not that all populist parties make all of these claims, but only that these claims are often made by populist politicians in word and deed, and that they therefore are worth exploring as part of a discussion of the potential reasons for supporting populism. Of course, this raises the issue of what the threshold for calling someone a "populist" is. How many of the claims must a party or politician make in order to qualify as populist? Populists come in degrees, and how populist a party or politician is can be seen in terms of how many of these claims they make and how strongly they formulate them. Unfortunately, I cannot come closer than saying that I would not call anyone a populist who did not show in word or deed that they believed in most of these claims. None of the claims on its own makes one a populist; only the combination of most of them does so. Be that as it may, the contribution of this book is not classifying parties, but rather to consider the meaning and validity of a number of claims about recognition and democracy that are often raised by populists and their supporters.

If I were to give a one-sentence definition, I would say that *populism is a set of claims centered around the antagonism between the people and the elite as the fundamental circumstance of politics, the logic politics as an all-or-nothing battle, and democratic legitimacy as a question of the recognition of a part of the people as the only true people.*

Finally, I should mention that I have focused on the claims that make populism a distinctive interpretation of democratic politics, and not on what distinguishes it from ideologies that do not claim to be democratic,

---

[37] The idea that populism is leader-centric is found not only among more critical commentators such as Arato ("Political Theology and Populism") and Weyland ("Populism"; "Populism as a Political Strategy"), but also among theorists who promote populism, such as Laclau (*On Populist Reason*, 99–100; "Populism," 157) and Mouffe (*For a Left Populism*, 70).

such as fascism.[38] Populism, for example, importantly regards the holding of elections as required for political legitimacy, which fascism does not.[39] It is central for my purposes in this book that populists claim to be the true democrats. They routinely claim that the regime in which they operate is not fully democratic and needs to be democratized by giving power back to the people.[40] As I have emphasized, my approach is to take this claim seriously and consider its meaning, appeal, and validity. At least part of the appeal of populism is that it wears the democratic mantle and that populist leaders claim to embody and implement the people's will.[41] Moreover, the appeal of populism is connected to the kind of recognition it promises to the people. When we acknowledge this, we have occasion to engage in a discussion of whether and to what extent people have democratic reasons of respect for accepting or supporting the claims of populism.

I.1.1   Populism on the Left and Right

An objection some may raise in relation to the suggested list of populist claims – as well as to a number of the arguments I make in the book – is that they fit right-wing populism better than they do left populism. One defender of left populism argues that the criticisms one can make of right-wing populism do not apply to left populism because the two "share nothing."[42] However, if left populism shares nothing with right populism, I see no reason to call both of them forms of *populism*. There has to be some overlap between the two in order for it to make sense to use a common label.

With regard to left populism, we are fortunate to have theorists who identify with the left, provide elaborate theories of populism, and endorse populism. I am thinking of Ernesto Laclau, who has developed the theory of populism, and Chantal Mouffe, who endorses this theory and promotes a left populist strategy.[43] In several places in the book, I shall refer to Laclau's theory of populism in order to show that my arguments apply to this too. In Chapter 6, I provide a detailed discussion and critique of

---

[38] For a good overview of the differences between populism and fascism, see Eatwell, "Populism and Fascism."

[39] Finchelstein (*From Fascism to Populism*, 4–5, 28–9, 99) argues that the acceptance of elections is the core distinguishing feature of populism compared with fascism. In Chapters 4 and 5, I suggest that populism has an ambivalent relation to elections, but I agree that elections are somehow a part of the populist view of democratic legitimacy.

[40] Canovan, "Trust the People!"; Canovan, "Taking Politics to the People."

[41] Mounk, *People vs. Democracy*, 8, 35, 50, 52.

[42] Stavrakakis, "Populism in Power," 275.

[43] See Laclau, *On Populist Reason*; Mouffe, *For a Left Populism*.

Mouffe's promotion of left populism. Laclau and Mouffe see populism not as an ideology, but as a "logic of articulation" (Laclau) or "discursive strategy" (Mouffe). However, I argue that their own articulation of populism in fact commits them to a number of more substantial claims. By engaging with the work of these theorists, as well as with studies of left populism in Latin America, I hope to show that my arguments apply not only to right-wing populism but also to left populism.

In the works of Laclau and Mouffe – which, by the way, may not be completely consistent – I do not find it difficult to locate examples of commitment to most of the claims listed above, even if they see those claims as articulations rather than essences.[44] However, there are two claims that do raise some difficulty. First, Laclau and Mouffe might have problems with claim (4), which states that the division between the people and the elite is moral and Manichean, and the people is in the right. For them, the division between the people and the elite is political rather than moral, which means they regard the frontier between the people and the oligarchy as created for political purposes of hegemonic conflict. However, the work of both Mouffe and Laclau does seem to imply that what they call the underdog or the people is somehow in the right, and that those in power or the oligarchy are wrong.

Second, Mouffe at least might deny that her populism is committed to claim (13), which says that the people can have only one legitimate representative and opposition to this representative is suspect and illegitimate. After all, Mouffe is renowned for the idea of agonistic pluralism, according to which "the opponent is not considered an enemy to be destroyed but an adversary whose existence is perceived as legitimate."[45] However, as I argue in Chapter 6, it is difficult to see how Mouffe's idea of agonistic pluralism can be consistently combined with Laclau's understanding of populism (which Mouffe claims to follow). Thus, Laclau explicitly notes that the populist construction of the people entails that the responsible power or elite "cannot be a legitimate part of the community."[46]

I should stress that the fact that left and right populism share a number of claims does not mean that there are no differences between them, or that their effects – for example, on democracy – are the same. It makes a difference which host ideology a populist party is connected to. However,

---

[44] For Laclau and Mouffe, "the people" is not an "essence" or an empirical referent but something that is articulated or constructed in discourse. See Laclau, "Populism," 160; Mouffe, *For a Left Populism*, 41, 62.

[45] Mouffe, *For a Left Populism*, 91. For an elaboration of Mouffe's view of agonism, see Mouffe, *Democratic Paradox*, 101–5.

[46] Laclau, *On Populist Reason*, 86.

in this book the focus will be on what I take to be the shared claims of different forms of populism, whether left, right, or center.

I.2   Overview of the Book

Beyond this Introduction, *Democratic Respect* is divided into six chapters. The starting point for Chapter 1 is empirical studies showing that feelings of misrecognition can explain much of the support for populism, and that these feelings drive the populist politics of resentment. While I accept and draw on the insight that the quest for recognition propels populism, I take issue with the literature that suggests that feelings of misrecognition and resentment are unconnected to facts and principles. Drawing on Axel Honneth's recognition theory, Peter Strawson's discussion of resentment, and John Rawls's idea of principle-dependent feelings, I argue instead that we should interpret the populist politics of resentment as a struggle for recognition based on distinctive moral experiences that are intimately connected to factual and normative beliefs. Resentment is based on the feeling that one is regarded and treated wrongly by other people, and it is an incipient demand to be regarded and treated differently. Thus, Chapter 1 provides an approach to populism and the politics of resentment that does not reduce them to ordinary citizens' unthinking or automatic emotional reactions or political entrepreneurs' manipulations of people. The proposed approach entails that we presume what I call a "participant attitude," which means that we take people's demands for recognition seriously by considering them on their merits, that is, by considering the factual and normative beliefs that give rise to the demands. Democratic respect does not require that we accept all demands equally, but it does require that we genuinely consider the validity of the claims people make on one another, rather than regarding them with an observer attitude as pathological cases in need of treatment.

While Chapter 1 sets out how to approach demands for recognition, Chapters 2 to 4 distinguish and evaluate different kinds of demand for recognition made by supporters of populism and found (explicitly and implicitly) in the claims of populism. If we can associate populist resentment with experiences of the violation of moral principles, we can ask which principles populist demands for recognition are based on, and whether they are valid democratic principles.

The aim of Chapter 2 is to distinguish between different kinds of demand for recognition and to assess their validity in light of fundamental democratic principles. Both of these tasks are missing from the existing literature on populism and recognition, which does not distinguish clearly between issues of recognition, respect, esteem, honor, dignity, and status, and thus cannot discuss their different normative implications. While "equal respect" is central to democracy on most accounts, it is important to acknowledge that not all demands for recognition are demands for equal respect. In particular, the type of respect that citizens and the government must display in democracies should not be confused with *esteem* for people's merits, identity, or way of life, but must consist in respect for citizens' status as citizens. Demanding and granting esteem for particular traits or ways of life, as populists do, is incompatible with a pluralistic society of free and equal persons. Further, it is crucial that we distinguish on the one hand between the notion of respect for status, understood in egalitarian terms as respect for the equal standing of all citizens or all human beings (democratic "dignity respect"), and the notion of respect for one's status as a superior (aristocratic "honor respect") on the other hand. Chapter 2 shows how demands for respect among populists tend toward the inegalitarian idea of "honor respect."

Although I argue that a democracy is a society of equality of respect and cannot supply equal esteem for everyone, I acknowledge that inequality of esteem can still pose a moral and democratic problem. This is because inequality of esteem under some conditions can convert into inequality of respect. Therefore, the second part of Chapter 2 argues that democratic respect depends on a form of *solidarity* that counteracts the ever-present danger that inequality of esteem might transform into inequality of respect. When inequality of esteem takes a form and reaches a degree that threatens the ideal of equal respect, there is a moral requirement to act in solidarity with those who struggle to be respected as equal participants in society. Acting in solidarity requires first that we aim to change the social circumstances that give rise to forms of inequality of esteem that turn into inequality of respect, and second that we only express disesteem and disagreement with vulnerable members of society in ways that simultaneously make clear that their way of life has a legitimate place in society and that they can participate in public life on equal terms with everyone else.

Chapter 3 turns from the quest for recognition among supporters of populism to the kind of demand for recognition that is inherent to populism as an ideology and a political logic. At the core of populism are the claims that only a part of the people is really the people and that the only legitimate option is to take sides with this part against the rest. I argue that populism so understood entails a unique claim for recognition, which sets it at odds with the ideal of respect for the equal standing of every last individual person. The populist claim for recognition arises from a totalizing framing of political conflict, according to which one can and should understand one uniform group in society – "the people" – to be the worst-off group *for all political purposes*. The populist claim for recognition is an exclusionary claim: We are something that you are not, that is, "the people." In contrast, I argue that in order to show equal respect for everyone, as well as solidaristic concern for diverse marginalized groups, it is imperative to focus on particular struggles for recognition and discuss who actually suffers the greatest injustice in each case separately. Moreover, it is the populist claim for recognition that explains its opposition to the deliberative aspect of politics, which stresses the importance of mutual critique and learning among citizens.

Chapter 3 goes on to contrast the populist claim for recognition with the kind of respect that Joel Feinberg argues is expressed in and through "the activity of claim-making" that is characteristic of a society with individual rights. The issue of rights is central to the discussion of populism, both because some populist politicians claim that we can have democracy without rights, and because some theorists of populism accept that illiberal democracy is essentially democratic. Going beyond Feinberg and with reference to Habermas, I argue that whether or not equal rights provide for respect and self-respect depends on how we as a society *understand* rights and how we *practice* the claim-making involved in having rights. In order to regard rights as establishing relationships of mutual respect, rather than as mere means to individual ends, we must adopt the participant attitude. Only by accepting the primacy of the participant attitude can rights struggles contribute to democratic respect.

The question of what kind of recognition populism supplies to the people connects to the question of how populists understand and practice "democracy." Chapter 4 examines and disputes the widespread assumption that populism is committed to a *procedural* conception of democracy that rejects all substantive standards and restraints on popular decision-making. I argue that populism cannot be regarded as essentially democratic and fully committed to the procedural aspect of democracy while it is only against constitutional constraints. Indeed, the fault I find with populism in terms of democratic respect is not that its understanding of democracy lacks substantive constraints on popular decision-making, but that it fails to appreciate the procedural value of democracy. In addition, populists have a very limited understanding of democratic procedures, focusing on aggregative mechanisms such as referendums and elections, while I argue for a more expansive understanding of democratic procedures that includes free opinion formation, activism, and deliberation in civil and political society.

This Introduction began with the claim that the debate over the meaning and value of populism is essentially a debate over how democracy should recognize the people. In this connection, Chapter 4 distinguishes between three different kinds of "democratic" recognition: (1) *procedural respect*, which demands that every citizen has an equal standing in political processes and procedures; (2) *outcome respect*, which demands that political outcomes should correspond to the people's opinions; and (3) *identification recognition*, which demands identification between the political leader and a homogenized people. I propose that the populist understanding of democracy fails to appreciate the importance of procedural respect, while it promotes outcome respect and identification recognition. The ideal of securing respect for the people through correspondence between public policy and people's opinions is incompatible with the circumstance of disagreement, which characterizes a free society, and leader-people identification has equally anti-pluralistic implications.

Chapter 5 focuses on how different democratic decision procedures – voting, majority rule, compromise, consensus, and public deliberation – relate to claims for recognition and democratic respect. Populism has its own interpretation and evaluation of these decision procedures and challenges us to explain and defend our view of them. Thus, the chapter proceeds by contrasting populist understandings and uses of different decision procedures with my democratic respect understanding of these. Populism is commonly seen as characterized by its adherence to the democratic principles of popular sovereignty and majority rule, and as only against liberal constraints on the will of the people as expressed by the majority. This chapter challenges that view of populism. First, among populism's claims we do not find a defense of majority rule that connects it to the sovereignty of *all* members of society, as we do, for example, in Rousseau. Second, if we understand majority rule as a principle that should regulate democratic decision-making over time, we will see that populists are not true majoritarians.

Populism claims to accept majority rule while completely rejecting the intrinsic value of compromise, another central feature of democratic decision-making. The second part of Chapter 5 discusses compromise as an attitude one can take when making decisions with one's fellow citizens. Populists regard compromise as a form of betrayal, weakness, and defeat, while I defend it as an important aspect of democratic respect. In the literature, there is a tendency to focus on the bad consequences of the refusal to compromise. By contrast, I argue that the rejection of compromise can also be *wrong in itself*. Political theorists have discussed whether the value of compromise is merely pragmatic or whether there can also be principled reasons for compromise. Populism's principled rejection of compromise shows why our defense of this practice must be principled and not merely pragmatic. Under certain conditions, the politics of compromise can be an important expression of democratic respect. The last part of the chapter connects the spirit of compromise to the notion of solidarity sketched in Chapter 2. I argue that compromise can be seen as a form of solidaristic inclusion of people with whom one profoundly disagrees.

Whereas the first five chapters of the book discuss the extent to which populist demands for recognition and populist ideas of democracy can be justified in light of the ideal of democratic respect, Chapter 6 considers the possibility that even if populism is in tension with our best conceptions of democracy and respect, it might nevertheless correct the deficiencies of actually existing democracy. The starting point of the chapter is that current democracies have many faults and are in need of correction. The chapter considers whether it is permissible to promote populism if it can correct some of the deficiencies of democracy. Thus, my question is not whether populist parties can correct democracy, as this question might be posed by an external observer. Instead, I adopt the participant attitude and ask whether we, or anyone, as fellow participants in democracy can endorse and promote populism because it has positive effects on a non-populist understanding of democracy. Applying the publicity condition first suggested by Kant and later expounded by Rawls, I argue that we cannot. We cannot *publicly* both endorse populism and say we do so because it improves democracy understood in non-populist terms. The publicity condition rules out the possibility of promoting one set of ideas (populism) for the sake of another set of ideas (non-populist democracy). The argument for promoting populism for the sake of non-populist ends cannot be made in public without frustrating those very ends.

1 Recognition and the Politics of Resentment

The current rise of populism is closely connected to the fact that many people feel disrespected by the surrounding society and the political system. Empirical studies show that people often feel attracted to populist parties because they feel stigmatized and dishonored, and have low subjective social status.[1] These feelings are part of and contribute to a politics of resentment directed against the political center, big cities, and certain elites.[2] On the one hand, populist parties express the frustration with and resentment of existing social and political practices; on the other hand, they provide their followers – "the people" – with the positive social identity and respect that they have lost.[3]

The aim of this chapter is to provide an approach to analyze the populist politics of resentment that considers people's emotional reactions but interprets them as connected to moral principles and demands. Thus, I understand support for populism as a struggle for recognition based on distinctively moral experiences that depend on factual beliefs and normative judgments. This approach entails that we presume what I call a *participant attitude*. This means that we take people's demands for recognition seriously by considering them on their merits, and that we assess whether they are demands that should be heeded in a democracy understood as a society of free and equal participants. We respect one another not by accepting all demands equally, but by genuinely considering the validity of the claims people make on one another, rather than regarding them with an observer attitude as pathological cases in need of treatment. This book promotes the participant attitude both as an approach in political theory and as part of a democratic ethos among citizens in general.

[1] See, for example, Gidron and Hall, "Populism as a Problem"; Hochschild, *Strangers in Their Own Land*; Spruyt, Keppens, and Van Droogenbroeck, "Who Supports Populism."
[2] Bonikowski, "Ethno-Nationalist Populism"; Cramer, *Politics of Resentment*; Fukuyama, *Identity*.
[3] On the last point, see Spruyt, Keppens, and Van Droogenbroeck, "Who Supports Populism."

The norm of "equal respect" is central to the meaning and justification of democracy.[4] Democracy is the only form of government in which political institutions are required to respect all citizens as equals, and it is this fact that explains its legitimacy and authority. In this chapter and the rest of the book, I connect this idea from democratic theory to the empirical observation that many people do not feel that society, and especially the political establishment, displays the required respect for them. Thus, my approach is to connect democratic theory and philosophy more closely to empirical explanations of current democratic discontent, and vice versa. In doing so, I will show that when used to describe the feeling of discontent among supporters of populist parties, "disrespect" – as well as related terms such as "dishonor," "contempt," and "disesteem" – does not necessarily refer to a lack of the *same kind* of respect as that which democratic theorists suggest we owe to one another, and which they think political institutions and practices should display and secure.

In other words, from the normative perspective of democratic theory and political philosophy, it is essential that we clarify whether feelings of discontent and resentment are rooted in the experience of violations of valid norms of equal respect, or whether they are rooted in other ideas or expectations that cannot be justified with reference to democratic norms. Thus, my aim in the following chapters is to investigate the meaning of different kinds of demand for recognition, and to determine which kinds can be understood as *democratic* demands and which cannot. This kind of investigation is especially relevant in a time when we lack a shared understanding of what we owe to each other as democratic citizens and of the underlying norms and social practices that sustain and constitute democracy. In other words, we need to think hard about the divergent forms of recognition at the current juncture when we may be losing (to the extent we ever had it) what we may call "the spirit of democracy."[5]

1.1   Populism as a Struggle for Recognition

As an explanation for "the populist tide," the Oxford historian Timothy Garton Ash writes: "Our societies have simply not delivered well enough on one of liberalism's central promises, summarized by the legal philosopher Ronald Dworkin as 'equal respect and concern' for each individual

---

[4] Anderson, "Democracy," 220; Christiano, *Constitution of Equality*; Richardson, *Democratic Autonomy*, 159; Rostbøll, "Democratic Respect and Compromise," 625; Valentini, "Justice, Disagreement and Democracy"; Waldron, *Law and Disagreement*, 108–18.

[5] The idea that different forms of government have different spirits goes back to Montesquieu, *Spirit of the Laws*. For an excellent contemporary use of this idea, see Näsström, *Spirit of Democracy*.

member of the society."[6] Many social scientists agree with Ash that support for populist parties and politicians can be explained by the fact that many people increasingly feel disrespected in various ways. The terminology differs, and while some commentators speak of "disrespect," others speak of "honor squeezes," "lack of positive social identity," and "low subjective social status."[7]

When Kantian political theorists and philosophers speak of "equal respect" or "respect for persons," we are speaking of a norm for how people ought to relate to one another – something we owe to one another, directly and through our political institutions.[8] It is not sufficient (or even necessary) to show that people *feel* disrespected – or that this explains support for populist parties – in order to conclude that some person(s) or institutions have failed to provide what they owe to others. If a person accepts their position as an inferior, they will not feel disrespected by being treated as having lower status; if a person believes they are superior, they will feel disrespected by being treated as an equal. Feelings of disrespect might provide pragmatic reasons for accommodation, but I am interested in intrinsic, principled reasons for respect. To assess the latter kind of reason, we need to know what exactly is meant by "respect" and "disrespect," as well as related terms such as "honor," "esteem," and "positive social identity." Thus, I shall review some of the relevant empirical studies and analyze how they understand these terms and what the people in question more precisely demand.

The recent surge in populism has been more pronounced on the right than on the left, except in parts of southern Europe.[9] For this reason, in the following I focus on supporters of right-wing populist parties. It is the feelings of resentment and disrespect among ordinary people that are of

[6] Ash, "Only Respect." To be precise, Dworkin's phrase is "equal concern and respect." For Dworkin ("Liberalism," 125–6), the principle of equal concern and respect is not a principle that is specific to liberalism as opposed to conservatism, but a broadly agreed upon principle of contemporary politics. On "equality" as a shared norm across the political spectrum, see also Dahl, *Democracy and Its Critics*, 84–7; Kymlicka, *Contemporary Political Philosophy*, 3–5.

[7] Cramer, *Politics of Resentment* ("disrespect"); Hochschild, *Strangers in Their Own Land* ("honor squeeze"); Spruyt, Keppens, and Van Droogenbroeck, "Who Supports Populism" ("lack of positive social identity"); Gidron and Hall, "Populism as a Problem" ("low subjective social status").

[8] Dworkin ("Liberalism," 125) argues that equal concern and respect is something that *the government* owes to everyone in its charge, and not something we as private persons owe to one another. While I agree that we do not owe, say, the same concern to other people's children as to our own, my understanding of "equal respect" extends beyond how the government should treat us to how citizens ought to relate to one another.

[9] Latin America, of course, has a strong tradition of left populism, including the "pink tide" of Hugo Chávez and Nicolás Maduro in Venezuela, Evo Morales in Bolivia, and the Kirchners in Argentina.

special interest here. Hence, I concentrate on what is sometimes called the demand side of politics.[10] This focus on feelings of disrespect and loss of status among groups of ordinary people, rather than on the "supply" provided by politicians, entails a presumption that there is a real desire and demand for recognition among people, and that this desire is not only the fabrication of political entrepreneurs.[11] Thus, the aim of the following chapters is to understand the exact meaning and discuss the normative grounds of different kinds of demand for respect among ordinary people, rather than how politicians exploit people's feelings.

With this aim in mind, it is instructive to begin with two intriguing and widely discussed ethnographies of the American Tea Party movement and right-wing supporters in rural America: Katherine Cramer's *The Politics of Resentment*, and Arlie Hochschild's *Strangers in Their Own Land*. Both authors have spent considerable time talking and listening to people attracted to populist politicians, and their studies provide in-depth portraits of those people and their opinions, feelings, and stories. Both books give empathetic accounts of people who feel misunderstood, ignored, and unfairly treated by political, cultural, and urban elites. Thus, while their vocabularies and emphases differ, Cramer and Hochschild highlight feelings of disrespect and loss of status as central explanations for support for populist politicians.[12] These studies provide great insights into the feelings of right-wing voters, but I shall suggest below that for our normative and democratic purposes, the exclusive focus on emotions and the neglect of the role of principle-dependent demands is a limitation, and that we need to more clearly distinguish between different kinds of demand for recognition.

Cramer's aim is to understand why rural people in the state of Wisconsin are against government regulation and support far-right candidates such as the then governor, Scott Walker. One of her main findings is "that animosity toward government is partly about feeling overlooked, ignored, and disrespected" by government, the political center, and urban people.[13] Cramer argues that the preference for small government has less to do with libertarian principles and more to do with identity and feelings of resentment.[14] Thus, what she calls the politics of resentment is in her interpretation about identity and hostile emotions toward other people

---

[10] Akkerman, Mudde, and Zaslove, "How Populist Are the People?"

[11] Cf. Spruyt, Keppens, and Van Droogenbroeck, "Who Supports Populism," 335.

[12] Eribon's *Returning to Reims*, an autobiographical and sociological study of French working-class voters who turned from voting communist to voting for the extreme right and the populist Front National, similarly stresses issues of recognition, collective identity, pride, and dignity.

[13] Cramer, *Politics of Resentment*, 40, cf. 52, 66, 105.

[14] Cramer, *Politics of Resentment*, 9, 24, 164–7.

rather than a matter of ideology or principles. However, Cramer also suggests that the resentment of her interviewees is rooted in the belief that they are "the victims of distributive injustice" regarding three different elements: resources, political power, and cultural respect.[15] She writes: "Many of the people I listened to in rural areas identified strongly as rural people and took it as given that rural areas do not get their fair share of political attention or decision-making power or public resources and have a fundamentally different set of values and lifestyles, which are neither understood nor respected by city-dwellers."[16] Cramer concludes that the people she talked to in rural Wisconsin want politicians who "understand and respect the way rural folks live and their daily concerns and desires."[17]

The theme of feeling overlooked, ignored, and misunderstood by the government, mainstream media, and other elites also features prominently in Hochschild's study of Tea Party supporters in Louisiana. The latter, she says, feel like "strangers in their own land" and "struggle to feel seen and honored."[18] Hochschild conceptualizes the emotions of her interlocutors in terms of an experience of an "honor squeeze."[19] As a result of structural and cultural changes, many people have lost the basis of the "honor" that was formerly provided by hard work, place, Christian morality, or being a heterosexual male. The people she talks to feel that their way of life and opinions are "held up to ridicule in the national media as backward."[20]

One woman in Hochschild's study explains her love of the conservative radio host Rush Limbaugh (to whom Donald Trump awarded the Presidential Medal of Freedom in 2020) with reference to her feeling that Limbaugh defends her against the insults of liberals: "Oh, liberals think that Bible-believing Southerners are ignorant, backward, redneck, losers. They think we are racist, sexists, homophobic, and maybe fat."[21] It is important to notice that there is no clear differentiation in Hochschild's description of her interviewees between feelings of disrespect for their way of life and political disagreements. What she describes is a feeling that there is an all-out attack on everything her interlocutors stand for and look like, as well as a defensive strategy of counterattack against and rejection of everything that is associated with the other side. However, from reading about her conversations with Tea Party supporters, it is clear that the latter not only have strong feelings and emotions, which

---

[15] Cramer, *Politics of Resentment*, 212, see also 12, 23, 55–84.
[16] Cramer, *Politics of Resentment*, 209.
[17] Cramer, *Politics of Resentment*, 223.
[18] Hochschild, *Strangers in Their Own Land*, 218.
[19] Hochschild, *Strangers in Their Own Land*, 144, 215–18.
[20] Hochschild, *Strangers in Their Own Land*, 221.
[21] Hochschild, *Strangers in Their Own Land*, 23.

is Hochschild's focus; they also have principles and norms that can help to explain some of these emotions.

Studies of countries other than the United States that are experiencing surges in support for populist parties, and studies using other methods, confirm the general findings of Cramer and Hochschild. For example, using comparative survey data, Noam Gidron and Peter Hall suggest that feelings of what they call low subjective social status and disrespect explain alienation from mainstream parties and support for radical and populist parties in contemporary European politics.[22] The feeling of low social status is described by Gidron and Hall both in terms of not being seen "as peers" and as a feeling of loss of former superior or privileged social standing.[23] From a normative point of view, as we shall discuss in more detail in later chapters, this constitutes a crucial difference when we come to evaluate the validity of such claims.[24] In a survey-based study of Flanders, Bram Spruyt, Gil Keppens, and Filip Van Droogenbroeck argue that an important explanation for the success of populism in the Dutch-speaking part of Belgium is that it meets the demand for a positive social identity among a stigmatized segment of the population.[25] By being included in the "the people" and esteemed by populist leaders, this group become able to "maintain their self-respect" and have a "positive social identity," while being able to blame others for their feelings of uncertainty and unease.[26]

Thus, empirical studies of supporters of populist parties converge on a similar causal narrative. People attracted to populism feel overlooked, disrespected, diminished in status, and lacking a positive social identity. These feelings fuel resentment and hatred of other people whom they hold responsible for their plight. These other people are mainly located in the political center, big cities, and the mainstream media, and are regarded as either "the elite" or undeserving groups whom the elite unfairly helps to get ahead.[27] Populist parties express and tap into this resentment by speaking of "us" versus "them," that is, by engaging in a form of identity polarization. According to this narrative, populists' talk of "the real people," and their praise of these people's hard work and common sense in opposition to the corrupt elites, helps their followers to regain lost feelings of social status and maintain their self-respect.[28]

---

[22] Gidron and Hall, "Populism as a Problem."
[23] Gidron and Hall, "Populism as a Problem," 1030, 1032.
[24] As I shall suggest below, resentment is an implicit claim or demand.
[25] Spruyt, Keppens, and Van Droogenbroeck, "Who Supports Populism."
[26] Spruyt, Keppens, and Van Droogenbroeck, "Who Supports Populism," especially 335, 344.
[27] Brubaker, "Why Populism?," 362–3; Hochschild, *Strangers in Their Own Land*, 137–9.
[28] In addition to the references in last few paragraphs, see also Fukuyama, *Identity*, 117–23, 159; Mudde, "Populism"; Müller, *What Is Populism?*; Mutz, "Status Threat."

Based on this background, we can say that supporters of populist parties are engaged in a struggle for recognition. They are reacting to a *changing recognition order*, where people "like them" have lost – or at least feel they have lost – their former status.[29] Recognition theory can help us gain a deeper understanding of these contentions.

1.1.1   Recognition, Social Change, and Political Struggle

As a theory of political conflict and change, the starting point for recognition theory is the idea that political struggles concern not only what one gets but primarily how one is regarded by other people.[30] That is, the motivation for political resistance or protest is not merely physical needs or material interests, but rather concerns one's standing in relation to other people. Experiences of humiliation and disrespect prompt people to fight back in order to gain the recognition from others that is needed for them to attain or maintain a positive view of themselves. Thus, recognition theory sees social struggles as caused by feelings of disrespect and as seeking to secure the recognition from others that is needed to gain or restore a positive self-relation, that is, self-respect and self-esteem.

It is a central contention in recognition theory that social and political struggles are based on distinctively *moral* experiences. The idea is that when people engage in social and political struggle, this is not simply to satisfy their material interests; rather, it is a morally motivated struggle to be treated and regarded properly by others. The point of political struggles is not just to get something but to show that you are *worthy* of getting something and *have the right to demand* something. Experiences of disrespect that cause social struggles are based on what the people in question believe they are owed. As Axel Honneth writes: "It is a matter of the disappointment or violation of normative expectations of society considered justified by those concerned."[31] When people's normative expectations are frustrated, they feel that they are treated as less worthy or valuable members of society than they ought to be. It is an experience of others or the surrounding society as treating them wrongly or unjustly.

The idea that political struggles are motivated by moral experiences of misrecognition rather than material interests should not be understood

---

[29] Zurn, "Populism, Polarization, and Misrecognition."

[30] In the following, I draw especially on Honneth, *Struggle for Recognition*, and Honneth's contributions to Fraser and Honneth, *Redistribution and Recognition?* For an excellent and critical introduction to recognition theory, see McBride, *Recognition*.

[31] Honneth, "Redistribution as Recognition," 129.

as if issues of redistribution were unimportant in recognition theory.[32] Rather, recognition theorists interpret conflicts over redistribution in a distinctive way. They understand them as conflicts over the standing and value of different people within socioeconomic relations. Conflicts over material resources, then, are seen as conflicts over who has the status to demand what, and who deserves to get what. These conflicts are moral conflicts and matters of recognition insofar as they are about different individuals' or groups' standing in relation to one another, about their respective worth as persons and the value of their contributions. The class struggle of workers, for example, is understood by recognition theory as less about economic deprivation and the satisfaction of material needs, and more a matter of *the normative recognition order* that determines workers' standing in the production process and the value of their labor.

So the point of applying recognition theory to the rise of populism is not to argue that the latter has cultural as opposed to economic causes. The point is that both cultural and economic developments can change the normative recognition order in ways that adversely affect the self-respect and self-esteem of some groups. Both sociocultural and economic changes can make people feel that they have lost the recognition from the surrounding society that they deserve. Both kinds of development can make people feel they have lost the respect and/or esteem that other people or society owe them.[33] When people blame their loss of status and esteem on the elite and minorities unjustly coddled by the elite, they may believe that they have reason to turn to populism.[34]

Sometimes, partly under the influence of Charles Taylor's influential "The Politics of Recognition," recognition struggles are seen as particularly related to contemporary identity politics, multiculturalism, and the politics of difference. However, my approach to struggles for recognition, which is more in line with Honneth's theory than Taylor's, does not limit the notion of struggles for recognition to these more recent developments. Most importantly, I see struggles for recognition not only as a matter of recognition of cultural differences. The more universalist Kantian politics of respect for dignity is also part of recognition struggles, as they are discussed in this book. Thus, I regard struggles for recognition as about demands for both respect for human dignity and esteem for particular identities. Moreover, as we shall see, I do not prejudge the question of whether demands for recognition are demands for equality.

---

[32] See especially Honneth's response to Fraser in Honneth, "Redistribution as Recognition," 135–59. See also Honneth, *Struggle for Recognition*, 166–7.

[33] I explain the important distinction between respect and esteem in Chapter 2.

[34] For a review of literature on explanations of populism that emphasize economic versus sociocultural grievances or their interaction, see Berman, "Causes of Populism," 73–7.

Our concern is exactly which kinds of demands for recognition populism entails, to what extent they are demands for equality, and thus whether they are *democratic* demands.

I said that political struggles are about how other people regard us. According to recognition theory, human beings see themselves through the eyes of their interaction partners. Human beings learn to relate to themselves via the values of other people, and they largely judge themselves by shared values. When people engage in social and political recognition struggles, it is because they mirror themselves not only in the values and norms of those they know but in the values and norms of the society of which they see themselves as part (what George Herbert Mead calls "the generalized other"[35]). Society is an institutionalized recognition order, which determines the standing of different groups and the worth of their identities and contributions. As members of a society, therefore, people are dependent on the particular manner in which inter-subjective recognition is institutionalized in their society.[36] And they struggle for recognition from society's shared culture and institutions.

The struggle for recognition from society's institutions is not merely symbolic but is also a struggle for power. When people struggle for recognition in the social status order, this can be a struggle for the power privileges that come with the standing of being a superior or an equal. In relation to populism, this means that we must analyze and assess what kind of power in relation to other persons the populist demand for recognition of "the people" entails. Is it a struggle to maintain the privileged standing and power of one group, or is it a (democratic) struggle to lift up one group in order to secure the equal political power of every last citizen?

People's feelings of disrespect seem to be particularly acute in times when they are experiencing fundamental *changes* in their society's recognition order. Thus, struggles for recognition and the related politics of resentment are not constants in history but are sensitive to changes in one's role, obligations, and standing in cultural, political, and economic relations in society.[37] The people most active in recognition-motivated social and political struggles are often the people who feel "their previously recognized self-understanding to be massively threatened by socio-political changes."[38] In other words, changes in the normatively integrated social order that undermine the recognition that a group used

---

[35] Honneth, *Struggle for Recognition*, 71–91.
[36] Honneth, "Redistribution as Recognition," 138.
[37] Zurn, "Populism, Polarization, and Misrecognition."
[38] Honneth, *Struggle for Recognition*, 167, with references to historical studies by Thompson (*Making*) and Moore (*Injustice*).

to get – and which they therefore believe themselves to deserve or be entitled to – are strong catalysts for social struggle. In order for it to be the basis of a political movement, it is essential that the feeling of disrespect be shared by a group and related to moral ideas of entitlement and desert.[39] Populism connects people with shared experiences and supplies ideas about who is to blame.

1.1.2   An Identity Politics of the Right

In recent history, struggles for recognition and the related idea of identity politics have been associated with the left and the struggles against oppression of minorities such as people of color, Muslims, the disabled, immigrants, and LGBTQ+ people. However, the populist right is also engaged in a form of identity politics, and some right-wing ideologues have embraced the language of identity, recognition, and even multiculturalism.[40] (Hochschild importantly notes, though, that her interviewees reject the language of victimhood even if they do feel like – and according to Hochschild in fact are – victims.[41])

Right-wing populist parties are successful with their identity politics, which seeks to strengthen and promote the identity of "the real people,"[42] because identity has become a problem for large groups of people. Struggles for the recognition of identities and cultures arise when people feel that their identity, culture, or status is threatened.[43] In the United States, especially older, less educated religious men who belong to the ethnic majority feel threatened in their identity and culture. Political scientists Ronald Inglehart and Pippa Norris suggest that support for right-wing populism can be explained by a "cultural backlash" among this group of people.[44] This cultural backlash began as a consequence of the cultural revolution of the 1960s, but it has been amplified by the feeling of economic insecurity caused by the economic recession that began in 2008, which hit the same group hard.[45] However, I argue first that

---

[39] Honneth, *Struggle for Recognition*, 162–4.

[40] Fukuyama, *Identity*, 117–23; Patten, "Populist Multiculturalism," 541.

[41] Hochschild, *Strangers in Their Own Land*, 131, 190, 215–16, 232.

[42] After the Brexit vote, the then leader of the UK Independence Party, Nigel Farage, called it "a victory for real people," and in 2008 the then vice-presidential nominee and Tea Party leader Sarah Palin talked of small towns as "the real America." For commentary, see Fukuyama, *Identity*, 159; Mounk, *People vs. Democracy*, 43; Müller, *What Is Populism?*, 19–25.

[43] Taylor, "Politics of Recognition."

[44] Inglehart and Norris, "Trump."

[45] See also Bonikowski, "Ethno-Nationalist Populism," 202; Gest, Reny, and Mayer, "Roots of the Radical Right," 1698, 1706; Gidron and Hall, "Populism as a Problem," 1032.

this reaction to the changing recognition order is rooted in a distinctively moral experience, and second that it is a response not only to cultural changes but also to changes in roles, obligations, and the distribution of material resources.[46] As Honneth writes, "intersubjective recognition is always shaped by the particular manner in which the mutual granting of recognition is institutionalized within a society."[47] Thus, struggles for recognition are not only about cultural identity, but just as importantly about demands for economic redistribution and political power.[48]

There is no doubt that struggles for recognition have contributed positively to the always-unfinished project that democracy is. Popular demands for recognition and respect have helped to make democracy more inclusive and egalitarian. Does that mean that struggles for recognition *always* deepen and improve democracy? Political theorists Jane Mansbridge and Stephen Macedo conclude with reference to some of the same empirical literature that I have reviewed not only that "populism typically includes 'a struggle for recognition'" but also that this can justify populism.[49] Their reasoning seems to be that (1) struggles for recognition are democratic, (2) populism is a struggle for recognition, and (3) therefore, populism is a democratic struggle.[50] I think this conclusion is too quick, because the argument's first and major premise fails to distinguish between different kinds of struggle for recognition. Not all forms of recognition are intrinsically democratic, and not all struggles for recognition have a democratic aim. Thus, we need to distinguish more carefully between different kinds of demand for recognition and assess their respective democratic credentials.

In order to evaluate different demands for recognition and their democratic credentials, we must go beyond some of the underlying assumptions as well as the conceptual framework used in the empirical studies reviewed in this chapter. First, the reviewed literature tends to focus on emotional and psychological factors, and to concentrate on how people feel. For our normative purposes, we should consider whether people's feelings of resentment and disrespect can be associated with moral principles. I argue that they can, which opens up the possibility of a normative discussion of the validity of these principles (see the next section). Second, the literature uses a number of different terms to describe what

---

[46] Zurn, "Populism, Polarization, and Misrecognition."

[47] Honneth, "Redistribution as Recognition," 138.

[48] On these issues, see the debate between Fraser and Honneth in *Redistribution or Recognition?*

[49] Mansbridge and Macedo, "Populism and Democratic Theory," 72.

[50] I acknowledge that I only address part of Mansbridge and Macedo's argument here. In Chapter 6, I discuss more fully their claim that populism can be a corrective to democracy.

the studied people crave and demand, including "respect," "recognition," "honor," "status," and "positive social identity." As we proceed, I want to narrow the question down to two kinds of demand: demands for respect for one's authority or status, and demands for esteem of one's character, merits, or way of life. The trouble is that all the abovementioned terms are used for both types of demand. I shall use "demand for respect" and "demand for esteem" as shorthand for these two types of demand. I see "the struggle for recognition" as a broader notion encompassing both types (see Chapter 2).[51]

1.2   Reactive Attitudes and Principle-Dependent Feelings

In the empirical literature on disrespect, loss of honor, and resentment, there is, as already mentioned, an emphasis on people's feelings and emotions *as opposed to* their principles and factual beliefs. The emotional aspect is highlighted, for example, by Hochschild, who searches for "the emotion that underlies politics" and suggests that an explanatory "deep story" of her Tea Party interlocutors is a *"feels-as-if* story," which, she claims, "removes judgment [and] fact."[52] We find a similar emphasis in Cramer when she argues that the Wisconsinites she listens to are driven by identity and feelings of resentment *rather than* by ideology and principles.[53]

I do not deny the importance of the affective dimension in political behavior, but I shall argue that it is a mistake to regard emotions and feelings of disrespect and resentment as unconnected to principles, reasons, and facts. From a normative and democratic perspective, citizens have good reasons to view one another in a different way than as moved only by unconscious and automatic responses to external stimuli. First, it is disrespectful in and of itself to view people as driven only by non-cognitive emotions and feelings. It entails viewing them as irresponsible creatures who cannot give reasons or supply principles for their political views and behavior. Second, if we want to maintain democratic dialogue, we must connect the emotions and feelings people have with principles that can be shared, contested, and discussed. One cannot argue with feelings directly, but we can argue about the principles that may be associated with them. And feelings such as disrespect and resentment

---

[51] This is in keeping with the use of the term by both Honneth (*Struggle for Recognition*) and Taylor ("Politics of Recognition"). However, in addition to "respect" and "esteem," Honneth includes "love" as a third component of recognition.

[52] Hochschild, *Strangers in Their Own Land*, xi, 135.

[53] Cramer, *Politics of Resentment*, 5, 24, 216.

are *moral* feelings that can be associated with principles, as we shall see later. Third, when we read the empirical literature, it is clear that the reported feelings of resentment are actually connected to people's belief that principles – for example, fairness and distributive justice – have been violated.[54] People do not feel resentment without judging, or without having a perception of the facts.

Drawing on Peter Strawson's paper "Freedom and Resentment," I want to suggest that we view populist resentment as what he calls a "reactive attitude." That is, I investigate what it would mean to view current resentments along the lines of Strawson's interpretation of reactive attitudes. According to Strawson, having reactive attitudes is central to "what it is actually like" to participate in interpersonal relationships.[55] It is an essential part of being involved in relations with other human beings that we react to their intentions and actions toward us with attitudes such as gratitude, resentment, moral indignation, forgiveness, and hurt feelings.[56] As human beings, we simply cannot ignore how other people relate to us and think about us. If someone does not respond to a question I address to them, normally I want to know if they simply did not hear me, or if they are deliberately excluding me from the conversation. If someone steps on my foot, I want to know if it was an accident, or if they malevolently wanted to hurt me. As Strawson writes, "it matters to us, whether the actions of other people ... reflect attitudes towards us of goodwill, affection, or esteem on the one hand or contempt, indifference, or malevolence on the other."[57] In the concise formulation of a recent commentator, "we care about how we stand in the other's world."[58]

Given our concern with recognition, one of the interesting observations in "Freedom and Resentment" is that there is an intimate connection between reactive attitudes such as resentment on the one hand, and interpersonal regard or respect on the other. Reactive attitudes, Strawson writes, "involve, or express, a certain sort of demand for interpersonal regard."[59] When we feel resentful of someone stepping on our feet or ignoring us in a conversation, we do so because of an implicit demand to be seen and heard, to be regarded as someone who *ought* to be seen and heard rather than ignored and disregarded. Moreover,

---

[54] Cramer, *Politics of Resentment*, 9, 209, 211–12; Hochschild, *Strangers in Their Own Land*, 139.
[55] Strawson, "Freedom and Resentment," 64.
[56] Strawson, "Freedom and Resentment," 62, 70.
[57] Strawson, "Freedom and Resentment," 63.
[58] Hieronymi, *Freedom, Resentment*, 7.
[59] Strawson, "Freedom and Resentment," 72.

having reactive attitudes and feeling resentment makes sense if and only if we regard others and ourselves as free and responsible persons. We blame and resent others' ill-treatment of us on the assumption that they are deliberately treating us badly and are free to refrain from doing so. And we demand to be seen and heard on the assumption that we have the *standing* to make such a demand.

Thus, resentment belongs to an attitude to human interaction – Strawson calls it "the participant attitude" – in which people view one another as free and responsible persons who make demands on and argue with one another.[60] Expecting to be treated in certain ways by others, and making demands in this regard, people presuppose their own authority to make such demands and the authority of the addressee to meet those demands.[61] Hence, resentment is both a demand for respect and an expression of respect. Stephen Darwall connects this point in Strawson to the moral idea of *human dignity* and writes, "the implicit aim of reactive attitudes is to make others feel our dignity (and, less obviously, their own)."[62]

1.2.1 Principle-Dependent Feelings

In Strawson, resentment and other reactive attitudes are *feelings*. However, for our purposes it is important to emphasize that reactive attitudes are *moral* feelings and not merely sensations. They are feelings that can be explained only with reference to a moral principle.[63] Reactive attitudes are provoked by violations of a moral principle. As such, and following John Rawls, we can call reactive attitudes "principle-dependent" rather than "object-dependent."[64] When supporters of populist parties feel resentment at being overlooked and disrespected, these feelings are dependent on and can be explained only with reference to violations of principles – for example, inclusion and fairness. These feelings cannot be explained or made sense of by the mere fact of being ignored or feeling pain (they are not merely object-dependent). This is because the latter states of affairs give rise to resentment if and only if someone is deliberately ignoring or disrespecting us – or if we believe they are

---

[60] Strawson, "Freedom and Resentment," 66.
[61] On the last point, see Darwall, *Second-Person Standpoint*, 5, 20–5.
[62] Darwall, *Second-Person Standpoint*, 85.
[63] For this understanding of moral feelings, see Rawls, *Theory of Justice*, 420–5.
[64] Rawls, *Lectures*, 45–8, 150–2; Rawls, *Political Liberalism*, 82–3; Darwall, *Second-Person Standpoint*, 95, 152, 220–1. The idea of a principle-dependent feeling goes back to Kant, who writes in a famous footnote in *Groundwork* (56, AK 4: 401n): "But though respect is a feeling, it is not *received* by means of influence; it is, instead, a feeling *self-wrought* by means of a rational concept."

doing so deliberately. If these things happen to us by accident (or to be precise, if we believe so), the feeling will be different. Hence, there is a difference between object-dependent feelings (pain and the state of not being responded to) and principle-dependent feelings (the feeling that a principle or norm has intentionally been violated).

Reactive attitudes such as resentment, then, are "reactions to the quality of others' wills towards us,"[65] not merely reactions to what *happens* to us.[66] We can feel what happens to us without any moral principles, but these feelings are object-dependent and can be described without moral principles (as when we feel hunger or physical pain).[67] But we can assess the quality of another's will and have reactive attitudes toward others only by associating our feeling with some moral principle regarding how people ought to relate to one another. Reactive attitudes are relational or second-personal: They are about how you and I interact with, treat, and regard one another. As such, they belong to – and can be explained only by – what may be called a relational view of morality, which focuses on the relations in which people stand to one another, how they interact, and what they owe to each other, rather than on states of affairs or well-being.[68]

When we feel resentment, we assume that others *know* that they are violating a principle. "That is not how to treat people, and you (should) know that" is implicit in the reactive attitude of resentment. As Strawson puts it, reactive attitudes "are precisely the correlates of the moral demand in the case where the demand is felt to be disregarded. The making of the demand *is* the proneness to such attitudes."[69] In other words, having reactive attitudes implies taking a participant attitude, in which we view it as common knowledge that people are prone to demand to be treated in certain ways and hold one another responsible for violations of legitimate expectations.[70] On these grounds, Gary Watson suggests that reactive attitudes are implicit forms of "moral address" and "incipiently forms of communication."[71] Having reactive attitudes, we assume that other people are

[65] Strawson, "Freedom and Resentment," 70.
[66] On the difference between what others will to us and what happens to us, see Nagel, "Agent-Relativity and Deontology."
[67] Rawls, *Lectures*, 46.
[68] We find such a view of morality, for example, in Anderson, *Imperative of Integration*, 16–21; Darwall, *Second-Person Standpoint*; Forst, "Two Pictures of Justice"; Scanlon, *What We Owe*. It is a fundamental Kantian idea that morality concerns "not what we should bring about, but how we should relate to one another" (Korsgaard, *Creating the Kingdom of Ends*, 275).
[69] Strawson, "Freedom and Resentment," 77, emphasis in the original.
[70] Darwall, *Second-Person Standpoint*, 74.
[71] Watson, "Responsibility," 122.

persons with whom we stand in moral and communicative relations – that they are fellow participants with whom we can argue and to whom we can address moral claims about what we owe one another.

I have proposed that when we have reactive attitudes, we hold others responsible in their relations to us for following principles that guide how one should interact with others. For reactive attitudes to make sense, we must presuppose both that these principles are common knowledge and that the involved participants are competent to apply them. Resentment only has a point if both the resenting person and the resented person know, and know that the other knows, that a sharable principle has been violated and that the resented person is capable of refraining from violating that principle. Moreover, when we take the participant attitude, we presuppose that the involved parties are claim makers and claim takers who can reason or deliberate with one another. In these ways and to that extent, I would say that participants who have reactive attitudes toward one another presuppose that they share a moral community with one another. In a moral community, there are principles that regulate how members stand in relation to one another, and members hold one another responsible for complying with those principles. Negative reactive attitudes such as blame and resentment do not involve expulsion of the target from the moral community, but are "the consequence of *continuing* to view [the blamed person] as a member of the moral community; only as one who has offended against its demands."[72]

1.2.2   Resentment as a Democratic Sentiment

On the basis of these insights from Strawson and his followers, we can and should reject approaches that understand the resentment of supporters of populist parties as emotional responses entirely unconnected to principles and facts. Such approaches make it difficult to view the people in question as fellow participants who make moral claims on us, and also make it impossible to discuss the validity of their claims. By contrast, if we regard resentment as rooted in the feeling that moral principles have been violated, and hence as an implicit form of moral address, we can and should respond to it as such. To respond to resentment as a form of moral address entails responding to it as a claim about how people ought to relate to one another. To be sure, in order for resentment to attain

---

[72] Strawson, "Freedom and Resentment," 77. Watson ("Responsibility," 125–8) rejects this conclusion with reference to the case of a radically evil person who is blamed but not seen as part of the moral community. I take this as a special case with less relevance for my purposes.

a moral character, it cannot just be about "me" but must relate to the violation of a more general moral principle.[73]

Notice here that a claim is not just the expression of a preference but involves an argument about who deserves what or about one's standing.[74] This does not mean that the claim to be treated differently should be accepted as it stands, but it entails a requirement to consider the claim *as a claim* that can and should be discussed, assessed, and decided upon. By viewing the resentful person as having a potentially rightful claim against us, we treat them as a free and responsible participant in common deliberation.[75] This common deliberation will not be about subjective feelings as such – that is, it will not be a case of people reporting their feelings to one another, as travelers report their experiences from foreign lands to one another. Rather, it will be a case of deliberation with fellow participants about the validity of sharable principles that give rise to feelings of resentment, as well as over whether valid principles actually have been violated. Thus, it will be a deliberation with both moral and factual components.[76]

Hence, I worry that the way in which the empirical literature typically posits feelings of resentment and disrespect as explanations of support for right-wing populism pushes us away from understanding the possibility of engaging with the principles that can be associated with and explain those feelings. For example, and as mentioned, it is central for Cramer to argue that support for populist politicians in Wisconsin is the result not of ideology and principles, but of identity and resentment.[77] She might here simply be confirming the finding that populist polarization in the United States has less to do with disagreement over policy than with hatred of "them."[78] However, this is not the same as saying that resentment is unconnected to principles. In fact, Cramer herself repeatedly notes that the resentment she observes is rooted in "a strong sense of distributive injustice," particularly injustice in the distribution of resources, political power, and cultural respect.[79] If people feel that something is *unjust*, and their resentment is caused by that feeling, then their resentment cannot be entirely separate from their principles or conception of justice.

To be sure, the principles or understandings of (in)justice that give rise to resentment are not normally rooted in a clear and coherent

---

[73] Strawson, "Freedom and Resentment," 70–6; see also Habermas, "Discourse Ethics," 48–9.
[74] See Chapter 3.
[75] For a similar point, see Schwarze, *Recognizing Resentment*, 8.
[76] Cf. Habermas, "Discourse Ethics," 49.
[77] Cramer, *Politics of Resentment*, 5, 24, 216.
[78] See, for example, Mason, *Uncivil Agreement*.
[79] Cramer, *Politics of Resentment*, 209, cf. 9, 211–12.

ideology or a philosophical conception of justice. Nor are they always based on clear policy preferences. But when you read ethnographies or news reports about the people in question (or talk to them yourself), it is quite clear that they do have some ideas about what justice requires and some principles regarding how we ought to relate to one another.

The fact that many supporters of populism feel resentment at the self interest and corruption of elites, at being ignored in and excluded from social and political life, and at being unfairly treated indicates a commitment to some widely shared principles of impartiality, inclusion, and fairness. In this way, the moral expectations that can explain some of the support for populism point to the possibility of finding some common ground, which makes common deliberation possible.[80] Democratic societies should take advantage of these commitments and discuss their meaning and implications. To be sure, people are not resentful of the exact same things, and this is (at least partly) because they have different ideas about right and wrong. (It might also be because of different perceptions of the facts and causal relationships.) Democratic respect requires that citizens discuss their differences of principle and on this basis determine which claims should be heeded, rather than treating anyone as beyond the reach of reason and common deliberation.

It might be objected to my vindication of resentment that "the politics of resentment leads people to view their insecure circumstances as the fault of guilty and less deserving social groups, and self-serving elites who coddle them, not as the product of broad social, economic, and political forces."[81] This objection raises two issues: First, which groups are blamed in the politics of resentment, and second, should blame be directed at particular persons at all, or rather at broader "forces"? Now, we cannot say both that populist resentment is directed at the wrong group (say, immigrants rather than economic elites) and that we should not blame any particular group but rather focus on broader structural issues. I do not think there is any contradiction involved in discussing social, economic, and political structures as well as who is to blame for maintaining those structures. Democracy is the proposition that we can and should hold one another to account for the circumstances and structures within which we live and act. We are often mistaken regarding who is accountable for our circumstances, but this does not mean that we should not try to find out who is responsible for those circumstances and hold them to account. The idea of mutual accountability is central to the

---

[80] Arato and Cohen, *Populism and Civil Society*, 48.
[81] Cohen, "Populism," 9.

notion of democratic respect promoted in this book – and resentment at being ignored and trodden on is part of its ethos and practice.

The *politics* of resentment may be detrimental to democracy, but this does not mean that *resentment* is necessarily an undemocratic sentiment. That is, we should not let a justified criticism of the strategies of political leaders who exploit people's frustrations and anger turn into a criticism of people's justified resentments. Thus, I think it is a mistake to make a sharp contrast between addressing the concerns of populist voters "as free and equal citizens" on the one hand and as "pathological cases of men and women driven by frustration, anger, and resentment" on the other, as Jan-Werner Müller does in his influential book *What Is Populism?*[82] My analysis above shows that it is possible simultaneously to regard people as driven by resentment *and* as free, equal, and responsible citizens. When we view people with a participant attitude and as having principle-dependent feelings, we are not treating them as pathological cases, but rather as members of a shared moral community. People can have good reasons for their resentment, and resentment can be a reasonable reaction to unfair or disrespectful treatment.

Some scholars argue that resentment makes politics personal and turns attention away from the discussion of policy, which is what politics should be about.[83] It is true that resentment is often personal: It is "me" or "people like me" who the resentful person feels is/are treated unfairly and not respected. But democracy is also about such relational issues. Part of the justification of democracy is exactly that it is the only form of government that respects everyone as free and equal persons – and if it is failing in that respect, people are displaying a democratic sentiment by feeling resentment at how they are treated. But of course, not all feelings of resentment and disrespect can be explained and justified by democratic and egalitarian principles. (Nor is it Strawson's argument that reactive attitudes will always reflect a specific set of ideal principles, but only that in any human society people will have some set of moral expectations and reactions.[84]) My task in the following chapters will therefore be to provide some ideas that can contribute to a public discussion regarding which feelings of resentment can be rooted in democratic principles and which cannot, and hence when demands for recognition should be heeded and when they should not.

Before I turn to an explication of the participant attitude, let me say a word about how I connect recognition theory and Strawson. In short, I see them as both overlapping and complementary. They are overlapping

---

[82] Müller, *What Is Populism?*, 103.
[83] Müller, "Capitalism in One Family"; Weale, *Will of the People*, 114.
[84] Hieronymi, *Freedom, Resentment*, 25–9.

both in the centrality they give to recognition or interpersonal regard in social life and in interpreting the related emotions in moral and evaluative terms. Strawson can complement recognition theory with his fine-grained phenomenology of reactive attitudes and his notion of the participant attitude. Recognition theory can complement Strawson with its historical sensitivity and its more political focus on collective struggles. In relation to our analysis of populism, it is important to stress, as recognition theory does, that feelings of disrespect and resentment are not emotions that each person experiences on their own; rather, they are felt to be, and politically articulated as, shared with others.

1.3   The Participant Attitude

On the one hand, this book uses the participant attitude as an approach to political-theoretical argument, and on the other hand it promotes this attitude as a basic aspect of the democratic ethos among citizens in general. Laying the groundwork for subsequent chapters, the previous section used the participant attitude as a way to interpret the resentment and struggles of supporters of populism as expressions of distinctively moral reactions. These reactions entail claims or demands for interpersonal regard that we ought to discuss on their merits.

In relation to the notion of democratic respect, there are three aspects of the participant attitude in particular that I would like to highlight. First, the participant attitude is an attitude of involvement rather than detachment. When you take the participant attitude, you view yourself as an involved participant interacting with other participants. You are not detaching yourself from the practice of human relationships in order to explain, manipulate, or exploit them. You are simply regarding yourself as part of human interactions, as one participant among others. As an engaged participant in normal human relationships, you have certain expectations and reactions regarding how others see you and relate to you. To be sure, human beings also have and use the capacity for detachment, but the latter requires that they employ a special "resource" or ability – the ability to suspend the participant attitude in favor of the observer attitude.[85] Hence, it is the observer attitude that requires that we do something extraordinary. To view others as objects of benevolent treatment or strategic manipulation, or as movable by threats and rewards, requires that we detach ourselves from the participant attitude and take an observer attitude. It is part of the ethos of democratic respect,

---

[85] For a discussion of this "resource" or ability and why employing it cannot become the rule in human relationships, see Hieronymi, *Freedom, Resentment*, 18–35.

as I understand it, to see oneself as an involved participant among other participants, and it can harm democracy if the detached attitude of the observer becomes the rule in our political relationships.

Second, when we take the participant attitude, we view each other as responsible members of a moral community. Reactive attitudes are expressions of *moral* expectations and demands: They concern how we *ought* to relate to and regard each other. In a moral community, as mentioned, there are principles that regulate how members stand in relation to one another, and members hold one another responsible for complying with those principles. The participant attitude and its presumption of a moral community only imply that there are expectations and reactions based on common principles, not that these principles are ideal or democratic. Thus, the fact that people take a participant attitude toward one another does not mean that a community has ideal or valid common principles. The importance of the participant attitude is different: Participants view everyone involved as "a term of moral relationships,"[86] which is a necessary condition for discussing and finding shared principles for the community. Moreover, the idea of being part of a community points to the crucial issue of people's standing within this community and how they regard one another. These issues are essential for democratic respect, which has as a basic requirement that we view all involved as responsible members of a shared community with common principles.

Third, when we take the participant attitude, we presuppose that we can reason with other participants and influence them in this way, rather than only causing wanted behavior by subjecting others to external pressure and influence. In other words, the freedom and responsibility presupposed by the participant attitude includes the idea of reason-responsiveness. Participants view themselves as actors in the active and reflective sense of persons who deliberate about what to do and are capable of acting on reasons, rather than as bystanders who can only record their own preferences and behavior as if the latter were something that happened to them. Adopting the participant attitude, they see their own and others' actions as indications of the quality of their will, as something they have freely and reflectively decided to do, rather than as effects of external causes. This aspect is crucial both for democratic ideas of common deliberation and for the democratic norm of mutual accountability. Without presumptions of deliberate and deliberative action, public deliberation and accountability lose their meaning.

Now, it might be objected that many resentful people do not see the objects of their resentment in the way Strawson suggests. In response,

---

[86] Strawson, "Freedom and Resentment," 73.

I would like to make clear that the question is not what people actually believe about one another, but what makes their attitudes to one another *intelligible*.[87] Unless people presuppose certain things about the objects of their reactive attitudes, such as freedom, responsibility, and understanding, these attitudes become unintelligible, and their demands lose their point. It is simply meaningless and pointless to feel resentment toward and address demands to things that lack free will or understanding. Hence, the idea is that it does not make sense to feel resentment toward someone unless you presuppose that they can understand and respond appropriately to the demands you make on them.

When I propose that we use the Strawsonian framework and the participant attitude to understand supporters of populism, I am proposing that we approach their resentment as an intelligible demand to be treated differently. We can only ask the question of whether people's resentments are valid if we presuppose that they are not pathological or senseless, but are forms of moral address within a moral or political community. In other words, I suggest that we take a participant attitude to people's resentments, which means that we treat them as intelligible demands to be met with proper regard. I also propose that such an attitude toward other people is an essential aspect of a democratic culture and the spirit of democracy. Democracy requires that citizens, as a rule, view one another as free, equal, and responsible participants.[88] However, meeting other people's resentments and demands for recognition with a participant attitude and democratic respect does not mean that we have to accept their demands as legitimate, only that we consider and discuss their validity on their merits. Some resentments and demands for recognition are themselves not rooted in respect for others as free, equal, and responsible co-citizens.

1.3.1 Charity, Respect, and Racial Resentment

It is important not to confuse my approach, based on the Strawsonian participant attitude, with the charitable ethnography that we find, for example, in Cramer and Hochschild. This book is not an empirical study, and its contribution is not to generate new empirical findings. However, it is the aim of this book to listen to and engage with what followers of populism believe and say, with their grievances and demands (as these have been reported in other studies). Thus, there is an aspect of

---

[87] Darwall, *Second-Person Standpoint*, 24–5, 53–6, 74–9; Watson, "Responsibility," 122–4.

[88] I write "as a rule" because there are exceptions where we as democratic citizens can suspend the participant attitude and take the observer attitude.

charity – or better, respect – in my approach, insofar as it proceeds from the assumptions that people make intelligible demands for recognition and that they have reasons for their demands. However, the participant attitude approach does not assume that people's grievances and recognition demands are necessarily legitimate. Nor does the assumption that people have reasons for their feelings and demands mean that they have *good* reasons. What distinguishes my approach from Cramer's and Hochschild's is exactly that I discuss the validity of the demands made by supporters of populist politicians and parties.

Cramer sees her ethnographic approach as respectful of the people she met in Wisconsin because she *listened* to them, rather than going there to tell them "what is right and good."[89] Her study, she writes, "operate[s] on a belief that all people are, at root, good and deserving of respect."[90] The participant attitude approach and my understanding of respect shares the idea that we should listen to others, including those with whom we disagree. However, the notion of democratic respect that I defend in this book does not assume that people are at bottom good or that their claims are always valid. First, as I (in a Kantian vein) ague in Chapter 2, democratic respect is independent of whether or not we regard others as *good* persons (which is a matter of esteem). Respect is something we owe to others by virtue of their humanity, not their good qualities. Second, democratic respect does not exclude criticisms of other people's beliefs. It requires that we listen to others and seriously consider their claims before we decide on their validity. But it does not require that we refrain from expressing disagreement or engaging in critical dialogue. It is important for Cramer to stress that her method of listening "conveys respect" for the people she studies.[91] However, it is remarkable that she is not interested in the principled arguments her subjects might give for their political opinions, but only in their underlying feelings and identities. I find it more respectful to engage critically with people's reasons and principles, as fellow participants in democracy.

These points are especially relevant in relation to the issue of racial resentment, which clearly is part of the success of much right-wing populism, including Trump's in the United States.[92] Hochschild's study has

---

[89] Cramer, *Politics of Resentment*, 37, 40.

[90] Cramer, *Politics of Resentment*, 225.

[91] Cramer, *Politics of Resentment*, 40.

[92] On white racial resentment and the election of Trump, see Anderson, *White Rage*, 161–80. Mutz ("Status Threat," E4332) argues that the election of Trump can be explained partly by a "racial status threat," which "is not racism of the kind suggesting that whites view minorities as morally or intellectually inferior, but rather, one that regards minorities as sufficiently powerful to be a threat to the status quo."

been criticized in this respect for displacing the discussion of racialized inequality and for legitimizing the grievances of her white interlocutors. If the resentment and demands for recognition by white Tea Party and Trump supporters are based on a desire to protect racialized privileges, they are not making legitimate demands, as one critic of Hochschild emphasizes.[93] This criticism of Hochschild is based both on evidence that the white subjects of her study are not in fact the people who are worst-off (the African-American population in Louisiana is in general worse off) and on the moral premise that there is no legitimate claim for the protection of racialized privileges. It is exactly this kind of assessment of the legitimacy of the demands made by different groups that my focus on the moral experiences and principles behind people's feelings of resentment enables us to make. It is why I have stressed that people's resentments must be assessed in terms of whether *valid* principles have *actually* been violated.

In Chapter 2, I return to how populist resentment is based on demands for recognition of the superior status of one group, "the people," rather than on a principle of equal status for individual persons or citizens. Sometimes the identity and superiority of the people in populism is racialized, but it does not have to be. From the perspective of recognition theory, we should look at society as a normatively integrated order that assigns status and worth to individuals and groups. If the resentment of a group can be explained by its desire to protect its privileges under conditions of a changing recognition order, rather than by a commitment to equal treatment, it is clearly not a democratic sentiment that can be the basis of legitimate demands for recognition. Still, we should also avoid another pitfall, which is to suggest that because a group are privileged in one respect (as whites are in the United States), then none of their grievances or claims can be legitimate. In Chapter 3, I argue that populism is characterized by its application of the same division of society for all political purposes, as if the same two groups were respectively worse and better off in all respects. We should not apply the same logic to the claims of white groups, as if they were better off in all respects just because they belong to a group that is better off in one respect; rather, we should distinguish among their discrete claims and judge them separately on their merits. In order to show equal respect for everyone, we should consider particular political struggles for recognition and justice and discuss who is owed what in each case separately.

[93] For a criticism of Hochschild's lack of attention to racialized inequality and its relation to her charitable ethnography, see Bhambra, "Brexit, Trump, and 'Methodological Whiteness,'" 222–7.

1.4   Pragmatic versus Moral Responses

I should make clear that my primary concern in this book is not the possible pragmatic or instrumental value of showing people "respect" in order to avoid them lending their support to populist political leaders and parties. Some commentators seem to take such a pragmatic approach, as when Ash suggests that "only respect for the 'left behind' can turn the populist tide."[94] Whether or not respect for people who feel that they have been left behind, are strangers in their own land, or have low subjective social status will reduce support for populist leaders is an empirical question, and not one this study can definitively answer. Moreover, the trouble is that sometimes you can make people feel better about themselves and enhance their self-respect and self-esteem – two notions I shall distinguish later – by giving them something that they are *not* owed as equal citizens or persons. Hence, my question is not whether or how we can counteract populism by making people *feel* respected, but rather which demands for respect should be heeded *as a matter of principle* or on intrinsic grounds. The intrinsic grounds I have in mind are based on an understanding of democracy as "a society in which people are related to one another as social equals, as opposed to social inferiors or superiors."[95] More specifically, I shall understand "social equals" in terms of citizens being free and equal *participants*.

Crucially, we misunderstand the demand for recognition (respect and/or esteem) if we respond to it in a purely instrumental way, as a means to achieve a desirable state of affairs (here, a reduction of support for populism). If you display respect for someone *in order to* achieve a desirable state of affairs, you are not actually respecting them. You are treating them as a means rather than an end in themselves, violating one of Kant's formulations of the categorical imperative.[96] Similarly, if you praise someone in order to achieve some external end, this is not actually a form of esteem. There is something condescending and demeaning in treating both respect and esteem as means to a valuable end, which turns them into their opposites.[97] I turn to the difference between respect and esteem in Chapter 2, but here I stress that they are both forms of recognition that lose their meaning and value if they are treated as mere means. Thus, our question in this book is not the efficacy of recognition

---

[94] Ash, "Only Respect."
[95] Kolodny, "Rule Over None I," 196.
[96] Kant's formulation (*Groundwork*, 80, AK 4: 429) is: "So act that you use humanity, whether in your own person or in the person of any other, always at the same time as an end, never merely as a means." See also Hill, *Respect, Pluralism, and Justice*, 93.
[97] See Taylor, "Politics of Recognition," 68–70.

(respect and esteem) to combat populism, but rather the meaning and validity of different kinds of struggle and demand for recognition.

As argued above, resentment belongs to the participant attitude, where we hold one another responsible for our actions. The same is true of feelings of recognition and misrecognition, respect and disrespect, esteem and disesteem. When we view recognition, respect, or esteem as a *treatment* against populism, we are no longer taking the participant attitude toward others but adopting an "objective attitude" toward them, or as I prefer to put it, an "observer attitude" (to avoid the connotation that its opposite, the participant attitude, is merely subjective). Strawson describes the objective attitude as one where we treat other people precisely as objects of treatment, rather than as persons toward whom we can have reactive attitudes.[98]

Respecting or esteeming fellow citizens for the sake of a socially desirable goal such as reducing support for populist parties is not "the right kind of reason" for respect or esteem.[99] As Darwall puts it, "to be a reason of the right kind, a consideration must justify the relevant attitude in its own terms."[100] To respect or esteem someone with the aim of turning the populist tide is clearly not to respond to a demand for respect or esteem on its own terms. As we shall see, respect is a response to another person's status or standing, while esteem is a response to their merits, qualities, or character. Thus, recognition requires that we recognize the other person *because of* their status (respect) or merits (esteem); it cannot be a response to some other concern without ceasing to be a form of recognition.

For something to be the right kind of reason for recognition, it has to be capable of being shared and made public among participants. I return to the precise meaning and democratic significance of publicity in Chapter 6, but it should be clear enough that the only reason for respect and esteem that can be made public is that you actually respect and esteem the other. It is self-defeating publicly to announce that your reason for showing other people respect or esteem is the socially desirable consequences of doing so. In that case, no one will be or feel respected or esteemed.

To avoid misunderstanding, my point is not that pragmatic responses to populism can never be justified. My point is that such instrumentally conceived responses cannot properly be called forms of recognition,

---

[98] Strawson, "Freedom and Resentment," 66.
[99] Darwall, *Second-Person Standpoint*, 15–17, 120; Strawson, "Freedom and Resentment," 61–2.
[100] Darwall, *Second-Person Standpoint*, 16.

respect, or esteem. Supporters of populist parties may or may not have unfulfilled legitimate demands for recognition, and it is important to be able to understand and discuss the content and validity of their demands. Thus, my aim is to gain a better understanding of what populist demands for recognition are demands for, and to discuss whether and why they should be heeded. Gaining a better understanding of these issues is crucial for my thesis that we are witnessing a crisis of understanding of the normative requirements of democracy, as well as my aim to provide some conceptual clarifications in that regard. The first step here is to distinguish more clearly between respect and esteem, and to develop a notion of solidarity that is fit for a pluralistic society, which I do in Chapter 2.

2   Respect, Esteem, and Solidarity

In Chapter 1, I reported that there is a significant empirical literature that connects the rise of populism to widespread feelings of disrespect. On this basis, I argued that we can see populism as part of a struggle for recognition and make use of some of the resources of recognition theory. In addition, I argued that we should not understand feelings of resentment at a lack of recognition from the surrounding society as blindly emotional and unconnected to facts and judgment. Rather, the politics of resentment and struggles for recognition have their roots in a distinctively moral experience: the feeling that one is treated wrongly. If we can associate populist resentment with experiences of the violation of moral principles, we can ask what those principles are. That is, we can ask which principles populist demands for recognition are based on, and whether those principles are valid democratic principles. Hence, it is the aim of this chapter to distinguish between different kinds of demand for recognition and assess their validity in light of fundamental democratic principles.

Consider in this connection that the empirical and explanatory literature uses a variety of related but different terms to describe what supporters of populist parties crave and demand, including "respect," "honor," "status," and "positive social identity." Thus, we hear that populism's supporters "struggle to feel seen and honored"[1]; that they feel "overlooked, ignored, and disrespected"[2]; that they experience "status threat"[3]; that they express feelings of "low subjective social status"[4]; and that populist parties give "stigmatized groups a positive social identity [and a way to] maintain their self-respect."[5] All of these ideas relate to the struggle for recognition, but they are not all demands for the same

---

[1] Hochschild, *Strangers in Their Own Land*, 218.
[2] Cramer, *Politics of Resentment*, 40, cf. 52, 66, 105.
[3] Mutz, "Status Threat."
[4] Gidron and Hall, "Populism as a Problem."
[5] Spruyt, Keppens, and Van Droogenbroeck, "Who Supports Populism," 335–6.

thing, and they are not all demands that are compatible with what I call democratic respect.

A democracy, in Elizabeth Anderson's concise formulation, is "a community in which people stand in relations of equality to others."[6] This means that "citizens make claims on one another in virtue of their equality, not their inferiority [or superiority], to others."[7] Anderson suggests, moreover, that a democratic community in which "we collectively heed our mutual claims on one another in constructing rules and goals for those parts of our lives that we live in common with our fellow citizens ... embodies relations of mutual respect."[8] While the understanding of democratic respect promoted in this book agrees that we should pay attention to and consider all claims made by our fellow citizens, our question is about which claims can be made "in virtue of our equality" and which cannot.

Not all claims for respect, esteem, honor, and so forth are or can be made in virtue of our equality, and thus not all such claims are democratic. This point is overlooked if we understand resentment and recognition as purely emotional and psychological issues without connecting them to moral and democratic principles. Moreover, our question is not what makes people feel good about themselves, but what we owe to one another in a democracy understood as a society of free and equal participants. This question requires that we make finer distinctions between different kinds of recognition. Therefore, this chapter asks: What kinds of demand for recognition can citizens make on one another while honoring the ideal that they must stand in mutual relations of equality?

In answering this question, my approach is more Kantian than recognition theory tends to be. As I see it, recognition theory is more valuable for *explaining* struggles for recognition than it is for *normatively evaluating* different kinds of demand for recognition. Recognition theory is too concerned with what makes people feel good about themselves – what Honneth calls "a positive relation-to-self"[9] – and therefore fails to explain cases in which we do *not* owe people the recognition that secures this kind of psychological state. In other words, recognition theory is more concerned with psychological needs than with questions of justice – or it reduces the latter to a matter of fulfilling the former, which means that it treats every recognition deficit as a problem.[10] However, as I shall argue,

---

[6] Anderson, "What Is the Point," 289.

[7] Anderson, "What Is the Point," 289.

[8] Anderson, "Democracy," 220.

[9] Honneth, *Struggle for Recognition*.

[10] For a similar point, see McBride's (*Recognition*, 6–7, 115–19) criticism of what he calls "the recognition deficit model."

and as I suggest the case of populism shows, it is not always wrong for demands for recognition to go unfulfilled.

I cannot discuss the terminology used in all the different empirical studies; instead, I begin my analysis by highlighting a normatively important difference between respect and esteem. This distinction will help us to better understand what kinds of demand citizens can make on one another as free and equal participants in democracy. I argue that a democracy is a society of equality of respect, but that citizens cannot demand to be esteemed for their particular qualities or way of life. Still, inequality of esteem can be a moral problem because of its tendency to translate into inequality of respect. Therefore, we need a kind of solidarity that counteracts the ever-present danger that inequality of esteem might turn into inequality of respect. Along the way, I also discuss the concept of "honor," which among right-wing populists often is bound up with protection of hierarchical privileged standing, but which can be democratized in a modern understanding of dignity.

2.1   Respect versus Esteem

In everyday language, we use "respect" in two different ways.[11] First, we say that we respect someone for their merits or their character – for example, as an *excellent* teacher or a *good* person. I respect you for your hard work, your dedication, your good deeds, and the like. This use of "respect" entails appraisal, and to respect others in this sense is to praise or esteem their achievements. People may also seek – and others may supply – esteem for their particular way of life or culture, as good, admirable, and worthwhile. We esteem someone because of their success in meeting certain standards of excellence.

Second, we may respect someone for their position, standing, or status – for example, as a *teacher* or as a *person*. If a student respects someone *as their teacher*, or if I respect someone *as a person*, we are not praising their merits or achievements; we are recognizing their standing or status vis-à-vis us. I respect that you are the teacher, I respect that you are a person and not a thing, and the like. In this case, we recognize what the person *is* and not what they have done or achieved. This means that we are not applying any standards on which respect is conditional. Moreover, while the first kind of respect is always for something

---

[11] For different versions of this distinction, see Bird, "Status, Identity, and Respect"; Darwall, *Second-Person Standpoint*, 122–6; Darwall, "Two Kinds of Respect"; Jones, "Equality, Recognition and Difference"; McBride, *Recognition*; Runciman, "'Social' Equality."

particular or something that distinguishes one member of a genus from other members of it, respect in the second sense is for a property that is shared across everyone who belongs to the genus (all citizens or all human beings, for example).

For convenience of exposition, I shall refer to the first kind of respect as "esteem" and reserve the term "respect" for respect for status or standing. In short, esteem is merited by conduct or character, while respect can be demanded based on status or standing. I use "recognition" as a broader term that includes both respect and esteem.

Unfortunately, the key difference between esteem (for merits, character, and way of life) and respect (for status) goes unnoticed in the empirical literature on supporters of populism. For example, in the important work of Noam Gidron and Peter Hall, it is argued that supporters of populist parties are often people who "feel deprived of the roles and *respect* normally afforded to full members of [society]."[12] Elsewhere in the same article, they mention "the quest for *social esteem* as a crucial motivation for action,"[13] without mentioning the difference between respect and esteem. However, their examples concern what I call esteem rather than respect. Thus, they write that populism's supporters feel socially marginalized because of "the loss of a valued economic position or from the perception that cultural elites no longer attach value to one's views."[14] The latter is not about lack of respect for one's standing as a person or a citizen, but about lack of esteem for one's particular traits, achievements, or views. Gidron and Hall highlight the importance not of objective social status, but of the "*subjective social status* of citizens – defined as their beliefs about where they stand relative to others in society."[15] For our purposes, it is imperative to stress that where one feels one stands relative to others in society can be a matter of respect as well as of esteem, and that it makes an important normative difference whether it is one or the other.

Now, the failure to distinguish between respect and esteem might not (only) be a shortcoming in the empirical literature; it might also be a fact about many people's understandings and feelings of disrespect and lack of status. In a democracy as a society of equal and plural participants, I argue, it is absolutely crucial that we do not confuse lack of esteem for people's particular identity, achievements, or views with lack of respect for their equal standing as co-citizens. Later in the chapter, however,

---

[12] Gidron and Hall, "Populism as a Problem," 1028, emphasis added.
[13] Gidron and Hall, "Populism as a Problem," 1033, emphasis added.
[14] Gidron and Hall, "Populism as a Problem," 1031.
[15] Gidron and Hall, "Populism as a Problem," 1031, emphasis in the original.

I shall argue that disesteem cannot always be disentangled from disrespect, and that this fact calls for expressions and acts of solidarity with other citizens' particular (legitimate) ends, identities, and cultures.

As several philosophers have pointed out, respect for persons (and for other forms of status, such as citizenship) is something that conceptually and in principle can be equally demanded by everyone, while esteem for merits or qualities cannot be so.[16] To take the latter first, it simply makes no sense to demand equality of praise or esteem. As W. G. Runciman put it some time ago, "universal equality of praise is equivalent to no praise at all."[17] We seek praise and esteem for what is *particular* about us, and not for what is universally shared. Esteem involves making distinctions between better and worse. Moreover, being praised gets its meaning and value from being recognized as *deserving* praise – from being regarded as having *done* something that merits esteem. There is no value in being praised for one's efforts, merits, or character if everyone can *demand* to be equally praised just by virtue of their equality and independently of anything they have done.

To turn to "respect for persons," this has historically not always been an egalitarian idea.[18] However, since the enlightenment and with Kant, "respect for persons" has come to be understood in universalistic and egalitarian terms, and with many hard-fought struggles for recognition, we are approaching a situation where everyone (all human beings) will have come to equally enjoy the status of being a person, at least in principle. (Or at any rate, many have come to understand and appreciate the idea of respect for persons as an egalitarian idea, even if its realization falls short.) In contrast to esteem, respect is something that a person can demand independently of anything they have done; they simply have to *be* a person. Respect differs from esteem "in that it can be mandated and not just warranted by its object."[19] I can demand that you respect me as a person, but not that you evaluate my achievements positively. Thus, the demand for respect for one's status or one's personhood (or humanity or citizenship) is a demand that intelligibly can be a demand for equality. Status can be (demanded to be) equalized, while praise or esteem cannot.

Above, I said that esteem is something we can show for people's merits, character, or achievements. I also said that we can esteem people

---

[16] Bird, "Status, Identity, and Respect"; Darwall, "Two Kinds of Respect"; Jones, "Equality, Recognition and Difference," 32; Runciman, "'Social' Equality."

[17] Runciman, "'Social' Equality," 223; see also Barry, *Culture and Equality*, 270.

[18] Bird, "Status, Identity, and Respect"; Darwall, "Respect as Honor"; Green, "Two Worries."

[19] Darwall, *Second-Person Standpoint*, 120.

for their culture, way of life, and identity. But does it make sense to speak of culture and identity as achievements and objects of praise or esteem? The notion of "identity" is especially tricky here. Some might say that identity is not an achievement, but something people just have or are ascribed – by themselves or others (think of ethnic or sexual identity, for example). But people often do think of the identities that are connected to their culture or way of life as objects of appraisal, and as deserving of esteem. They might think, for example, of their religious or occupational identity as something for which they are owed esteem – as based on a good and worthwhile religion or occupation. I do not think it is a mistake to think of cultures and the identities connected to them as objects of appraisal – and as such of esteem and disesteem. Cultures are achievements and can be appraised as good and worthwhile, or not. My point, rather, is that esteem for cultures and cultural identities is not something anyone can *demand* in virtue of their equality as citizens or as a requirement of what I call democratic respect. To put it differently, esteem is not what we owe to one another in virtue of democratic equality.

I have argued that esteem by its very nature cannot be equal and for this reason is not something people can demand of one another in a democracy. When we turn to issues of culture and identity, which are so prominent in contemporary political struggles, then we should also note that we cannot demand esteem for these from others. If I do not share your culture – for example, your religion – I am not doing anything wrong in not praising or valuing it. Indeed, it would be wrong of you to demand that I do so, because it would be equivalent to demanding that I give up my own religion or culture.[20] In other words, demands for esteem of one's culture cannot be reciprocal, and they thus violate a fundamental requirement of democratic respect.

Perhaps society can be criticized for having too narrow an idea of what can constitute a valuable form of life. Moreover, it might be said that we do not always have to give up our own culture or ideas of the good life in order to appreciate that other people's forms of life can also be worthwhile. I think that is true, but I do not think it contradicts the point that people cannot demand of one another that they mutually esteem each other's forms of life. Some forms of life cannot be esteemed equally by those who are committed to them, such as the life of the deeply religious person and the life of the atheist. Neither of these persons treats the other wrongly by not being able to praise or find value in the other's life.

---

[20] See Rostbøll, "Impartiality, Deliberation, and Multiculturalism."

2.1.1 Kant and Dignity Respect

The distinction between respect and esteem outlined above is only formal and does not say anything substantive about what is involved in the status that is to be respected or the excellences that should be esteemed. For our purposes, it is not necessary to say anything about the excellences to be esteemed,[21] but I need to indicate what I mean by "respect for persons," which is central for democracy. While I cannot provide anything like a theory of respect for persons, I will mention some core aspects of the idea, beginning with Kant but also adding some further ideas.

In the Kantian tradition, "respect" is something that one can demand because of one's status *as a person*. A person is something that by its very nature is "an end in itself" and "may not be used merely as a means," writes Kant.[22] A person "is exalted above any price" and "possesses a *dignity* (an absolute inner worth) by which he exacts *respect* for himself by all other rational beings in the world. He can measure himself with every other being of this kind and value himself on a footing of equality with them."[23] I interpret Kant's idea that a person is above any price and can demand ("exact") respect from us as meaning that other people have an authority in relation to us that is independent of any appraisal of their merits on our part. In other words, Kantian respect does not depend on esteem. We owe respect to other persons simply because of their standing as persons, their dignity.[24]

The standing grounded in dignity is not just the standing of not being subject to ill-treatment; more importantly, it is the standing of someone who has *the right to make demands* in their relations with others. "Dignity" is the name for the authority to demand certain actions of others in relation to oneself and our common world, as well as the standing to demand respect for this very authority.[25]

Kantian dignity respect, then, concerns how we perceive and relate to others. It is fundamentally about regarding others as beings capable of thinking and acting on the basis of reasons, as persons who can make up their own minds on a rational basis, and whom we should therefore treat as such by engaging with them through arguments rather than force.

---

[21] In a democracy we do not need to agree on what constitutes a good and worthwhile life or the excellences connected to this question. However, we do need to agree on the excellences or virtues that are required for the ideal of democratic respect. Hence, I focus on the meaning of respect for persons and dignity respect that are part of that ideal.

[22] Kant, *Groundwork*, 79 (AK 4: 428).

[23] Kant, *Metaphysics of Morals*, 557 (AK 6: 434–5).

[24] See Hill, *Respect, Pluralism, and Justice*, 87–118.

[25] Anderson, "Democracy," 220; Darwall, *Second-Person Standpoint*, 13–14, 121; Rostbøll, "Autonomy, Respect, and Arrogance," 632–3.

Kantians often say that this entails viewing others as *autonomous* beings, which means seeing them as free and responsible beings who can give – and act on the basis of – reasons and principles.

Showing respect for dignity is not just a matter of including certain facts about others in one's deliberations about how to treat them, as an observer might do; it is a matter of relating to them as fellow participants in a community where the members hold one another accountable. When persons respect one another's authority to make claims on each other's conduct, they hold each other mutually accountable. This means that demands for dignity respect cannot be unilateral: One cannot demand respect without respecting the other, and one cannot hold the other accountable in a respectful way without making oneself equally accountable. Note that we are not just saying that demands for respect ought not to be unilateral; we are saying that respect cannot be had or shown without mutual accountability. Mutual accountability is *constitutive of* dignity respect. As Darwall writes, "we respect one another ... by making ourselves mutually accountable."[26] I add that this requires that we regard ourselves as having the standing of fellow participants in a community where we hold one another mutually accountable.

In the political domain, citizens are respected as autonomous and mutually accountable when the political process "publicly address[es] each citizen as someone capable of joining in public discussion [and] solicit[s] the participation of every citizen as a potential agent of political decision."[27] We do not just respect others by refraining from engaging in certain acts toward them; in a democracy, we respect them by inviting them to express their opinions, by engaging with their ideas and arguments, and by counting their votes. Dignity respect is not only about our standing as subjects of law; just as importantly, it is also about our equal standing as *authors of law*. The political process fails in terms of democratic respect if it gives to some a lawgiving standing that it fails to provide equally to all citizens. I want in particular to highlight that our political culture fails in terms of dignity respect if citizens in their interactions fail to solicit the participation of everyone equally. Democratic respect, as I understand it, requires that we invite each other in and encourage everyone's participation in matters of common concern.

We see here that showing respect for others requires taking what in Chapter 1 I called a participant attitude. People who respect one another regard each other with a participant attitude of mutual accountability, rather than an observer attitude where one sees others as determined

---

[26] Darwall, "Respect as Honor," 14.
[27] Richardson, *Democratic Autonomy*, 63.

by external causes and aims to explain or manipulate them in ways that disregard their standing as autonomous beings.

For respect to be had, it must be shown. But how do we show one another respect? It might be argued that how we show respect for one another is socially and culturally dependent – different times and different cultures have different ways of expressing respect, even respect for equality. Yet clearly there are some cases that we can agree are expressions of disrespect within a given time and place: For example, no one could sincerely and reasonably deny that segregation in the United States was a sign of disrespect for Black people.[28] Other cases are more difficult – for example, whether caricatures of the Prophet Muhammad in contemporary Europe show respect or disrespect for Muslims, to take a much-discussed case that I have written about elsewhere.[29]

Rather than explicating concrete guidelines for how persons show respect for one another, I have made the more abstract suggestion that we express respect for others by treating them as fellow participants and authorities in common deliberation. This understanding of respect includes the possibility of recursively discussing disagreements on exactly what should be taken as disrespectful treatment.[30] The key to being treated with respect is being listened to and included as a fellow participant in discussions of issues of common concern, including discussions of what is of common concern and what it means to be treated with equal respect. Thus, we express respect for others in action by soliciting their participation, considering everyone's claims equally, and treating them as fellow authorities in common deliberation. We fail to respect others not only when we fail to listen to their concerns, but also when we address them in ways that discourage their political participation, and when we treat them as having nothing of value to contribute to discussions of common concern.

Earlier, I said that respect does not depend on esteem. This is important for understanding the standing and rights people have in relation to one another in a democracy, as I see it, because it means that we do not need to evaluate other people's merits, character, or culture in order to respect them as equals. The respect we owe to each other as citizens and the respect the state owes us is unconditional. As Habermas writes, "the right to equal respect, which everyone can demand [...,] has nothing to do with the presumed excellence of his or her culture."[31] Indeed, the

---

[28] Green, "Two Worries," 228.
[29] Rostbøll, "Autonomy, Respect, and Arrogance."
[30] Benhabib, *Claims of Culture*, 12–13, 181; Rostbøll, "Freedom of Expression," 12–13; "Use and Abuse," 416–20.
[31] Habermas, "Struggles for Recognition," 129.

idea of mutual respect is endangered if it becomes entangled or conflated with the idea of esteem for merits or ways of life. Esteem by its very nature requires discrimination and the assessment of better and worse, which is foreign to and undermines the egalitarian Kantian notion of respect for persons. If we make respect dependent on esteem, there is a danger that we will only respect what we actually find praiseworthy. Since society cannot meaningfully assess the acts, characters, and cultures of all citizens as equally praiseworthy, the demand for esteem actually turns out to be a demand for discrimination rather than equality.[32]

Nothing I have said indicates that people should not be free to struggle to be esteemed for their merits, character, or culture. I have only argued that they cannot *demand* such esteem from others, and that no one, including the government, has a duty to distribute esteem equally. Note here that when people demand to be equally considered for their merits in some sphere where this makes sense, this is not a demand for equal esteem, but a demand for equal status in a competition that can have an unequal outcome. Thus, one can complain about being unfairly treated if one's efforts and merits are not considered on equal terms with others' efforts and merits in areas where this makes sense. But this is best understood as a complaint about not being respected as an equal, not as a complaint about not being equally esteemed.

It might be objected that while society cannot esteem all ways of life equally, it can accept that a plurality of ways of life has value. To do the latter, a society would not have to make discriminations between better and worse forms of life but could regard different ways of life as incommensurable. This objection could take the form of a Berlinian value pluralism according to which there are many forms of value and these cannot be compared or put into a hierarchy.[33] While I agree that a society can accept that many different forms of life have value, I want to make the following observations. To accept incommensurability is to accept that there is no common standard according to which we can esteem ways of life. Thus, on this view, it also does not make sense to speak of equal esteem of different ways of life. Indeed, I am unsure if it makes sense to say that people esteem one another across incommensurable ways of life. The idea that there are many valuable forms of life is a different idea than esteem, and the expression of the former idea accomplishes something different than what we have discussed under the heading of esteem. Moreover, while some aspects of a way life might be incommensurable because they refer to different standards of

---

[32] Offe, "'Homogeneity' and Constitutional Democracy," 135.
[33] Berlin, "Two Concepts of Liberty," 167–72.

excellence or goodness, other aspects refer to common standards. That living in a small town is good for some does not exclude the possibility that living in the city is good for others, but the belief that God created the world does exclude atheism, and the political opinion that the right thing to do is to close the borders excludes the opposing view that justice requires a more open asylum and immigration policy.

2.1.2   The Good, the Right, and Toleration

The distinction between esteem and respect is connected to another important distinction in neo-Kantian theory, namely that between the good and the right.[34] I am concerned with questions of "the good" when I ask what constitutes a happy and fulfilling life for me or for us (people like me). Thus, questions of the good arise from within the first-person perspective of an individual person or a "we." I am concerned with questions of "the right" when I ask how I should conduct myself in relation to others, and how a plurality of persons should stand in relation to one another. Questions of "the right," then, concern how a plurality of persons, each of whom has their own conception of the good, should conduct themselves and stand in relation to one another. The right is what I have called a relational or second-personal issue, while "the good" is first-personal. We might say that issues of esteem relate to the good, while issues of respect (for status) are issues of right (or justice). The significance of the distinction is that it requires that people differentiate the issue of what is good for them (individually or as a cultural group) from what is right for them *in relation to others* who might not share their understanding of the good and fulfilling life.[35]

The distinction between questions of the good life and questions of right or justice is essential to make sense of the meaning and practice of toleration.[36] To understand this, consider that the concept of toleration is characterized by three components. (1) *Objection*: A belief or practice

---

[34] For the distinction between the right and the good, as well as the idea that the right has priority over the good in his own theory, see Rawls, *Theory of Justice*, 21–30. Habermas (*Between Facts and Norms*, 94–9) draws a similar distinction between "the moral" and "the ethical."

[35] Habermas ("Reply to Symposium Participants," 393, emphases in the original) argues that what matters in public deliberation is the perspective taken by participants: "Each participant must turn away from the *ethical* question of which regulation is respectively 'best for us' from 'our' point of view. They must, instead, take the *moral* point of view and examine which regulation is 'equally good for all' in view of the prior claim to an equal right to coexist."

[36] According to Forst ("'To Tolerate Means to Insult,'" 232), the distinction between individual ethical beliefs about the good life and moral norms that everyone must accept "may be the greatest achievement within the discourse of toleration."

must be regarded as objectionable before we can speak of tolerating it. We do not say that we "tolerate" beliefs that we affirm or to which we are indifferent. (2) *Acceptance*: When we tolerate a practice, it is because there are certain moral reasons that trump the reasons for objection. These reasons for acceptance require that we accept the practice, without making us agree with it. (3) *Rejection*: Any conception of toleration involves a specification of its limits. This is the case because the normative reasons for acceptance will simultaneously entail reasons for rejection. For example, if the reason for acceptance is grounded in a norm of equal respect, this entails a rejection of practices that violate the norm of equal respect.[37] The distinction between the good and the right helps to explain how we at one and the same time can object to something and nevertheless have reasons to accept it. Reasons of objection concern the good, while reasons of acceptance and rejection concern the right. I can object to your notion of the good life while still accepting your right to live according to it. But if the practice of your conception of the good violates principles of right, I have reason to reject it as intolerable.

Of course, the distinction between the good and the right does not solve the substantial problem of which practices should be tolerated and which practices are beyond the limits of toleration. These substantial problems depend on a theory of right or justice.[38] Nevertheless, the distinction between the good and the right, like that between esteem and respect, is necessary for understanding the possibility of the discourse and practice of toleration and mutual respect. In practices of toleration, "the attitude of respect overrides our negative esteem judgment and restrains us from acting on that judgment," as Cillian McBride succinctly puts it.[39]

2.2   Honor Respect

Above I mentioned that the idea of "respect for persons" has not always been an egalitarian idea. It only became so during the enlightenment and with Kant. Yet it is important to stress that respect for standing or status (and not just esteem) *can be and still is* also used in an inegalitarian and hierarchizing manner. As I have emphasized in the distinction between respect and esteem, the former is independent of particular merits and achievements, and it *can* be a demand for treatment as an

---

[37] Rostbøll, "Compromise and Toleration," 27.
[38] According to Forst ("Limits of Toleration"), the three components characterize the *concept*, but there are different *conceptions* of toleration that specify the reasons for the three components in different ways because of different normative theories. Thus, a conception of toleration is normatively dependent on a theory of justice.
[39] McBride, *Recognition*, 52.

equal. Nonetheless, "respect for status" can be both for the status of the other as an equal and for the other's status as a superior. In relation to populism, it is of particular interest to understand and interrogate the widespread use of "honor" and "status" in the empirical literature on its supporters. Thus, when commentators explain support for populist politicians or parties in terms of feelings of disrespect, dishonor, and loss of status, we should consider two different questions. First, are the people in question demanding esteem for their merits and culture, or are they demanding respect for their status? Second, if it is the latter, are they demanding respect for their status as equals, or as superiors?

When Hochschild, for example, speaks of the experience of "honor squeezes" among the Tea Party and Trump supporters that she studies, this seems to include aspects of both a lack of esteem for their achievements and a disrespect for their status.[40] The perceived lack of esteem from the surrounding society that she reports concerns, for example, a lack of esteem for their hard work, self-reliance, and moral character. The loss of respect for status connects to issues of belonging to a social group – such as white people or Christians – that has lost its privileged standing in the social hierarchy.

I would like to call attention to the idea that while "honor" under some circumstances may be psychologically connected to esteem, and while contemporary societies still give public "honors" for excellence, there is also a use of "honor" that is connected to a form of respect for status, which is independent of esteem. In order to understand "honor respect," as distinct from both esteem and dignity respect, consider how "respect for persons" is used – speaking in simplified and ideal-typical terms – in aristocratic societies.[41] Respecting someone in the honor culture of *l'ancien régime* was about bestowing on them a higher status or rank in the hierarchy.[42] Honor respect, in this usage, acknowledges and creates orders of rank. Honor here, by definition, is something that not everyone can have. As Montesquieu wrote in the mid-eighteenth century, "the nature of *honor* is to demand preferences and distinctions."[43] In this regard, honor is like esteem: They both respond to (perceived) differences.

The traditional idea of honor may be understood as one where what we have called respect and esteem are not clearly differentiated; it is a blend of the two. Thus, the honor showed to the nobility was simultaneously a form of respect and esteem.[44] However, the traditional idea of honor

---

[40] Hochschild, *Strangers in Their Own Land*, 215–18.
[41] In the following, I draw on Darwall, "Respect as Honor."
[42] Taylor, "Politics of Recognition," 26–7.
[43] Montesquieu, *Spirit of the Laws*, 27, emphasis in the original.
[44] Honneth, "Redistribution as Recognition," 140–1.

differs from esteem insofar as it is not something one can merit or earn: It is not something that is deserved by its object, but something that some people can *demand* from other people. This is why we distinguish aristocracy from meritocracy. In an honor culture, who is owed honor respect is socially constituted, in the sense that it is dependent on actual social relations and on who manages to attain honor respect from whom.[45]

My suggestion is that we should further explore the possibility that in the reported feelings of loss of status and honor among some supporters of right-wing populism, we find vestiges of an honor culture that differs in normatively important ways from both lack of esteem and lack of egalitarian dignity respect. That is, we should examine the possibility that some people turn to populist parties not because they are not praised for their achievements or have lost their status as equals, but rather because they have lost or fear losing some form of superior and privileged status in the social hierarchy.

For example, when some white people feel resentment about being disrespected and losing status, this can be understood as an issue of loss of honor respect for their "status" as whites – a loss of their racialized privileges.[46] As shown by law professor Cheryl Harris, whiteness has traditionally constituted a superior status in American culture and law, and some feel that they have to protect this status against cultural and legal changes.[47] Similarly, Joel Anderson argues that in much of US history, "white identity functioned as a form of racialized *standing* that granted all whites a superior social status to all those who were not white," and that the loss of this standing "due to the victories of the civil rights movement ... led to anger, anxiety, and resentment among many whites, and a desire to restore that standing."[48] The same may be said about being heterosexual, Christian, and a man in many countries. Being white, heterosexual, Christian, and a man are regarded as forms of status when one sees them as providing special privileges and honors that others, including the government, should respect. Populists often provide a kind of protection for the privileged status of their followers.[49]

---

[45] Darwall, "Respect as Honor," 11, 16, 28–9.

[46] Bhambra, "Brexit, Trump, and 'Methodological Whiteness,'" 227. See also Mutz ("Status Threat"), who provides evidence that Trump's election victory in 2016 can partly be explained by a feeling of "racial status threat" among white Americans.

[47] Harris, "Whiteness as Property."

[48] Olson, "Whiteness," 704, emphasis in the original. Gest, Reny, and Mayer ("Roots of the Radical Right," 1698–9) argue that a similar racial politics can be found in the European context.

[49] In a recent article, Smith and King ("White Protectionism in America") have shown how Trump's rhetoric and policies articulate a vision of white protectionism.

These forms of status are obviously not forms of status as an equal to everyone else in society, and recognition of them is recognition of superiority. Honor respect, as understood here, then, contributes to rank-ordering rather than equality. In a democracy as a community where people stand in relations of equality with one another, claims made in virtue of alleged superiority in status clearly have no legitimate place.

Our brief discussion of honor respect suggests that for a demand for recognition to be democratic, it is not sufficient that it be a demand for respect for status (rather than esteem for merits); it must also be made in virtue of one's equality with all other members of society – and all other human beings in society must be regarded as members. In a word, while respect for status can be an egalitarian and democratic norm, it is not necessarily so.

In contrast to a loss of honor respect, when people feel that they are being overlooked and ignored and that political elites are "not listening to what [they] have to say,"[50] or when they "struggle to feel seen"[51] and feel "that they have been pushed to the fringes of their national community and deprived of the roles and respect normally accorded to full members of it,"[52] these feelings can be understood in terms of a lack of respect for their status as equals – for example, as citizens or persons. Demands to be paid attention to, listened to, considered, and regarded as a full member of society are all demands that can be made in virtue of one's equality, and as directed to others as sharing an equal standing in the community. In short, these are demands people can make *as persons* or *as equal citizens*, or as I prefer to put it, *as free and equal participants in democracy*.

By merely observing people's feelings of disrespect or their struggles for recognition, we cannot know what exactly they are missing and demanding – or what populist politicians supply. There are at least three possibilities, which I have explained in this section. First, the people in question may feel a lack of and demand esteem for their merits and ways of life (esteem). Second, they may miss and demand respect for their standing as equals (democratic dignity respect). Third, they may feel they have lost and demand the restoration of respect for their status as superiors (aristocratic honor respect). While in a democracy we can demand respect from one another, we will go wrong if we do not differentiate between these very different kinds of demand. In a pluralistic society where we respect the fact that people value different forms of life, we cannot demand that others esteem our cultural particularities. And in a society of equals, we cannot demand honor respect that upholds

---

[50] Cramer, *Politics of Resentment*, 40, 52.
[51] Hochschild, *Strangers in Their Own Land*, 144.
[52] Gidron and Hall, "Populism as a Problem," 1028.

hierarchies of rank. The respect that we can demand from one another in a democracy must be compatible with mutuality and equality.

In the analysis above, I have focused on supporters of *right-wing* populist parties to the exclusion of an analysis of left-wing populism and its supporters. This focus raises two questions. (1) Are the issues I have raised concerning esteem and honor really about (support for) populism, or rather about (support for) far-right ideology, notably ethnonationalism and the protection of racialized privileges? (2) Does the preceding analysis and discussion have any relevance for the evaluation of left populism? First, I do think that it matters for the kind of esteem and honor respect that supporters seek that the parties in question are not just far-right parties but also make populist claims. When supporters are referred to as "the real people," they feel both that they can be proud of their way of life and collective identity (esteem) and that they have a *special* standing in the polity (honor respect). The populist claims, moreover, justify these feelings and demands *as democratically legitimate*.

Next, as I aim to show in Chapter 3, it is inherent to populism, as a set of claims and a logic, that it must provide esteem for the collective identity of one group to the exclusion of other groups. As left populists such as Laclau and Mouffe also accept, the populist articulation of the people homogenizes an otherwise diverse group in order to create the collective identity of "the people."[53] Moreover, all forms of populism, left and right, entail that only some citizens have the standing and legitimacy of the people who should rule. This does not mean that there are no differences between left and right populism, or that they are equally exclusionary. Host ideologies do make a difference, and some of the arguments above would have to be adjusted to fit left populism. However, my contention is that all forms of populism provide esteem and honor respect for one group in society in ways that are incompatible with the democratic norm of awarding equal respect for the dignity of each and every citizen.

2.2.1   Democratizing Honor

I have submitted that the hierarchical notion of honor may not have entirely disappeared from contemporary struggles for recognition. Some people feel resentment not just at being treated as inferiors but also at

---

[53] Laclau ("Populism," 157) describes the logic of populism as "homogenising." See also Chapters 3 and 6 in this volume.

having lost – or at fearing losing[54] – the honor and respect that comes with socially constituted superior standing. We will now consider another way in which the older notion of honor is still with us.

According to Jeremy Waldron, the older notions of rank and honor have not been obliterated by the modern notions of dignity and respect. Rather, the resources of the older ideas are put to work in the new ideas. Like the older idea of high rank, the modern idea of dignity, which emerged in the late eighteenth century, conveys ideas such as authority and deference, as well as the prohibition of humiliating and degrading treatment. Thus, Waldron's hypothesis is that "the modern notion of *human* dignity involves an upwards equalization of rank, so that we now try to accord to every human being something of the dignity, rank, and expectation of respect that was formerly accorded to nobility."[55] In other words, what we respect, and the way we are supposed to respect the dignity of every human person today, is comparable to how people were formerly supposed to respect or honor the high rank of the nobility.[56] What has changed with the modern idea of human dignity is not so much how we show respect – although that has changed as well – but that respect is now something that is owed to everyone in virtue of their humanity.

Waldron's account agrees with the idea that respect is for someone's status – the normative status expressed in the idea of human dignity. Moreover, his compelling story can explain why everyone today has the normative expectation of being treated as having a *high* status or rank. The demand for respect is a demand not just to be treated as equal to everybody else, but to be treated as of *equal and high* rank. The upward equalization of rank expressed in the idea of human dignity entails an extension of formerly high-status treatment to every human person.

Waldron's hypothesis is relevant for our discussion of the supposed feeling of "honor squeeze" and "status threat" among populism's supporters. This feeling can be seen as a feeling of loss of the respect and deference from others required by the enjoyment of high rank. Waldron's story suggests that the feeling of lack of respect for high rank can refer either to a high rank that is enjoyed by one sector of the population only or to a high rank that has been universalized to include everyone. To be sure, some people might feel that if everyone is included in the high rank,

---

[54] Mutz ("Status Threat," E4338) argues that Trump's election victory can be explained by high-status groups' fear of losing their dominant position in society: The election was "an effort by members of already dominant groups to assure their continued dominance."

[55] Waldron, "Dignity and Rank," 33.

[56] Waldron ("Dignity and Rank," 34) takes this idea from Vlastos ("Justice and Equality," 54), who writes that "first-class citizenship [has] been made common [and established] a 'rank of dignity' in some ways comparable to that enjoyed by hereditary nobilities of the past."

then it is no longer a high rank. However, the idea expressed by the idea of human (as opposed to aristocratic) dignity is exactly that high status can be awarded to everyone and remain a high status or rank. It is the idea that "we all look up to each other from a position of upright equality."[57] The point is that the feeling of lack of respect is similar, while from a normative point of view it matters greatly whether the complaint concerns a lack of deference for a higher rank reserved for some or a lack of deference for a status and authority shared equally by everyone.

Similarly to Waldron, Honneth writes that "the premodern concept of honor," which assured honor by hierarchy, today has been "*democratized* by according all members of society equal respect for their dignity and autonomy as legal persons."[58] Perhaps what is required in the current situation is not so much to overcome or ridicule people's sense of honor, then, but to democratize and equalize it. People who have a sense of honor will demand to be treated with respect and will feel resentment at being treated with disrespect. Whether or not this sense of honor serves democratic ends will depend on the "honor code" they adhere to, that is, who they believe has honor (only some, or everyone equally) and what this means for how they ought to be treated. Honor codes are not necessarily moral or egalitarian, but they can be transformed to be so.[59] Thus, if we can democratize the honor code and turn people's desire for honor into a demand to be treated not just as of high but also as of equal rank, we will have met an important challenge in contemporary struggles for recognition.

2.3   Democratic Respect in the Real Word Requires Solidarity

Shortly before the 2020 US election, the sociologist Richard Sennett explained the strong support for Donald Trump through the notion of a "zero-sum game" of honor, of which he and Jonathan Cobb had "glimpsed the origins" fifty years before among the white working class in Boston, Massachusetts.[60] This zero-sum game entails the idea that "to affirm the honor of our group, we have to denigrate the honor of your group."[61] Similarly, in his 2003 book *Respect in a World of Inequality*,

---

[57] Waldron, "Law, Dignity, and Self-Control," 60.

[58] Honneth, "Redistribution as Recognition," 141, emphasis added.

[59] For the notion of "honor code," and for an argument that the quest for honor can also serve laudable moral ends and effects, see Appiah, *Honor Code*. See also Krause's *Liberalism with Honor*, which argues that honor is an important motivational source of political agency and can have egalitarian effects.

[60] Sennett, "Even if Donald Trump Loses"; Sennett and Cobb, *Hidden Injuries of Class*.

[61] Sennett, *Respect*, 55.

Sennett describes the predicament of contemporary society as one of "scarcity of respect," and he writes that we interact "as though there were not enough of this precious substance to go around."[62] On the one hand, Sennett says that contemporary society singles out "only a few for recognition,"[63] and on the other hand, he implies that the fight for respect does not have to be a zero-sum game.

The distinction between respect and esteem, which is absent from Sennett's analysis, shows that recognition as esteem might indeed be a zero-sum game, while recognition as respect for status *can* be mutual and egalitarian. A group can in principle attain respect for their status as citizens or human beings without denigrating other groups. Indeed, while the attainment of esteem requires the outdoing of others, respect in the Kantian sense requires equality and mutuality. Yet Sennett's work also shows how difficult it can be, in a class society and a world of inequality, to equally respect "those destined to remain weak,"[64] and that people often feel they have to struggle to prove their worthiness of respect from others.[65] In other words, Sennett's work suggests that under some social conditions, equal respect for dignity cannot be separated from the struggle for esteem for one's achievements and contribution to society.

The conclusion of our earlier discussion was that the type of equality that characterizes a democratic society is equality of respect rather than equality of esteem. In a democracy, people can demand to be respected as equal persons and citizens, but not to be equally esteemed for their merits, character, or way of life. In this section, I want to argue that even if we accept this conclusion, as I think we should, inequality of esteem can still be a moral problem, and it is not something that contemporary democratic societies can simply ignore.[66] When inequality of esteem takes a form and reaches a degree that threatens equal respect, our ideal of democratic respect requires that state and civil society respond and act in solidarity with those who struggle to be respected as equal participants in society. This means that we must go beyond the idea that the norm of respect calls only for acceptance of and noninterference with difference, and that we must include among our democratic obligations – make part of our democratic ethos and recognition order – some kind of positive concern that people's (legitimate) ways of life should not stand in the way of recognition of (respect for) their equal standing and participation in society.

---

[62] Sennett, *Respect*, 3.
[63] Sennett, *Respect*, 3.
[64] Sennett, *Respect*, 263.
[65] Sennett and Cobb, *Hidden Injuries of Class*, 27, 30, 246.
[66] On this point, see also Fourie, "To Praise and to Scorn."

The question is what kind of concern we can show for others' ways of life while still being true to democratic equality and mutual respect.

The Strawsonian idea of the participant attitude and the Kantian notion of respect are both relational notions. That is, they concern how people stand in relation to one another and how they treat one another. Thus, the ideal of taking a participant attitude to others and the ideal of mutual respect already presuppose some kind of shared community. We are participants in a shared community with shared norms, and we respect one another as members of this community. I want now to argue that these ideas already point to an idea of solidarity as a form of mutual concern for the inclusion of others.[67] In other words, the idea of solidarity that I promote in what follows is normatively grounded in the idea of mutual respect among equal participants. However, solidarity is not just another word for mutual respect. It is something like the cultural, political, and social advancement and performance of equal respect. Thus, I see solidarity as a response to the real-world difficulties of actually realizing a society in which people respect each other as equals. In particular, solidarity is a response to the ever-present danger that inequality of esteem might transform into inequality of respect.

2.3.1   Inequality of Esteem and Solidarity

When Sennett writes that contemporary society singles out only a few for recognition, he means that it has a very narrow understanding of what counts as a successful and valuable life. Societies characterized by extreme competition and high levels of economic inequality will leave many people feeling that their lives are not recognized by others as socially valuable, but also that this lack of social esteem affects their ability to be respected as equal citizens. In other words, when the parameters of a valuable life narrow, there is a danger that inequality of esteem turns into inequality of respect. The problem is that those who are seen as useless in the economic system – "those destined to remain weak," as Sennett puts it – will not only see themselves as less esteemed but will feel like second-class citizens. They will feel not only that their way of life is not esteemed by others, but that their ends and their opinions are not as important as the ends and opinions of everybody else. This is detrimental to the ideal of democratic respect promoted in this book.

Even if a society is more egalitarian and/or has a broader idea of what counts as a valuable life, it is difficult to imagine a society that is not

---

[67] On the idea that mutual respect can be "thickened" into a notion of solidarity, see also Laitinen, "From Recognition to Solidarity."

biased toward some forms of life over others. The public culture, social institutions, and economic system will always be more conducive to some kinds of life than others. Participants in the last decades of debate over multiculturalism, gender, and sexuality have argued that the public culture and institutions of contemporary societies in North America and Europe are biased in favor of Christian, patriarchal, and heterosexual ways of life.[68] For supporters of right-wing populism, by contrast, the feeling seems to be that the public culture has become biased in favor of urban, secular, academic, and cosmopolitan ways of life.[69] In the multiculturalism literature, the fact that society is never neutral is connected to issues of majority versus minority cultures and power inequalities. However, it is also important to include the socioeconomic dimension, especially when we are discussing the rise of populism. As mentioned in Chapter 1, economic relations are part of struggles for recognition.[70]

Economic modernization – including globalization, automation, the dismantling of manufacturing, financialization, and urbanization[71] – is not neutral between different ways of life, and nor are processes of secularization and the turn toward so-called post-materialist values.[72] At least to some extent, the latter favor people who are engaged in cognitive labor and have more urban and cosmopolitan identities. Some people might see these developments as inevitable and/or as welcome forms of progress. However, we should not be blind to the fact that they contribute to what I earlier referred to as a new recognition order (see Chapter 1). Some people will not just feel that they are losing out and being left behind by these developments; they will have very good reasons for these feelings. In these circumstances, I suggest, society owes them expressions and acts of solidarity that make it clear that they have a legitimate place in society. This will be a matter not of showing esteem for their choices, opinions, or achievements, but rather of publicly expressing as well as legally and economically ensuring that the latter do not affect their standing as free and equal participants in society.

In most contemporary liberal and constitutional democracies, the problem is not that people are not formally allowed by the state to live

---

[68] For an early and influential formulation of this position, see Young, *Justice*.
[69] Bonikowski, "Ethno-Nationalist Populism," 202; Fukuyama, *Identity*, 119–20; Inglehart and Norris, "Trump."
[70] See also Gidron and Hall, "Populism as a Problem."
[71] See, for example, Berman, "Populism Is a Symptom"; Brubaker, "Why Populism," 368–79; Cohen, "Populism"; Cramer, *Politics of Resentment*; Gest, Reny, and Mayer, "Roots of the Radical Right"; Gidron and Hall, "Populism as a Problem"; Hochschild, *Strangers in Their Own Land*; Inglehart and Norris, "Trump."
[72] On post-materialism, see Inglehart, *Silent Revolution*; Inglehart and Norris, "Trump."

according to their own conceptions of the good. Civil rights give them the freedom to do so. Nor can people complain that others do not value their culture; in a pluralistic society, we cannot expect or demand that all people value the same way of life. But there might be a valid complaint in the sense that some ways of life are not seen by others – political elites, the media, and the entertainment industry, for example – as having a legitimate public presence. We have a democratic problem if some people have reason to feel that the public realm is not open to them, that the public does not want to see or hear them, or that they do not belong to the public. This is a problem not only with dominant cultural expressions of disesteem and disagreement, but also with social-economic conditions that express and encourage forms of unequal esteem that are hard to prevent from turning into inequality of respect.

In his recent book *The Tyranny of Merit*, Michael Sandel describes and criticizes what he takes to be the central kind of inequality of esteem that characterizes many contemporary societies. He shows how "the myth of merit" ("you can make it if you try") promoted by contemporary liberal and social-democratic political elites has eroded the social esteem of the working class.[73] By focusing on not only the necessity but also the intrinsic value of higher education, so-called center-left political leaders – from Tony Blair, Gerhard Schröder, and Bill Clinton to Barack Obama – have defined a rather narrow ideal of what counts as a good and successful life. The message has been that being successful and having a good life require having a higher education and being able to participate in the global knowledge economy. According to Sandel, the flipside of this message – which has both an expressive and a policy aspect – is that people with less or no education feel humiliated, and feel that there is no "dignity" in their own occupation and way of life.

We have to be very clear in defining exactly what the problem of inequality of esteem consists in, before we discuss what can be done about it and what kind of solidarity it calls for. For Sandel it is a moral evil *in itself* that those left behind by globalization "sensed that the work they did was no longer a source of social esteem [... and that it] no longer signified a valued contribution to the common good."[74] Based on this assessment, he writes: "Any serious response to working-class frustrations must ... put the *dignity of work* at the center of the political agenda."[75]

We find an approach similar to Sandel's in Axel Honneth's earlier discussion of solidarity, which he places under a discussion of esteem – his

---

[73] Sandel, *Tyranny of Merit*.
[74] Sandel, *Tyranny of Merit*, 199.
[75] Sandel, *Tyranny of Merit*, 205, emphasis added.

third form of recognition (the other two are love and respect). According to Honneth, solidarity should be understood as an interactive relationship in which people "esteem one another symmetrically ... in light of values that allow the abilities and traits of the other to appear significant for shared praxis."[76] Only in this way is "one given the chance to experience oneself to be recognized, in light of one's own accomplishments and abilities, as valuable for society."[77]

There is much evidence that people who feel that their work and their abilities are no longer recognized (socially esteemed), or who do not feel that their contributions to society are as highly valued as they used to be, turn to populist parties. Sandel refers to some of this evidence in his discussion.[78] But, as I have said repeatedly, this causal connection is not sufficient to normatively justify that kind of esteem.

While I agree with the criticism of meritocracy and that we need to show solidarity with people who lose out in its competition for esteem, I have some reservations about the route taken by Sandel and Honneth. In particular, I think it is a mistake to say that it is a moral evil in itself if the social esteem of particular kinds of trait and occupation changes and that we need to reestablish social esteem for (certain kinds of) work. The problem is related to what we have already said about the idea of esteem, namely that esteem loses its point unless we make discriminations. Sandel and Honneth respectively note that the kind of esteem that they speak of requires a substantive idea of "the common good" and "a community of value" in light of which people's work and abilities can be seen as valuable. However, in order for people to feel and indeed be esteemed for their contributions in light of the values constituting the common good, these common values must include some indication of what counts as a valuable contribution to society – and what does not. Any scheme of valuation that is clear and strong enough for some people to actually feel socially esteemed will make other people feel less socially esteemed.

Sandel's focus on "recognizing work" and his idea of promoting the "dignity of work" are troublesome from the perspective of democratic respect, for two reasons. First, an understanding of the common good that recognizes work will have less social esteem for those who do not or cannot work. We see this in the type of esteem that populists show for their potential supporters – and fail to show for those not regarded as part of the people. Populist recognition is a kind of esteem that rank-orders, by denigrating not only the elite but also those below or outside

---

[76] Honneth, *Struggle for Recognition*, 129.
[77] Honneth, *Struggle for Recognition*, 130.
[78] Sandel, *Tyranny of Merit*, 199.

of the esteemed people.[79] Typically, populists have pitted hardworking people not only against a corrupt elite but also against less deserving groups below them.[80] Second, I worry that Sandel's understanding of the dignity of work counteracts the politically and socially fragile idea that respect for dignity is unconditional and associated with people's humanity, rather than their achievements or contributions. The phrase "the dignity of work" can be used to mean different things, and if it is used to mean that no kind of work can take away the worker's human dignity, I have no objection.[81] But this is not how Sandel understands the dignity of work. He sees it as a matter of social esteem for one's contributions to the common good.[82]

In short, Sandel's use of the phrase "the dignity of work" reveals a misguided acceptance that social esteem for a way of life is a precondition for the person's dignity. Thus, instead of fighting to maintain the independence of respect and dignity from esteem and contributions, an approach such as Sandel's collapses that distinction. If we make dignity dependent on social esteem for work or ways of life, we will not succeed in establishing a society of equal dignity.

Honneth's position is more sophisticated, and I cannot go into it in detail. However, I want to challenge the close association Honneth draws between solidarity and esteem in *The Struggle for Recognition*, which I referred to above. In his subsequent discussion with Nancy Fraser in *Redistribution or Recognition?*, Honneth actually accepts that esteem for *culture* is not something one can demand – for reasons similar to those I have provided.[83] In Honneth's scheme, esteem (as the third kind of recognition) is related not to culture or ways of life, but to people's particular contributions to society as achievements. However, he also argues that the development of the welfare state entailed a legal "incorporation of the sphere of social esteem" through social rights that guarantee "a minimum of social status and hence economic resources independently of the meritocratic recognition principle."[84] But if we see the welfare state as a matter of guaranteeing a minimum of status to everyone independently of their merits, this shows that the solidarity expressed

---

[79] Brubaker ("Why Populism," 362–4) notes that populists differentiate "the people" not only from the elite above, but also from people below or on the outside.

[80] Hochschild, *Strangers in Their Own Land*; Kazin, *Populist Persuasion*; Müller, *What Is Populism?*, 23–4.

[81] The idea of the dignity of work has a complex history, among other places in Christian thought (Martin Luther King, for example, spoke of "the dignity of labor"). My objection to Sandel concerns his specific use, where the key is to enhance the social esteem of work.

[82] Sandel, *Tyranny of Merit*, 197–222.

[83] Honneth, "Redistribution as Recognition," 161–70.

[84] Honneth, "Redistribution as Recognition," 147.

through the provision of social rights is not a matter of esteem but of respect. This comes closer to how I view solidarity, that is, as a matter of acting to ensure that status is independent of esteem.

The mistake of Honneth and Sandel, I think, lies in regarding the individual experience of lack of esteem as a moral evil in itself, and in Honneth's case in regarding solidarity as a form of esteem that can mitigate that evil. My argument, by contrast, relies on regarding equality of respect as the core moral ideal and considering inequality of esteem as a problem only if it becomes entangled with or translates into inequality of respect. Thus, rather than enhancing esteem for specific ways of life, including occupations, the task of solidaristic action and policy is to keep practices of equal respect independent of inequalities of esteem.

My proposal regarding the need for a certain kind of solidarity with people who are victims of some kinds of disesteem, then, depends on the acknowledgment that even though the distinction between respect and esteem is analytically clear, it is vulnerable in actual practice. Under some conditions and in some forms, lack of esteem is difficult to differentiate from being treated as if one's ends were of less than equal importance in society. It is unavoidable, I think, that (dis)respect will have a contextual and symbolic element.[85] Sometimes, therefore, expressions of disesteem and disagreement are received as expressions of disrespect, that is, as expressing the belief that the target does not have an equal right to coexistence or that their concerns are not of equal importance to those of other people. In these cases, the government and other citizens have an obligation to make it apparent that their lack of esteem for certain ways of life is not an expression of disrespect. This is where the type of solidarity I speak of becomes relevant and necessary.

Solidarity, as I see it, is required for and aims to secure the social conditions for upholding the separation of respect and esteem in the real world. When some people feel that they do not have an equal and legitimate place in society and the public sphere, it is not sufficient to point to their equal legal status or refrain from interfering with their pursuits. Sometimes the state and other citizens need positively to express and perform their commitment to equal respect. The kind of solidarity that lies in positively expressing one's commitment to equal respect does not require equal esteem, but it does require an acknowledgment of and appropriate response to the consequences of inequality of esteem for relations of mutual respect. While solidarity in my understanding is not about promoting equality of esteem, it requires that we consider first how to change social circumstances (such as severe economic inequality

[85] See Green, "Two Worries," 228.

and meritocratic extremism[86]) that give rise to forms of inequality of esteem that turn into inequality of respect, and second, how we express disesteem and disagreement in ways that are not associated with inequality of respect.[87]

2.3.2   Solidarity as Active Inclusion

Rather than responding to the crisis of recognition – which fuels populism – with solidarity as a kind of esteem for particular people's occupations, way of life, and opinions, I propose instead that political actors respond with a kind of solidarity that expresses their legitimate place in society and aim to secure their opportunities for equal participation in society. This kind of solidarity goes beyond liberal toleration but does not require equal esteem for all traits, achievements, and ways of life. Liberal toleration means that the tolerated party is allowed by the state to live according to their own conception of the good without interference, while esteem is a positive appraisal of their way of life as good and worthwhile. For society to recognize different ways of life as legitimate options, more is sometimes required than refraining from interfering in people's lives.[88] For example, when economic modernization and cultural developments are shifting away from rural or small-town life and making "a blue-collar way of life [go] out of fashion,"[89] society and government need positively to show concern for people's way of life and listen to their grievances. Somehow, the surrounding society and public policy must show people that their way of life – their occupation, religion, and locale, for example – is a legitimate option and does not detract from their status as free and equal participants in society.

Expressions and acts of solidarity as I understand them are ways of declaring that society respects the object as an equal whose ends and particular lives are equally important as the ends and lives of everyone else in society. Here solidarity is understood as a form of mutual concern where we afford other people's ends "some non-instrumental weight in [our] practical reasoning."[90] That is, when we think about how to treat others, we give weight to their ends because they are *their* ends, and not because we share those ends or have an interest in their realization. This does not require that we abandon the notion of equal respect in favor

---

[86] O'Neill, "Philosophy and Public Policy."
[87] Cf. Fourie, "To Praise and to Scorn."
[88] Cf. Galeotti, "Rescuing Toleration," 91–2.
[89] Hochschild, *Strangers in Their Own Land*, 218.
[90] Mason, *Community, Solidarity and Belonging*, 27.

of esteem for others' ends, but it does require that respect is expressed positively and explicitly – and that disesteem and disagreement are not expressed in ways that delegitimize other people's equal participation in society and politics. If the aim is to show others that their way of life has a legitimate place in society, under some conditions this requires that the surrounding society and government should publicly express exactly that conviction. While it is a difficult and context-dependent question how this can be done, I would like to propose that it is an obligation that falls particularly on people who have great influence on the common culture, such as politicians, the media, and the entertainment industry. The ways in which these speak about and portray different groups in society, as well as their depictions of the good and successful life, significantly affect whether people feel that their own way of life is a legitimate option and that their opinions should be equally considered.[91]

My proposal is that privileged groups and government policies should respond to the feelings of lack of recognition and status that supporters of populism often express with solidaristic action, which shows that the latter's ways of life are legitimate options in contemporary society – if indeed they are legitimate. We act in solidarity with others by actively inviting them in and soliciting their participation in society and the public sphere. Thus, I understand solidarity as a form of active expression and an act of inclusion in society and in political processes of opinion and will formation.[92] In short, I see solidarity in terms of acts and policies of *active inclusion*.

Solidarity as active inclusion is not uncritical acceptance of any and all ways of life or political opinions as equally right and legitimate. Not all ways of life are legitimate options in a democratic society, because not all ways of life are consistent with equal respect and plurality.[93] Obvious examples include the way of life of criminal groups such as the Mafia, and racist groups such as the Ku Klux Klan and the Proud Boys.[94] Some populist leaders legitimize the actions of such groups, but that is obviously a violation of democratic respect. An example of the latter was Trump's comment that there were some "very fine people on both sides" at a rally organized by white supremacists in Charlottesville, Virginia, in 2017.

---

[91] These issues are well described in Eribon, *Returning to Reims*.
[92] This understanding of solidarity is similar to that promoted by Brunkhorst in *Solidarity*.
[93] As Laitinen ("From Recognition to Solidarity," 134) puts it: "Equal respect draws the boundaries for normatively acceptable forms of solidarity."
[94] I take it that being part of groups such as the Mafia, the Ku Klux Klan, or the Proud Boys qualifies as a way of life and is part of the engaged people's identity, which is not true of all cases of criminal activity.

Legitimization is not something citizens can demand as a right. The kind of inclusion I speak of here entails a kind of legitimization of people's particularity, their specific ends, culture, or political opinions, and we cannot demand respect for the latter in the same way that we can demand respect for our personhood or humanity. Solidaristic inclusion might sound more like esteem than respect, because it refers to people's particularities rather than our shared humanity. However, the judgment that is involved in solidarity as inclusion is not about whether the involved people's ends are truly good or worthwhile; rather, it is a judgment regarding whether these ends are compatible with other people's standing as equal participants in the political community. Thus, inclusion is based on a respect judgment rather than an esteem judgment. Inclusion as a positive act of solidarity and respect lies precisely in the judgment of ends as compatible with the shared democratic community of equals. Moreover, the aim and justification of solidarity as inclusion is to maintain and reinforce the equal standing and mutual respect of citizens.

Political conflict is not excluded by but is often required by solidarity as active inclusion. It is a political struggle to create more inclusive cultural, social, and economic circumstances. Opposition will have to be overcome. However, when we see mutual respect as the core normative commitment, the goal of solidaristic struggles must be to restore or create relations of mutual respect with everyone rather than upholding antagonistic relations.[95]

Solidarity as active inclusion is the publicly expressed and acted-upon judgment of one person or group that another person's or group's way of life is a legitimate option in society. There are some requirements for this judgment to count as a form of solidarity and for it to express genuine respect. First, inclusion as a form of legitimization has to involve an *actual and sincere judgment* and cannot be arbitrarily given. As an expression of respect, including particular others as legitimate participants depends on the fact that others take them seriously, consider their case on its merits, and see their way of life as a legitimate option for what they take to be intrinsically good reasons. This means, second, that solidarity as inclusion of particular others requires *critical engagement* with the recognition demands made by the object group. If we do not critically engage with people's claims, we cannot reach a judgment about their validity. Third, the judgment and the critical engagement with other people's claims must take place as part of a *shared and public process of deliberation*. If there is no such common deliberation, the community cannot attain common knowledge regarding why some ways of life are

---

[95] Laitinen, "From Recognition to Solidarity," 144.

deemed legitimate – and others are not. In Chapter 3, I argue that this deliberation should not be about ways of life as undifferentiated wholes, but must be about more specific claims.

As I have said, populism is characterized by the rejection of all competitors as illegitimate, and when in power, populists "will not recognize anything like a legitimate opposition."[96] Thus, for populists, political opponents are not just people with whom they disagree, but rather people who have no legitimate place in the political community. Because populists exclude rather than include political opponents, one could say that they fail to act in solidarity with the latter. Nevertheless, we should not be blind to the possibility that many supporters of populism are driven by the feeling that they themselves are treated as if they have no legitimate place in the political community. When they feel that their way of life and their political opinions are misunderstood or not seen and heard, the issue need not be that they regret that others – "the elite" – do not agree with them or esteem their culture; they may also be asking to be recognized (respected) as having a legitimate presence in the political community.

I began this section by proposing that even if people cannot demand equality of esteem, our societies cannot just ignore inequalities of esteem. The problem is that under the nonideal conditions in which we live, disesteem is sometimes indistinguishable from disrespect. That is, sometimes the lack of agreement with and negative evaluation of other people's opinions and way of life transmute into a situation in which some fail to show others that they all have a legitimate presence as fellow citizens and parts of the political community. Oftentimes, the problem is not so much the absence of positive expressions of the legitimization of others' views or culture, but rather, the presence of negative expressions of delegitimization. Examples of delegitimization are expressions of mockery, ridicule, and scorn. In addition, people might feel that they have no legitimate place in the political community if others ignore them, show no interest in them, and/or do not listen to them. In these cases, we as participants in democracy must show one another that we are concerned about the particular identities, occupations, locations, and projects of our fellow citizens. My proposal is that we do so by engaging with one another's claims in common deliberation, and by showing one another that all ways of life that – after common scrutiny – can be shown to be compatible with the equal standing of others have a legitimate place in the community.

---

[96] Müller, *What Is Populism?*, 20. This characterization of populism is found not only in critical accounts such as Müller's, but also in the sympathetic account of Laclau (*On Populist Reason*, 86).

It is crucial in this connection that expressions of disesteem and disagreement must refer to a specific and well-defined action, attribute, or
opinion, and not to other individuals or groups as a whole. Disesteem
and disagreement must be about people having failed to achieve some
standard of goodness or rightness. If others humiliate or scorn someone
beyond their achievement in relation to a standard, then this, as Runciman notes, is "strong *prima facie* evidence of an inequality of respect."[97]
Solidarity as inclusion does not entail that anyone should refrain from
expressing their disagreements with other people's opinions regarding
standards of right and wrong, nor that they should refrain from expressing their objections to certain cultural practices as mistaken. What it
requires is that we do so in a way that does not turn into an expression
that the other has no legitimate place in the community, and that we seek
to secure the social conditions for a plurality of ways of life.

Part of solidarity as active inclusion, then, is a form of civility in interaction with other citizens. It is about addressing others in a way that
makes them feel like peers and equal participants. It is about speaking to
others in a way that invites them into the conversation and encourages
them to participate, rather than pushing them out. It is about showing
others that they have a legitimate and equal place in society and the
public sphere.[98]

It might be said that supporters of right-wing populism will have none
of this civility. Populists reject "political correctness" and are attracted
by the frank political speech that is often said to characterize populist
politicians.[99] Thus, it could be objected to my proposal that we do not
show other people respect and solidarity by providing something that
they reject. Yet if it is true that supporters of right-wing populism complain about not being seen and heard, about being ridiculed and scorned,
as we have seen that the ethnographic literature suggests,[100] then they
actually do demand a kind of civility from others. To be sure, people
disagree on the exact requirements of civility, but I think it is a mistake
to assume that anyone rejects the norm entirely. The resentments and
feelings of disrespect that we have discussed only make sense if people

---

[97] Runciman, "'Social' Equality," 225.

[98] Mounk (*People vs. Democracy*, 190–1) proposes that this includes politicians "speaking
the language of ordinary people [...] and eschewing the preferred locutions of highly
educated elites." Eribon (*Returning to Reims*, 122–6) suggests that the explanation for
the French working class's turn to the populist right is that the socialist left no longer speaks the language of the governed but of those who govern, and only the right
defends their collective identity and dignity.

[99] Brubaker, "Why Populism," 366–7; Moffitt, *Global Rise of Populism*, 57–63.

[100] See the section "Populism as a Struggle for Recognition" in Chapter 1.

actually do demand of one another the minimum of civility that lies in people listening to one another.[101]

2.4   Democratic Solidarity

Solidarity as a form of active inclusion based on a normative commitment to equal respect can be placed between two other conceptions of solidarity. At one extreme, in at least part of the literature on recognition, solidarity is seen as a form of mutual esteem, and as requiring some degree of "community of value."[102] This view is incompatible with what I have said about esteem, pluralism, and disagreement, as I already explained in my objections to the position of Sandel and Honneth above. Solidarity, as I understand it, is needed precisely when there is no community of value in the sense of a shared view of what should be esteemed and regarded as good or worthwhile ways of life. It is an active way of including people who disagree in the shared life of society.

At the other extreme, solidarity is seen as a matter of *taking sides*. On this view, "solidarity will most often pit us against individuals or groups who represent divergent positions."[103] My understanding of solidarity, by contrast, is exactly about avoiding pitting people against each other.[104] More precisely, solidarity as active inclusion is about keeping the political and cultural struggles between different groups within the limits that are appropriate for seeing all involved, despite their differences, as legitimate members of and participants in a shared political community.

Solidarity is sometimes seen as something we owe only to those who suffer the gravest injustice – "the victims," as it were. This is the position, for example, of Avery Kolers in *A Moral Theory of Solidarity*. He argues that justified solidarity involves taking sides with the victims and deferring to their views.[105] Like my own view, Kolers's view of solidarity is Kantian. Thus, he understands solidarity "in terms of basic respect as the duty not to stand by while another is treated as a second-class citizen."[106] In relation to our discussion, we might ask whether solidarity as inclusion is something we owe only to those fellow citizens who are losing out in the current struggle for recognition, those who fail to attain the esteem

---

[101] Some demands for civility might work to silence dissent and can rightly be criticized for this. However, this criticism itself relies on the value of the minimum of civility that lies in not silencing others. For a nuanced discussion of these issues, see Bejan, *Mere Civility*.

[102] Honneth, *Struggle for Recognition*, 129.

[103] Kolers, *Moral Theory of Solidarity*, 39.

[104] Cf. Hussain, "Pitting People against Each Other."

[105] Kolers, *Moral Theory of Solidarity*.

[106] Kolers, *Moral Theory of Solidarity*, 108.

necessary to be respected as equals or who are simply not respected as equals. In our polarized context, the problem with this suggestion is that it does not consider the possibility of disagreement on the issue of who the victims are. On the one hand, the recognition order of any society is clearly biased in favor of some ways of life over others, which means that acts of inclusion are most important in relation to people whose way of life and basic standing is most threatened in society. People in powerful and privileged positions who feel secure in their identities and status do not need active acts of others to be included. On the other hand, current struggles for recognition show that there is no agreement on who the victims of the greatest injustice are, or whose way of life the current system favors. Moreover, each person has multiple identities, some of which make them vulnerable and others less so. Whose identity and status are most threatened, and who suffers the greatest injustice in the contemporary United States: rich, urban, gay people, or poor, white, Christian rural people?[107]

To view solidarity as a matter of taking sides with the victims and deferring to their opinions does not take us beyond populism, but tends to confirm its worldview. A defining feature of contemporary populist politics is exactly that it seeks to frame political conflict in terms of a grand societal division between victims and perpetrators: the good people versus the bad and responsible elite.[108] Some political theorists even defend populism as a solidaristic struggle (on behalf) of the underdog against the powerful or the oligarchy.[109] My objection to this construal is that it entails the idea that there is one monolithic group in society – "the people" – who can be regarded as the victims or the worst-off group *for all political purposes*. However, as Kolers himself argues, "there is no one who counts as worst off in all contexts."[110]

Kolers argues that justified solidarity is about taking sides with the group that "suffers (the greatest) inequity *relative to the structure of the political conflict*."[111] Here it is imperative, I think, not to reduce all political conflicts to one overall societal conflict between two broad identity

---

[107] Or who is more underprivileged, a poor Black man in Detroit or a poor white man in a trailer park in Louisiana? See Sindberg's ("Kendt sociolog") interview with Hochschild. See also Sandel (*Tyranny of Merit*, 203): "Attributing 'white privilege' to disempowered white working-class men and women is galling; it ignores the struggle to win honor and recognition in a meritocratic order that has scant regard for the skills they have to offer."

[108] Mudde, "Populism," 29.

[109] For a defense of populism as a construction of the people as the underdog fighting those in power, see Laclau, *On Populist Reason*, Chapter 4; Mouffe, *For a Left Populism*, 5, 10–11. See also McCormick, *Machiavellian Democracy*.

[110] Kolers, *Moral Theory of Solidarity*, 5, cf. 103–4.

[111] Kolers, *Moral Theory of Solidarity*, 106, emphasis added.

groups, which is what populism does. Rather, to show solidarity with the least well-off, we should focus on particular political struggles for recognition and justice, and discuss who actually suffers the greatest injustice in each case separately. Moreover, it is essential that we keep in mind that solidarity is an active way of expressing and promoting the norm of equal respect, which means that there are limits to the opinions to which solidaristic action should defer.[112] The way in which populism divides society into the suffering people and the oppressive elite fails to acknowledge both the fact that this construction and demarcation of the real people will always exclude the valid claims of some groups and the fact that the claims of "the people" whose side populist politicians take are not necessarily claims for (or consistent with) equality. By contrast, solidarity based on equal respect must necessarily be a discriminating solidarity, which means that it must be a solidarity based on principles and judgments in relation to actual circumstances.

While the practice of solidarity as active, context-sensitive inclusion has to take account of whose identities and ways of life are most threatened in contemporary society, it is not conducive to a democratic culture of mutual respect and common deliberation about equal treatment to build dichotomies where society is divided into two monolithic groups of oppressors and oppressed, victims and perpetrators. In the next chapter, I suggest one way to avoid such dichotomies.

It might be objected that the suggestion that we look at different struggles for recognition separately in order to assess who actually suffers the greatest injustice in each case will make popular struggles impotent. Some political theorists defend populism exactly as a way of connecting different political struggles and making them powerful.[113] My position is not opposed to different disadvantaged groups uniting their struggles or building coalitions against common opponents. My worry is that populists build coalitions in a way that groups people together arbitrarily rather than in terms of who actually suffers the greatest injustices. Moreover, "the people" on whose side the populist leader stands must be and are homogenized: They are understood as victims or the powerless in relation to a shared, homogenous identity. The designation of a group as victims, oppressed, or the underdog is a consequence of the populist articulation of the people, rather than its cause. This means, moreover, that the populist cannot allow the possibility that some members of the people oppress other members of the people, or that some members of the group designated as the elite are underprivileged in some respects.

[112] Kolers agrees with this.
[113] Laclau, *On Populist Reason*.

Finally, when the populist leader takes sides with the people, this is a form of "solidarity" that excludes the possibility of showing any kind of concern or respect for those who are not on the right side, that is, the side of the populist's people.

2.4.1   The Priority of Democratic Solidarity over Partisan Solidarity

Under current conditions, which are characterized by profound disagreements on the meaning of respect and on who is disrespected, the type of solidarity that our democracy is lacking is not one that takes sides or pits one group against another. In this connection, we may distinguish between partisan solidarity on the one hand and democratic solidarity on the other. Partisan solidarity is a type of support that you show for one group *against* other groups in society, because you think members of the first group are victims of injustice perpetrated by the other groups. Democratic solidarity, by contrast, is a kind of concern that you show for all members of society as equal participants in a form of cooperation that transcends your particular partisan commitments and beliefs about who the victims and perpetrators of injustice are. Partisan solidarity is necessary to motivate and organize fights against injustice, and I do not reject its value. My argument, however, is that partisan solidarity is not the only form of solidarity required by democratic norms or to make democracy work – and that in our current predicament, the more urgent need is to strengthen the democratic solidarity that does not depend on prior substantive agreement about who the victims of injustice are. Solidarity as active inclusion is exactly a type of democratic solidarity that acknowledges that citizens disagree about who is most in need of partisan solidarity.

This does not mean that we should not be concerned with the question of who in society are victims of injustice. On the contrary. Democratic solidarity is a way of including everyone in common deliberation in order that citizens together can determine who actually suffers the greatest injustice. In contrast to partisan solidarity, we do not take it for granted that we already know who the victims are and whose views are right. We give everyone the opportunity – an opportunity that has both political-cultural and economic aspects – to be heard in the common conversation about justice. Democratic solidarity is about making everyone authors of shared social and political institutions.

As a democratic and normative notion, solidarity as inclusion does not entail that all positions are legitimate, but it requires that the community considers which positions fall within the broad range of views that are compatible with the general idea of democratic equality with which

I began this chapter. So in showing concern for all legitimate ways of life and including all legitimate positions, we are still taking sides: We are taking sides with democracy.[114] However, taking the side of democracy and equal respect is not a threat to pluralism and disagreement, but rather their precondition. To take the side of democracy is to respect cultural pluralism and political disagreement.

It is sometimes argued that solidarity necessarily entails identifying with one group *against* another group. On this view, solidarity is connected to shared identity and a particularistic community, and it is claimed that community, identity, and solidarity all require some form of exclusion, or an "other" in relation to which the community can constitute itself.[115] However, it is important here to distinguish between drawing a distinction on the one hand, and excluding concrete others on the other.[116] Democratic solidarity, as I understand it, does require that we differentiate between democratic and nondemocratic ideas, and that we side with the former; but this does not mean that showing democratic solidarity requires that any concrete persons be excluded from the community. (The idea that solidarity requires exclusion may be a product of tying it too closely to the idea of esteem and community of value.)

Andrea Sangiovanni has suggested that solidarity entails acting with others with the common goal of overcoming adversity. He argues that joint cooperation and action are required to sustain common political institutions in order to overcome "a special kind of adversity[, namely] the ever-present danger of *civil dissolution*." With reference to Kant's "Doctrine of Right," Sangiovanni argues that allowing the state to dissolve "would necessarily involve us in wronging others 'in the highest degree.'"[117] Kant's assumption is that people can stand in rightful relations to one another only under a common will or in a public legal order (such as a state), and therefore people have a natural duty to leave the state of nature. They "do wrong in the highest degree by willing to be and to remain in a condition that is not rightful."[118] Sangiovanni's point is that if we have a duty to leave the state of nature because it is necessary to overcome the morally relevant adversity of that condition, we also

---

[114] By using the phrase "taking sides," I am not implying an arbitrary or decisionistic choice. The choice in favor of democracy can be reasoned and rationally justified.

[115] We find the particularistic view of solidarity both in the liberal nationalism of, for example, Miller (*On Nationality*) and in the post-structuralist (and populist) view of Mouffe (*Democratic Paradox*, 13, 41; *For a Left Populism*, 71).

[116] For an elaboration of this point, see Abizadeh, "Does Collective Identity."

[117] Sangiovanni, "Solidarity as Joint Action," 354.

[118] Kant, *Metaphysics of Morals*, 452 (AK 6: 307–8). See also Rostbøll, "Kant, Freedom"; "Kant and the Critique."

have a moral obligation to transform unjust institutions and to maintain existing just institutions. Solidarity on this account aims to overcome the threats to just institutions, and it is grounded "in our joint action *as authors* of political and social institutions."[119]

The understanding of respect promoted in this book assumes that people can only stand in relations of equal and mutual respect in a democratic society and when they share democratic institutions. This is why I call it democratic respect. My understating of solidarity is normatively grounded in this notion of respect. I see solidarity as a response to the fact that democratic respect is a very demanding and fragile ideal in the real world. Relations of equal respect are in constant danger of being undermined by social, economic, and cultural changes. This is because these changes affect the recognition order on which democratic respect is dependent. Without active engagement and adjustments, we cannot uphold relations of equal respect when other parts of the recognition order change in terms of roles, obligations, and material conditions. Solidaristic action is called for exactly in order to protect and uphold relations of equal respect – as free and equal participants in society and politics – in the face of changes in materially and culturally expressed esteem.

Democratic solidarity, then, is justified by the acknowledgment of the socioeconomic, cultural, and political preconditions of a society of equal respect. That is, it is grounded in the acknowledgment of the fact that a society of equal respect is hard to achieve and maintain in the real world. There are several aspects to this acknowledgment.

First, central to the idea of solidarity is the acknowledgment of mutual dependence and that the participants share each other's fates.[120] When people act in solidarity, they do so not only for their own sake or only for the sake of others, but for "us together."[121] Thus, solidarity is based neither on egoism nor on altruism, but on a form of reciprocity. The idea of reciprocity involved in solidaristic action is not just an abstract moral ideal but is based on the belief that people in actual social relations are dependent on each other and can only achieve the aims in question if they acknowledge their obligations of mutual support. Solidaristic reciprocity means both that the parties involved should all benefit from social cooperation and that they must accept that cooperation has costs that must be shared – sometimes significant costs.[122] As citizens, we are

---

[119] Sangiovanni, "Solidarity as Joint Action," 356, emphasis changed.
[120] Sangiovanni, "Solidarity as Joint Action."
[121] Laitinen and Pessi, "Solidarity," 2.
[122] Sangiovanni ("Solidarity as Joint Action," 356) emphasizes that solidaristic action includes "the disposition to incur significant costs."

mutually dependent on one another to establish and maintain a society, an economy, and a political culture that provide a valuable place for everyone. Democratic solidarity is grounded in the acknowledgment that society, the economy, and political institutions are joint social products.[123] They are produced and reproduced by all of us as joint authors. Solidarity is required because none of us can live in a democratic society unless we ensure that everyone also has the ability to do so on free and equal terms. A society where some members cannot achieve equal respect is not a democratic society.[124] This is why we have a democratic obligation to actively include everyone in society and solicit their free and equal participation in the political process.

Second, solidarity cannot be passive or negative; it demands action.[125] As I said above, solidarity is more demanding than toleration as the requirement not to interfere in other people's legitimate pursuits. The action required by solidarity can take many different forms, and it can happen outside the state in civil-society action, or it can happen through the state. It can take cultural and symbolic forms, as when the surrounding society (the state and other citizens) positively expresses and shows people that their ends are of equal importance to the ends of others and that their opinions have an equal right to be heard and considered. It can take form of social and economic policy, as when the state establishes social rights that (to repeat a quote from Honneth) provide "a minimum of social status and hence economic resources independently of the meritocratic recognition principle."[126] Or as in the case where social primary goods are distributed according to Rawls's difference principle, which expresses the solidaristic idea of no one "wanting to have greater advantages unless this is to the benefit of others who are less well off."[127]

Finally, I see solidarity as a response to the fact that we never fully live in a democratic society of equal respect but must continuously aim to create it. Inequality of esteem always threatens to translate into or "justify" inequality of respect, and solidarity is needed to combat this. Economic inequalities always risk being used to establish political power inequalities, and solidarity is required to combat these oligarchic

---

[123] As Sangiovanni notes ("Solidarity as Joint Action," 356), his "argument shares with the socialist an emphasis on joint social production (in the widest sense that includes the production and reproduction of political institutions such as the state)."

[124] Brunkhorst (*Solidarity*, 2) traces this idea to the French Revolution and quotes Article 34 of the Revolutionary Constitution of 1793: "There is oppression against the social body when a single of its members is oppressed."

[125] Kolers, *Moral Theory of Solidarity*, 28–9 Chapter 3.

[126] Honneth, "Redistribution as Recognition," 147.

[127] Rawls, *Theory of Justice*, 90. Rawls (*Theory of Justice*, 90–1) himself regards the difference principle as corresponding to the idea of "fraternity."

tendencies. Inequalities in education ("cultural capital") is turned into unequal opportunities in society in general and politics in particular, and solidarity is required to combat this as well. Thus, to demand solidaristic action is to insist that we must always be alert to and counteract the myriad ways in which different forms of inequality undermine the aim of establishing a democratic society of equal and mutual respect. A society of mutual respect has legal, social, economic, and political preconditions, and the action of continuously upholding and strengthening these is what I call democratic solidarity.

Before we end, let me consider the objection that my discussion of solidarity upholds a false narrative of populist parties as representing those who have been left behind, a narrative that populist politicians themselves strategically promote. The problem with this narrative, it might be said, is that it overlooks the facts that populist parties (1) are not exclusively supported by the worst-off members of society and (2) often promote policies that are not to the advantage of the worst-off. In response to this important objection, I should stress that I am not arguing for *special* solidarity with the people who feel or express the most resentment or who support populist parties. My discussion of these groups of people is a consequence of the fact that resentment, respect, and populism are the topics of this book. Of course, groups other than supporters of populism may be both less seen and heard *and* more truly victims of injustice.[128] The idea of democratic respect and solidarity is that we must listen to and learn from *everyone* and not assume that we already know which groups have valid claims. Democratic solidarity is a part of a political culture where we respect disagreement, give room to a plurality of ways of life, but also discuss in common what justice requires. To act in democratic solidarity with people is to support them to overcome the obstacles – including political disagreements and inequality of esteem – to their being treated as sharing the high and equal rank of everyone else.

---

[128] Bhambra, "Brexit, Trump, and 'Methodological Whiteness.'"

3 Rights and the Populist Claim for Recognition

In Chapter 2, I analyzed and assessed the different kinds of demand for recognition that empirical studies indicate drive supporters of populist parties. I emphasized the important normative differences between demands for respect and for esteem, as well as between the egalitarian notion of respect for dignity and the hierarchical notion of respect for honor. Moreover, I advanced an idea of democratic solidarity as a kind of common action that aims to overcome inequalities that threaten the respectful inclusion of everyone as free and equal participants. In this chapter, I turn from the quest for recognition among populism's supporters to the kind of demand for recognition that is inherent to populism as a set of distinctive claims. In this connection, I shall present and discuss what I call *the populist claim for recognition*.

Most contemporary writers on populism agree that the core feature of populism is the way in which it divides society into two qualitatively different and antagonistically opposed groups, the people and the elite. Populism involves the claims that only a part of the people is really the people and that the only legitimate option is to take sides with this part against the rest. In what follows, I argue that populism so understood entails a unique claim for recognition, which sets it at odds with the ideal of respect for the equal standing of every last individual person. The populist claim for recognition is an exclusionary claim: We are something that you are not, "the people." Moreover, it is the populist claim for recognition that explains its opposition to the deliberative aspect of politics, which stresses the importance of mutual critique and learning among citizens. Finally, the chapter contrasts the populist claim for recognition with the kind of respect that is expressed in and through individual rights claims. Adopting a participant attitude, we can see rights as establishing relationships of mutual respect, not as mere means to individual ends. In this way, rights struggles can contribute to democratic respect.

3.1   The Populist Claim for Recognition

Interpreting populism as making a claim for recognition is part of approaching it through what I have called the participant attitude. When we view each other as fellow participants, we regard the positions taken by one another as expressing certain normative expectations about how we ought to regard and relate to each other. Adopting the participant attitude in relation to populism, we see it as making *a claim addressed to us*, and we ask what it asks of us, what it asks us to accept, what it asks us to believe and to do. A claim is not just an expression of a preference or an automatic emotional reaction; it is an assertion of a right to something, a demand for something as due.

With Habermas we might understand the populist claim for recognition as a "validity claim," that is, as asserting the truth and/or rightness of something. According to Habermas, people who engage in communicative action *necessarily* regard one another as raising such claims, and they presuppose that the parties involved are capable of understanding and responding to them.[1] The point here is neither that all uses of speech qualifies as communicative action where people aim to reach an understanding about what is true and right, nor that populist politicians necessarily make clear assertions in their communication.[2] My proposal is rather that it is valuable for understanding and evaluating populism as well as a requirement of democratic respect to approach populism *as if* it raises a validity claim addressed to us as fellow participants.

As I argued in Chapter 1, populist resentment can be seen as a moral feeling based on principles and a perception of the facts. Part of the appeal of populism, I think, lies in the fact that many people believe the populist attack on the elites to be morally *justified*. The populist claim is that the people are not getting what is due to them, what they have a right to, or what they deserve. Supporters of populism believe that they are the victims of injustice, that they are being wronged, and that the elite is responsible for their plight.[3] The populist claim is a confirmation of these beliefs: that it is *true* that the people are oppressed, and that it is *wrong* for the people to be oppressed.

Put in these very general terms, the populist claim for recognition sounds unremarkable. Clearly, it is wrong for the people to be oppressed; it is wrong for anyone to be oppressed. However, we should remember

---

[1] Habermas, *Between Facts and Norms*, 17–21; Habermas, *Theory of Communicative Action*, 22–44. Cf. Rostbøll, *Jürgen Habermas*, 26–7.

[2] Richardson ("Noncognitivist Trumpism," 656–60) shows that Trump gives his listeners lots of speech but very few assertions.

[3] Cramer, *Politics of Resentment*, 12, 23, 55–84, 212; Laclau, *On Populist Reason*, 85–7.

that for the populist, "the people" does not refer to everyone – not to all of humanity, but also not to the legally defined citizenry. The populist people is necessarily only a section of the population. So who is this people, how is it demarcated? It might be tempting to say that the people is the section of the people that is oppressed or marginalized – the underdog.[4] But to see the people as the oppressed part of a population creates a problem for populism, because populists also hold that the people is the part of the population that should rule. If the part called the people actually manages to become the rulers, as is its due, it is no longer oppressed and hence no longer "the people." Thus, the populist claim cannot be that "the oppressed" should rule. Populism needs a more enduring and stable understanding of the people.[5]

It might be suggested that "the people" could be defined in economic terms. The point would then be that "the poor" should rule, and that one can remain poor while ruling. However, this solution entails that it possible to be oppressed in some respects (poor) and not oppressed in other respects (the ruling group). It would be to deny the very core of populism, which is the claim that we can and should divide society into *one* dichotomous relation of top and bottom. The populist claim has to be that there is one identity group that constitutes the people, and that this people can be defined independently of who actually possesses political power. (Or one would have to accept that the people can never be in power, and that populism can only be oppositional.[6])

It is central to the populist claim that *the same division* between people and elite can and should be applied *for all political purposes*. It is *the same group* who is the victim of all of society's injustices and who has privileged access to the true and the right. The core populist claim is that there is only one societal conflict, and it is between the people and the elite.[7] According to Laclau's influential view, "populism requires the dichotomic division of society into two camps."[8] As per his theory of populism, the identity of the people is the product of a *radical*

---

[4] Laclau (*On Populist Reason*, 87) understands "the people" as "the oppressed underdog."
[5] As Canovan ("Taking Politics to the People," 34) writes, in populism, "'the people' must be understood as an entity, a corporate body, with a continuous existence over time [.... A] prime characteristic of 'the people' is unity. So are boundaries: the contrast between 'us' and 'them', between those who are and are not included in the notion of 'the people', is a crucial aspect of the ideological picture."
[6] It is true that that populists who have taken over government control often speak as if they are still in opposition and someone else still possesses the real power. But this fact does not mean that populists do not claim that "the people" should rule, and thus it still requires an identification of the people that is independent of actual power relations.
[7] Rosanvallon, *Le siècle du populisme*, 78–9.
[8] Laclau, *On Populist Reason*, 83.

construction in which the different demands and grievances of many different groups are united into one constitutive antagonism to the elite.[9] Whether or not actual populist leaders and their followers see the people as a construction, my point is that they *publicly claim* that there is only one political opposition in society and that all politics should take place along this frontier. Populism is the claim that all differences and conflicts align in and can be reduced to one grand opposition between two identity groups.

It follows from this claim that internally among "the people" there is neither oppression nor disagreement, and that the populist claim for recognition is only directed upward against the dominance of the elite. Populists speak and act as if "the people" all have the same interest, the same desire, and the same political opinion – and as if these are realized by getting rid of the elite and giving power (back) to the people.[10] All differences are reduced by the populist to that between the people and the elite: Internally each group is treated as homogenous. Defenders of populism such as Laclau and Mouffe might object that this is just how populists speak and perform, and that populists can allow differences and plurality among the people (as long as "the people" is articulated as an empty signifier).[11] If we adopt the participant attitude, however, the important question is what claim the populist leader addresses to the world.[12] And the populist leader claims to represent and embody the people in terms that express the latter's unity and homogeneity, rather than in terms that allow for the existence and value of internal differences, conflicts, and disagreements among the people.[13]

Populism, I think, is first and foremost a claim for recognition of the people. We have already discussed at great length the different ways in which (supporters of) populism can be seen as engaged in a struggle for recognition. Now we can add a further dimension to our analysis and discussion. Based on what I have already said, let me briefly list some elements of what the populist claim for recognition is a claim for. First, it is a claim for recognition that "the people" and they alone are victims of injustice. Second, it is a claim for recognition (esteem) of the value of "the people's" way of life and opinions as good and right. Third, populists claim that the group they call the people has a special and high

---

[9] Laclau *On Populist Reason*, 72–128; Stavrakakis, "Populism and Hegemony," 547.

[10] Rosanvallon, *Le siècle du populisme*, 43–5.

[11] Laclau, "Interview with Ernesto Laclau," 263; Mouffe, *For a Left Populism*, 62.

[12] See also the discussion of publicity in Chapter 6.

[13] McKean ("Toward an Inclusive Populism," 802) criticizes Laclau's populism for its "practical closure of identity[, which] requires a homogenizing and polarizing logic that renders everything interior to the system the same and everything exterior to it different."

standing that must be respected as such.[14] This claim includes, fourth, the idea that "the people" is the true and only legitimate ruler. Fifth, the populist claim for recognition is of "the people" as a collective subject and a unified identity group.

In what follows I would like to highlight and explain two dangers to democratic respect posed by the populist claim for recognition. Both dangers connect to the fact that populism seeks recognition for a homogenously conceived collective subject and identity group. First, the populist claim for recognition entails that the confrontation between different groups and parties must be one where you either accept or reject *everything* the other group stands for. The dichotomic division of society into two camps requires that the camps be regarded as exclusive identity groups with entirely separate ways of life, values, and opinions. Populists view one way of life as deserving of protection *in its entirety* and the other way of life as deserving of destruction *in its entirety*. This view is grounded in the claim that one group can be regarded as the innocent victim and the other as the responsible perpetrator for all political purposes. There is no possibility here of discussing and distinguishing between the validity of discrete claims that the diverse members of the groups make. There is only one claim to consider and one decision to make: Whose side are you on?

I argue instead that in order to show equal respect for everyone, as well as solidaristic concern for the inclusion of everyone in society and politics, it is imperative to focus on particular political struggles for recognition and justice, and to discuss who actually suffers the greatest injustice in each case separately. Democratic respect requires that we approach people's way of life as composed of multiple and diverse claims. When we relate to one another as free and equal participants in democracy, we should consider the specific and disaggregated claims made by others, rather than reducing them to homogenous identity groups, each of which makes one grand unified claim.

The second danger of the populist claim for recognition is that it undermines the possibility of recognizing individual rights claims. It has often been noted that populists are impatient with legal procedures and deny that the will of the people should be constrained by respect for individual rights.[15] This description of populism is often connected to

---

[14] Rosanvallon (*Le siècle du populisme*, 33, my translation) puts it well: "The term ['the people'] allows both the expression of anger and at the same time membership of a particularly noble group."

[15] Müller, "Populism and Constitutionalism"; Canovan, "Trust the People!" 8; "Taking Politics to the People," 39.

its anti-liberalism and to the notion that populism promotes a form of illiberal democracy or democracy without rights.[16] I return to the issue of the relationship between democracy and rights in Chapter 4. In this chapter, I want to propose that there is a logical connection between the populist claim for recognition and its hostility to individual rights (or to the equal rights of minorities[17]). In short, populism *is* the confrontation of the demand for recognition of the people as a collective agent with respect for the rights claims of individual persons. In other words, the way in which populism claims we must recognize and respect the people, as a unified entity with one will, is by its very nature antithetical to the kind of respect that is expressed in and through individual rights. Later in this chapter I provide what I think is a normatively attractive interpretation of the meaning and value of individual rights, which I confront with the populist claim for recognition.

3.2   Protecting "the People's" Way of Life

Supporters of populist parties are often driven by the feeling that their way of life is under siege and in danger of disappearing.[18] Populist politicians promise to protect the people's status and way of life against the destructive forces brought down on them by "the elite." The pioneering populism scholar Margaret Canovan suggested two decades ago that populism is a kind of "redemptive politics" that promises a bright and perfect future.[19] However, commentators on contemporary populism stress that it is more concerned with protecting the status quo or bringing back the good old days.[20] Rogers Brubaker, for example, argues that a central element of contemporary populism is protectionism.[21] This protectionism can be (1) *economic*: protection against threats to domestic producers, workers, and debtors posed by foreign companies, workers, and creditors; (2) *securitarian*: protection against threats of terrorism and crime; (3) *cultural*: protection against threats posed by foreign cultures,

---

[16] Mounk, *People vs. Democracy*, 29–52; Mudde and Rovira Kaltwasser, *Populism*, 80–6; Müller, *What Is Populism?*, 44–60.

[17] Mudde ("Three Decades," 10) notes that it is minority rights that populist radical right parties are skeptical of.

[18] Wuthnow, *Left Behind*, 6, 43. According to Wuthnow (*Left Behind*, 43), it is "the communities upholding their way of life" that many people in rural American feel are in danger.

[19] Canovan, "Trust the People!"

[20] Rosanvallon, *Le siècle du populisme*, 72–4.

[21] Brubaker, "Why Populism," 366. On support for populism as related to defending and protecting one's collective identity, see also Eribon, *Returning to Reims*, 126; Smith and King, "White Protectionism in America."

values, and religions. All three kinds of protectionism can be seen as united in the protection of people's current way of life, culture, or collective identity.[22] It is this aspect of populism – *populism as protection of "the people's" way of life* – that provides the focus of my analysis of the populist claim for recognition.

Populist politicians, then, promise "the people" that they will protect and maintain their way of life. This promise entails a claim on other members of society (and beyond), namely the claim that they should recognize (respect *and* esteem) that way of life. However, "a way of life" has many aspects, and if in the struggle for recognition we treat a group's way of life as something to be accepted or rejected *as an indivisible whole*, we risk accepting either too much or too little. We risk accepting too much if we "recognize" an entire way of life with all its claims for esteem, respect, and honor. First, it is unclear what it actually means to recognize an entire way of life. Do we respect people's right to engage in it, or do we esteem their way of life as worthwhile and their norms and beliefs as right and true? I discussed the important differences between these ideas in Chapter 2. Second, if we tolerate and accept all the beliefs and practices comprising a way of life, we fail to consider the legitimacy of the different claims involved in them. Are the associated claims all consistent with democratic respect and the free and equal participation of everyone in society?

To illustrate the variety of claims made in the name of one's way of life, consider how Hochschild suggests that her Tea Party interviewees felt "culturally marginalized," among other things, because "their views about abortion, gay marriage, gender roles, race, guns, and the confederate flag all were ridiculed in the national media as backward."[23] At the same time, Hochschild describes other, more innocent beliefs as essential aspects of her interlocutors' way of life, including the value of manual labor, love of rural living, and deep religious faith. It is clear that the different aspects of this way of life involve very different claims on others. It is important in this connection to keep in mind the differences between beliefs we might agree with or at least tolerate (what I just called innocent beliefs) on the one hand, and the controversial beliefs mentioned in the quotation. The latter are beliefs about how our common relations and society should be organized, and they involve issues of basic rights and human equality. While a democracy should respect the right to express these beliefs, I see no reasons of democratic respect or solidarity to esteem, agree with, or legitimize practices and opinions that fail to respect fundamental democratic principles of human equality.

---

[22] I shall use "way of life," "culture," and "collective identity" interchangeably.

[23] Hochschild, *Strangers in Their Own Land*, 221.

What we see in this example is that when populist politicians promise to protect and maintain a way of life, they commit themselves to the acceptance of a broad and complex set of values, beliefs, and practices. Moreover, considered as a whole, a way of life is not something that the surrounding society or other citizens can simply be indifferent to or tolerate without making discriminations. The reason for this is that ways of life have propositional content and involve a number of claims on others and society in general.[24] That is, a way of life involves ideas about right and wrong, true and false. These validity claims are not just about the good life for individuals themselves, but also concern interpersonal norms regarding how people ought to relate to one another. Ways of life include claims on others and seek to impose duties on others. Insofar as people's ways of life have propositional content, they cannot be equally right, and insofar as they include norms about how to organize common affairs, they become rivals in defining what the right norms for society are.[25] This is why I say that we accept too much if we accept a way of life as a whole without considering the content of the specific and disparate claims made in and on behalf of the respective identity group.

Equally, the surrounding society should be careful not to delegitimize a group and its way of life as a whole because some of its claims are undemocratic and intolerable. Society can still show solidarity with the same group's concerns to protect the options of, for example, manual labor, rural living, and religious faith. Moreover, even if the members of a group share some features that have long given them a privileged status (say, whiteness and Christian faith), this does not mean that they necessarily belong to the dominant and oppressive group in all respects. For example, many supporters of right-wing populist parties are not privileged in terms of social class and education.[26] By treating a group as having *no* valid claims, society or other groups fail to act in solidarity with that group's legitimate ends.[27] Hence, while in Chapter 1 I argued that it would be too quick to conclude that just because a group are engaged in a struggle for recognition, they are engaged in a *democratic* struggle, here I argue that it would likewise be rushed to assume that supporters of

---

[24] For a similar point in relation to the multiculturalist demand for equal recognition of all cultures, see Barry, *Culture and Equality*, 270.

[25] Cf. Waldron, "Cultural Identity and Civic Responsibility," 161.

[26] On the United States, see Inglehart and Norris, "Trump." However, Mudde (*Far Right Today*, 78–80) argues that successful far-right parties have a more diverse support base than the stereotypical white working-class man.

[27] As Cohen ("Populism," 31) argues, the challenge is to find a way to be solidaristic with the legitimate grievances of supporters of populism without sacrificing allegiance to democratic equality.

right-wing populist parties have *no* valid claims for respect and solidarity just because most of them belong to traditional dominant groups such as whites, Christians, and heterosexuals.

If we treat a group's way of life as a unified whole and reject it *tout court*, we risk disrespecting its members. We can disesteem and object to particular aspects of a way of life without violating democratic principles, and we can rightly reject some of its claims, but we should be aware that because people's identities are closely bound up with their way of life, an all-out rejection of their way of life will be felt as a rejection of *them*. This is another reason why I stress that any way of life has many different aspects and includes different types of claim on others. We might rightly reject some of the aspects and claims of a culture (or way of life) that we do not share (racism, to stay with an obvious but still important example); other aspects we might merely object to as mistaken or foolish, but within the limits of toleration (for example, some religious beliefs and practices); still other aspects we are likely indifferent to (say, dress codes).[28] To portray ways of life as something to be protected or rejected as undifferentiated wholes, as well as to view one group as the victim for all purposes, amounts to a failure to consider people's specific claims on their merits. Furthermore, this way of framing political relations undercuts the possibility of distinguishing between claims we object to but which are still tolerable and claims that should be rejected as intolerable because they fail to respect other people's rights as equal participants in society.[29]

In addition, both the demand to have one's culture recognized as a whole and the rejection of a culture as a whole tend to ossify, freeze, or reify people's culture and identity.[30] Right-wing nostalgic defenses of "real people's" way of life and progressives' rejection of the same both engage in a form of identity politics where culture and identity are treated as given and unchangeable. In this confrontation, you either win or lose everything. There is no room to entertain the possibility that a culture or identity might develop or be partly transformed. Nor is there any room in this form of enclave thinking for dialogue across groups. The latter requires that we see

---

[28] Of course, many people do not accept others' religious practices; nor is everyone indifferent to dress codes. These issues have been hotly disputed in the multiculturalism debates over the last few decades. Thus, some might disagree with my examples, but I still think we have to accept the suggested differentiations. There is always something in other people's cultures that we, on reflection, either accept or are indifferent to.

[29] For the distinction between objection and rejection in practices of toleration, see Chapter 2.

[30] This is a much-discussed issue in the literature on recognition, multiculturalism, and identity. For an excellent example, see Appiah's (*Ethics of Identity*, 105–10) discussion of "the medusa syndrome." Hirvonen and Pennanen ("Populism as a Pathological Form," 39) show how populism limits progress by ossifying identities.

ways of life as composite wholes with many different and ever-changing aspects. For a culture to change in a way that is responsive to public deliberation requires that citizens discuss and assess *the specific and different claims* made by those who share the culture in question. Treating cultures as unchanging wholes inhibits mutual learning and social progress. What many societies need at the current conjuncture is precisely to figure out how everyone can find a place and feel at home in a changing recognition order, and this can be done through neither a complete rejection nor a complete acceptance of any existing way of life.

In the populist demand to protect the way of life of the authentic people, there is no question of considering individual claims or opinions: Everything "the people" stand for must be accepted, and everything the opponent stands for must be rejected. This totalizing demand for recognition makes it impossible to engage in a politics of mutual respect, which requires that we distinguish between different kinds of claim for recognition. All-out rejection of an opposing identity group amounts to disrespect for its bearers' status as free and equal participants in the political community, and does not qualify merely as a legitimate expression of disapproval, disesteem, or disagreement. It is a rejection of *them*. The problem with the populist framing is that it gives us only two options: Either we respect and esteem the entire way of life of the group populists call "the people," or we have shown ourselves to be the enemy of the people. Either we accept *all* the demands of this group, or we have shown disrespect for them. What I call the populist claim for recognition is exactly the claim that the group populists call the people is the wronged (ignored, oppressed, silenced) party and therefore all their demands are just and should be accepted.

It is not only populists who reject their opponent's way of life in its entirety. Supporters of populism are often driven by the fact – or at least the perception – that *their* way of life is rejected in its entirety. As noted at the beginning of this section, many people turn to populist parties because they feel that their way of life is under siege and in danger of disappearing. Thus, we are caught in a negative dynamic where opposing identities and ways of life are rejected or accepted as undifferentiated wholes. The deeper problem is when we view one another as opposing enclaves with either generally good qualities or generally bad qualities. We cannot divide society up in this manner without undermining the possibility of, first, democratic respect for our differences and disagreements, and second, solidaristic action that aims to find a valuable and valued place for everyone in an ever-changing recognition order.

The division of society into two homogeneous groups, one with generally good qualities and the other with generally bad qualities, is central to the populist claim for recognition. The claim, moreover, is that the first group, "the people," can be regarded as victims of injustice for all political purposes. The consequence of this framing of political conflict is that in order to promote justice and democracy, we must accept everything that "the people" demand without discrimination. If we do not do so, we have not only failed to take sides with the victims, but we have also failed to respect the people. But even if a populist party responds to some valid grievances, by its own logic it has no way of demonstrating that these are the most important grievances to respond to, and much less that the group it designates as the real people are the victims in all respects.

Part of the literature on populism accepts that its supporters have legitimate grievances and regrets only that these grievances become channeled through populist parties. My point, by contrast, is that the grievances leading to support for populism are not necessarily all equally legitimate, and that we – citizens, politicians, and scholars – often fail to distinguish between those grievances that are based on principles consistent with democratic respect and those that are not.

Our challenge is to break out of the negative dynamic that characterizes the struggles for esteem and respect in the current changing recognition order. I do not want to suggest that we can ever put an end to the struggle for recognition, or that people can find a final and secure positive social identity. Indeed, finding a place in the recognition order and being respected as an equal participant in society is a continuous struggle that is part of the never-finished democratic project. Nonetheless, the struggle for recognition can take a wrong path, which I believe happens in times of populism. The struggle for recognition takes a wrong path when it follows a dynamic that is in principle incompatible with the possibility that every individual can be respected as an individual, and when it inhibits the possibility of mutual critique and learning.

In Chapter 2, I maintained that demands for esteem for one's particularities and honor respect for one's group are inconsistent with respect for the equal standing of all human beings. In this chapter, I argue that the framing of political struggles as a dichotomic struggle between different ways of life is incompatible with individual freedom and equality. The framing of political struggles as one grand antagonism between qualitatively different groups both eradicates the crucial distinction between esteem and respect, the good and the right, and makes it impossible to properly differentiate between and assess on their merits the various claims that are implicit in "a way of life." The populist claim for recognition also makes it impossible for citizens to engage critically with each other's political views, because it entails not just respect for the standing of the people but also esteem for everything connected to their way of life.

Indeed, I would argue that populism's hostility to more deliberative modes of politics can be explained by its understanding of what is
required in order to "recognize the people."[31]

3.3   How Rights Provide for Respect

I would like now to connect our discussion of claim-making and mutual
respect to the meaning and value of rights. In preceding chapters, I have
developed the notion of democratic respect as a question of recognizing
the authority of others to make claims on us. In what follows, I show how
a system of rights can provide every single citizen with the equal standing
of authoritative claim makers and claim takers that democracy requires.
The issue of individual rights is central to the discussion of populism, both
because populist *politicians* claim that we can have democracy without rights
("illiberal democracy" as Viktor Orbán calls it) and because some *theorists*
of populism accept that democracy without rights is "deeply democratic."[32]

The question made urgent by the rise of populism is not merely for or
against the protection of individual rights but also how we understand the
meaning, value, and practice of rights in democracy. I argue that whether
or not equal rights provide for respect and self-respect depends on how we
as a society *understand* rights and how we *practice* the claim-making involved
in having rights. Thus, it is sufficient neither that a society has legal provisions for equal rights (say, a constitutional bill of rights) nor that political
movements and parties make their claims in the language of rights. In order
for rights to realize relations of mutual respect, citizens must also understand these rights in the proper way and take a particular attitude toward
one another in their rights-based claim-making. The value of individual
rights in terms of respect depends on an ethos in which citizens adopt the
participant attitude, where rights are seen as creating a specific kind of relation between persons rather than as a mere means for the egoistic person.
Rights are about what we owe to each other, about our mutual obligations.

Thinkers such as Honneth and Rawls have argued that the legal recognition of equal rights secures the social basis of self-respect. As Honneth
writes, the public character of legal rights "provide[s] one with a legitimate
way of making clear to oneself that one is respected by everyone else [...,]
that he or she is universally recognized as a morally responsible person."[33]

---

[31] On the rejection of the need for and value of public deliberation in populism, see Müller,
What Is Populism?, 25–32; Rosanvallon, *Le siècle du populisme*, 72–4; Weale, *Will of the
People*, x–xii. I return to issues related to democratic deliberation in Chapter 5.
[32] Mounk, *People vs. Democracy*, 8.
[33] Honneth, *Struggle for Recognition*, 120.

Similarly, Rawls writes that the public affirmation of equal rights means that "everyone has a similar and secure status *when they meet to conduct the common affairs of the wider society.*"[34] However, people can only feel secure in their status as equals when they meet others if they share a public culture characterized by a participant attitude of equal respect. It is not legal rights by themselves that provide recognition (respect) but people who do so, by mutually recognizing one another as rights bearers.

The fact is that while philosophers who argue that rights provide for mutual respect understand rights as relations and as involving obligations, citizens do not necessarily understand rights in this way. Citizens may understand rights as Karl Marx did in his critique of bourgeois society, namely as "the rights of ... egoistic man, of man as separated from other men and from the community."[35] Or they may understand rights as devices that protect one identity group against other identity groups, in the way populists aim to protect the life of one group against influences from other ways of life and interactions with outsiders. In order for rights to sustain respect and self-respect of the kind we have been discussing, we must understand rights differently, namely as establishing a specific kind of relationship between people, not as mere instruments for egoistic human beings or self-centered, protectionist identity groups.

So why should we reject the idea that rights are atomizing and merely instruments for the interests of egoistic man or protectionist identity groups? Why should we think instead that rights are relational and can provide for mutual respect among participants in a shared community? Consider here Joel Feinberg's proposal that rights are *claims* on others and therefore entail obligations.[36] According to Feinberg, for me to have a right to X is not merely a matter of me being free to X but entails the obligation (or duty[37]) of others to grant me X or not interfere with me in respect to X. I can be free to X if I am the only one around, if no one bothers to interfere with me, or if others benevolently decide not to interfere with me. But none of these cases amount to me *having a right* to X. I only have a right to X if I can claim the right to X in my relations with others, that is, if I can demand of others that they adjust their behavior in a way that respects my right to X. Rights give us standing and authority

---

[34] Rawls, *Theory of Justice*, 477, emphasis added.

[35] Marx, "On the Jewish Question," 42. Lefort ("Human Rights," 23, 32–3) argues that Marx fell into the trap of the dominant ideology when he understood rights as a disguise for bourgeois egoism, and that rights are in fact relational.

[36] Feinberg, "Nature and Value of Rights."

[37] While some philosophers distinguish between duty and obligation (for example, Rawls, *Theory of Justice*, 293 ff.), I shall not do so.

to make claims in our relations with others.[38] For this reason, we can say that rights are best understood not as the individual possessions of unconnected individuals, but rather as a type of relationship between persons. Indeed, rights are *constitutive* of a special kind of relationship between persons.[39]

According to Feinberg, "respect for persons ... may simply be respect for their rights, so that there cannot be the one without the other."[40] Importantly, it is the "activity of claim-making" implied by having equal rights that "makes for self-respect and respect for others"[41] – not merely the freedom to engage in the activities to which we have rights.[42] Respect and self-respect are relational issues that concern not just what we are free to do but the moral status we have among other persons and in the community. The corollary of you having the authority provided by your rights is the obligation (or "directed duty") on my (or the surrounding society's) part to be open to your claims.[43] Rights, therefore, do not separate people from one another but require that they regard each other as members of a community in which the members have mutual obligations.

A society constituted by a system of rights is based neither on egoism nor on benevolence. The egoistic person is characterized by always taking a first-person perspective and choosing what is good for them from that perspective. There is no guarantee that the egoistic person will prefer a society of rights and will not trade their rights for other valuable goods. For this reason, Anderson argues that the inalienable character of rights cannot be explained from the first-person standpoint of subjective preferences but requires that we take "the standpoint of the obligation holder."[44] People may and may not want rights, but this does not change the fact that others, as obligation holders, owe them respect as

---

[38] Darwall, *Second-Person Standpoint*, 140.

[39] Michelman ("Justification," 91) puts it vividly: "Why should rights be necessarily atomizing and alienating? A right, after all, is neither a gun nor a one-man show. It is a relationship and a social practice, and in both those essential aspects it is seemingly an expression of connectedness. Rights are public propositions, involving obligations to others as well as entitlements against them [.... T]hey are a form of social cooperation – not spontaneous but highly organized cooperation, no doubt, but still, in the final analysis, cooperation." See also Cruft ("On the Non-Instrumental Value," 451), who argues that basics rights are constitutive of "relationships that bind all humans together in fellowship as members of a shared proto-community."

[40] Feinberg, "Nature and Value of Rights," 252.

[41] Feinberg, "Nature and Value of Rights," 257.

[42] The activity of claim-making that Feinberg speaks of here should not be confused with the idea of validity claims mentioned earlier. A right is a valid claim, not a claim about what is valid.

[43] Darwall, *Second-Person Standpoint*, 142; Zylberman, "Why Human Rights," 324.

[44] Anderson, "What Is the Point," 319, 336.

authoritative claim makers. We owe to others respect for their rights in virtue of their dignity and their standing as free and equal participants in the political community, not to satisfy their subjective preferences.

Benevolence, for its part, is something a person or society give others as a free gift, but not something anybody can demand. Thus, a society based on benevolence is one where you can hope to be awarded certain freedoms but not one where you can claim them as a matter of right. Feinberg shows well why an imaginary benevolent society without rights would be lacking something important in terms of respect and self-respect: You might be able to do the same things in this society, but you would not be able to demand the same things of others or society, and you would therefore not have the standing and authority that are required for mutual respect.[45] Rights and mutual respect, then, are about not simply what people are free to do, but how we regard and what we owe to each other. The value of rights is that they make us independent of other people's subjective feelings about us – of their esteem, love, and benevolence.

Kant's rights-based moral and political theory is motivated precisely by a rejection of benevolence-centered moral theories and their aristocratic counterpart in political practice. As one commentator explains: "A society built around benevolence and kindness is for Kant a society requiring not only inequality but servility as well. If nothing is properly mine except what someone graciously gives me, I am forever dependent on how the donor feels toward me."[46] Yet, while freedom for Kant is about independence, this independence is only from other people's subjective feelings and choices (their ill- and goodwill), what he calls their private or unilateral will. Freedom for Kant is "independence from being constrained by another's choice,"[47] not independence from the political community or what he calls the common or omnilateral will. Indeed, Kant regards "the *dependence* of all upon a single common legislation" as a precondition of equal freedom.[48] Dependence on a private will violates freedom because a private will has purposes of its own, while dependence on a constitution is a precondition of freedom as independence, because it establishes "a collective general (common) and powerful will" that harmonizes the free choices of each without having purposes of its own.[49] Freedom in Kant is not freedom from others, but freedom in a

---

[45] Feinberg, "Nature and Value of Rights."
[46] See Schneewind, "Autonomy, Obligation, and Virtue," 311.
[47] Kant, *Metaphysics of Morals*, 393 (AK 6: 237).
[48] Kant, "Toward Perpetual Peace," 322 (AK 8: 349–50).
[49] Kant, *Metaphysics of Morals*, 409 (AK 6: 256). For a further elaboration of Kant's notion of freedom as independence, see Rostbøll, "Kant, Freedom."

person's relations to others. Hence, freedom is a kind of status one has in society, and it is constituted by individual rights.

Philip Pettit puts the idea well in explaining the republican conception of freedom: "Freedom requires independency on the will of others, even the goodwill of others. And for that deep and inescapable reason, free status is something that we can make available to one another as individuals only by collectively organizing ourselves in … a just and democratic state."[50] Rights, then, give us freedom as individuals, *and* they are part of a collective, cooperative enterprise. The respect provided by a constitutional democracy with a system of rights is one that regards each individual both as having the standing of an independent person with a will of their own and as a participant in a common will that must secure the equal standing of everyone.

3.3.1   Respecting People's Way of Life

Remember, we are concerned with the fact that a large group of people in contemporary society do not feel that their way of life is recognized. I have rejected the notion that society owes people esteem for their way of life, because universal equality of esteem is a nonsensical notion. What we owe others is respect for their status as equal persons or citizens, and solidarity in the face of respect-undermining adversity. Still, we can acknowledge the value that people attach to their way of life. That is, we can recognize that other people's way of life and identity matters very much *to them*.[51] This does not mean that *we* value their culture, but it means that we value and respect them as fellow citizens or persons who *have* a culture. What we respect here is their status as fellow citizens who have certain attachments and values (identities and cultures) that matter greatly to them. Indeed, the capacity to have "a conception of the good" and an identity that gives shape to one's "way of life" – "what one sees oneself as doing and trying to accomplish in the social world" – is part of what it means to be a person in Kantian theory.[52] If being a person includes the capacity to form one's own conception of the good, identity, or culture, then we should also recognize and respect the fact that such things matter to people exactly as persons. As Rawls writes, it is through the public affirmation of individual rights that citizens express "their recognition of

---

[50] Pettit, *On the People's Terms*, 184. Pettit is not explaining Kant here, but I think that the quoted explication of the republican conception of freedom fits perfectly with Kant as well. See also Rostbøll, "Non-Domination and Democratic Legitimacy," 435–6.

[51] Jones, "Equality, Recognition and Difference."

[52] Rawls, *Political Liberalism*, 31, cf. 18–20, 30–2; see also Rostbøll, "Kantian Autonomy and Political Liberalism," 348–50.

the worth all citizens attach to their way of life."[53] If people as equal persons (or citizens) should be able to form and pursue their own conception of the good and live according to their deepest beliefs or culture, then we should take these things seriously in the way we relate to them.[54]

When we connect respect for people's way of life to rights as claims, it becomes clear that we must consider more precisely what their actual claims are. Since a way of life consists of many different beliefs and practices, a demand for respect for one's "way of life" must also consist of a number of different claims. Some of these claims might be valid, while others might not be. A right is not just any claim but a *valid* claim, something others owe you.[55] The multiplicity of claims inherent in any way of life and the notion that a right is a valid claim entail that people cannot demand respect for and the right to engage in their "way of life" as such. Nor can others legitimately reject a way of life in all its many aspects. Insofar as, say, liberals and progressives reject a conservative and traditional way of life, because of its discriminatory aspects or because of its members' privileged status, they fail to differentiate different aspects of that way of life. To take other people's way of life seriously, as something that matters deeply to them and therefore should matter to us, requires that we do not reject all its aspects just because some of those aspects are intolerable or its bearers in some respects have a privileged status.

The conclusion of the preceding paragraph rests on a commitment to free and equal status, which means that those aspects of a culture that cannot be exercised with respect for equal freedom are beyond the limits of toleration. It is *the same norm* that requires us to tolerate others' free exercise of the legitimate aspects of their way of life *and* which puts limits on which cultural practices can be tolerated. It would be contradictory, and would undermine the moral-political culture of toleration, not to reject practices that do not recognize the norm that supplies the reason for toleration in the first place.[56]

Next, when we view respect and rights as securing the standing to make claims on others, respect for culture is not just a question of some (the elite, society, or state) *permitting* others to live according to their conception of the good life.[57] People *exact* respect from others, as Kant puts it,[58] and we assert our rights by making claims on others. The value

[53] Rawls, *Political Liberalism*, 319.
[54] Rostbøll, "Autonomy, Respect, and Arrogance," 634.
[55] Feinberg, "Nature and Value of Rights," 253.
[56] Rostbøll, "Compromise and Toleration," 27.
[57] See also Forst's ("'To Tolerate Means to Insult'") distinction between "the permission conception" and "the respect conception" of toleration.
[58] Kant, *Metaphysics of Morals*, 557 (AK 6: 434–5). See also Chapter 2 in this volume.

of rights lies precisely in the fact that we do not need others' permission to engage in our legitimate pursuits. Moreover, the dignity of the person lies not just in the right not to be ill-treated, or in being free to live according to one's culture, nor just in the authority to demand certain actions of others; most importantly, it lies in the standing to demand respect for that very authority.[59] The respect provided by viewing others as rights holders entails that everyone has the obligation to be open to, listen to, and consider others' claims on them and society. This obligation is one we have to the claim maker as a free and equal person, and not directly to their culture. But, as I have suggested, we must also acknowledge that others make their claims as persons for whom their way of life and identity matter deeply.

I just said that viewing others as rights holders entails that we must listen to and consider their claims. And earlier, we saw that Feinberg sees "the activity of claim-making" as central to the nature and value of rights. I want now to submit that these ideas indicate an intimate connection between rights as claims and common deliberation. The activity of claim-making constituted by a system of rights is an activity of addressing others and demanding a reasoned response from them. When people regard one another as rights holders, they respect one another as persons to whom they owe a hearing. Rights are related to common deliberation in three ways. First, rights as claim-making proceeds as a form of deliberation. Second, rights provide people with the freedom to engage in common deliberation.[60] Third, in respecting others as right holders we recognize that they have the qualities to engage in common deliberation.[61]

It might be asked whether the type of solidarity for which I argued in Chapter 2 is not a form of goodwill or benevolence. Solidarity as active inclusion under respect-adverse circumstances goes beyond respect for other people's right to engage in legitimate pursuits, to a positive expression that their ends or ways of life have a legitimate place in society. But note that the point of promoting solidarity as inclusion is not to suggest that people need others' permission, goodwill, or esteem to be free to engage in their legitimate pursuits. The right to do so is still independent of other people's esteem and benevolence. The point of solidarity is that a legal system of rights under respect-adverse conditions is insufficient

---

[59] Darwall, *Second-Person Standpoint*, 13f, 121; Feinberg, "Nature and Value of Rights," 252.

[60] We might discuss exactly which rights are required for the freedom to engage in common deliberation, but I think it requires an extensive set of individual, political, and social rights.

[61] According to Honneth (*Struggle for Recognition*, 120), "in the experience of legal recognition, one is able to view oneself as a person who shares with all other members of one's community the qualities that make participation in discursive will-formation possible."

for people to experience themselves as having a legitimate place in the social recognition order. Sometimes more is needed, as I think is evident from the resentment and struggle for recognition that many democracies are facing in the current wave of populism. Thus, my argument goes beyond the more legalistic approach of Kant to one that emphasizes the importance of informal attitudes.[62]

3.3.2   Rights and the Participant Attitude

One of the things we are learning, or at least are reminded of, as we observe the rise of populism and its transformation of democracy is how much a liberal democratic regime depends on a liberal democratic culture.[63] I have suggested an interpretation of the meaning and value of rights that emphasizes their relational character and the respect for the authority of members of the legal community as claim makers that rights entail. However, there is no guarantee that people will actually view their rights in this way. On the one hand, people might view their rights in the way that Marx said bourgeois society views rights: as nothing but instruments for the realization of egoistic aims. On the other hand, people might not feel that their rights provide them with the respect from the surrounding society that they need to maintain their self-respect. In this context, it is important to realize that how we understand individual rights depends on the *attitudes* we adopt toward both our institutions and the people with whom we share them. Therefore, I would like to argue that we cannot simply say that it is "the nature" of rights to provide for respect and self-respect, as Feinberg does.[64] Rights only do so if people view them in a certain way and adopt a certain attitude to their rights and the relationships they create with other people. Put differently, I am advocating a specific normative understanding of rights rather than merely describing what rights are.

In *Between Facts and Norms*, Habermas puts forward the idea that we can approach our rights from two different perspectives and with two different attitudes.[65] First, we can approach our rights as externally

---

[62] This does not mean that solidarity is only a matter of informal attitudes. As I have already mentioned, solidarity can also be institutionalized in redistributive policies and social rights.

[63] This is also one of the conclusions of Levitsky and Ziblatt, *How Democracies Die*. See especially their discussion of "the soft guardrails of democracy" in Chapter 7.

[64] As Wenar ("Rights") notes: "The statement that rights are claims is prescriptive for, not descriptive of, usage."

[65] Habermas, *Between Facts and Norms*, Chapters 1 and 3. For the distinction between the performative attitude of the participant and the objectivating attitude of the observer, see Habermas, *Between Facts and Norms*, for example, 18–20, 30–1, and 121.

given facts that we can take advantage of as means for realizing our ends. This approach entails the "objectivating attitude of the observer," who considers what is available to them as means for the realization of their individual (but not necessarily egoistic) ends. From this perspective and with this attitude, I can see why rights might be advantageous for me to have. However, I cannot see why I owe it to others to respect *their* rights, and nor can I see rights as securing self-respect. For the latter, we need a different perspective and attitude.

Thus, second, we may approach rights from the second-personal perspective of the participant, which concerns how we stand in relation to others and how we recognize one another. It is this perspective and attitude that I urge we should take throughout this book – because I think it is an essential aspect of the ethos of democracy – and which underlies the analysis of rights as relational claims in this chapter. From this perspective, rights are regarded not as externally given facts, but rather as something people recognize that they owe to each other. As Habermas puts it:

> Rights do not immediately refer to atomistic and estranged individuals who are possessively set against one another. On the contrary, as elements of the legal order they presuppose collaboration among subjects who recognize one another, in their reciprocally related rights and duties, as free and equal citizens. This mutual recognition is constitutive for a legal order from which actionable rights are derived.[66]

In other words, rights presuppose mutual recognition, and this mutual recognition constitutes a legal community of free and equal participants. Maintaining a system of rights is a way for the members of a political community to publicly recognize one another's freedom and equality. Moreover, people can only attain self-respect from their rights if they understand them as expressions of mutual recognition of equal standing among members of a shared, cooperating community.

We have seen that rights can be interpreted in relational terms, in which case their unique value lies in how the activity of mutual claim-making for which they call can make for respect and self-respect. Yet, I have also argued that the system of rights provided by a constitutional democratic regime does not *by itself* guarantee that people view their rights in this way. Indeed, it is also in the nature of legal rights, and part of their value, that they cannot obligate or force us to take a specific attitude toward our fellow citizens.[67] Legal rights provide citizens with the valuable freedom to take an observer attitude toward their fellow

[66] Habermas, *Between Facts and Norms*, 88.
[67] Habermas, *Between Facts and Norms*, 118–21.

citizens and their opportunities. That is, rights are also means to pursue one's own ends without constantly having to consider one's obligations to others. However, if citizens do not generally recognize that the system of rights that constitutes democracy depends on mutual obligations, and instead only see their rights with an observer attitude, I doubt that they can maintain democracy.[68] Consequently, our challenge is to establish a political culture that lives up to the meaning and value of rights as establishing relations of mutual respect among citizens.

It might be said that it is the very function of rights (legal and moral) to provide people with an area of personal freedom that precludes the requirement that rights be used for the good. Accordingly, it has been argued that having a right entails "a right to do wrong."[69] Moreover, as Waldron notes regarding the range of actions protected by rights, "individual choices are seen as crucial to personal integrity. To make a decision in these areas is, in some sense, to decide what person one is to be."[70] Hence, having rights entails a freedom to define and shape one's own identity. Does this point undermine my objection to viewing one's rights exclusively as a means for one's own ends? I do not think so. As those who defend the coherence of the idea that there can be a right to do wrong stress, this point does not make one immune from criticism of how one uses one's rights. Quite the contrary, it is exactly because there can be a right to do wrong that one can be criticized for one's use of one's rights. If I can have a right to make certain morally bad choices, this entails that there can be moral reasons to criticize my choices. If I have a right to choose something, I do not have to justify my choice in order to have the right to make it, but I might rightfully be asked to justify my action in other, not rights-related, moral terms. You can, for example, morally criticize my offensive or misleading public speech without denying my right to freedom of speech. The right to freedom of speech is not a sufficient reason to engage in all protected types of expression. "I have a right to say X" is not a sufficient reason to establish that it is good to say X, even if it is a sufficient reason for you not to interfere with me saying X.

My argument does not so much concern how people *use* their rights as how they *understand* their rights. Nonetheless, we can make a similar argument here as in the previous paragraph. Your right to regard your rights through the objectivating attitude of an observer and as mere means for your subjective ends is not a sufficient reason to understand your rights in that manner. We have moral reasons both to see rights as providing an

---

[68] See also Rostbøll, *Deliberative Freedom*, 161–6.
[69] Waldron, "Right to Do Wrong"; Jones, *Rights*, 204–7.
[70] Waldron, "Right to Do Wrong," 34.

area in which to define one's self and to be critical of those who only see rights in this way. As elements of a legal order, rights themselves cannot demand to be used or understood in a specific way, but we can still have good moral reasons to use and understand them in the way suggested. The reason to adopt the participant attitude and understand rights as relational claims is that this is necessary to understand the obligations we have to one another in terms of mutual respect. Mutual recognition of equal rights among people who regard each other as fellow participants is what constitutes and maintains a community of democratic respect.

The understanding of rights as forms of recognition of free and equal status includes respect for the authority of fellow citizens as claim makers. This point brings us back to the populist claim for recognition and the issue of acceptance versus rejection of people's cultures *as undifferentiated wholes*. Thus, when the surrounding society condemns the culture of a group of people – such as the way of life of potential supporters of right-wing populism – indiscriminately and as a whole, it in effect annuls the ability of those who share this culture to make claims, and it fails to respect their authority as equal claim makers. People whose entire way of life is under attack will not experience the public realm as open to them, others as wanting to see or hear them, or themselves as part of the public. As I have argued, people cannot demand that others or the public esteem their culture, nor can they require that others agree with the political opinions that are part of their culture, but they can demand that the public consider their claims and respect their authority as rights holders to make claims. We owe it to others as persons and fellow citizens to listen to their claims and consider whether they are valid or not.

To conclude this section, I want to set out four ways in which the populist claim for recognition contravenes the adoption of the participant attitude to our rights claims, where we presuppose that persons recognize one another as mutually accountable individuals with equal standing. The populist claim for recognition, remember, is the claim that we can regard one uniform and partial group in society – "the people" – as the worst-off group for all political purposes. First, the populist claim for recognition regards a particular group as "the people." But if only a part of the population has the standing of the (true or authentic) people, then the rest of the population is by necessity not recognized as having an equal standing in the political community. Thus, the populist claim for recognition lacks the mutuality and reciprocity of rights claims.

Second, "the people" provided with standing and recognition in populism are seen not as a plurality of persons, each of whom has their own claims, but as a macro subject with one voice and one will. Thus, the populist claim for recognition differs from individual rights claims by not being attributable to individual persons and not being about the standing of individuals. Or at least, it cannot be about the claims and standing of individuals as separable from and in potential conflict with "the people." Thus, the populist claim for recognition denies standing not only to its opponent (the non-people elite), but also to the separate individual persons who make up "the people."

Third, in order to create a collective people and distinguish it from the elite, populism depends on an identico-political construction where the two camps are distinguished as two qualitatively different *identity* groups.[71] But when politics is understood as an antagonistic conflict between two identity groups, it becomes impossible to separate demands for esteem and demands for respect. The populist claim to "respect" the people is simultaneously a demand that we accept their political opinions and esteem their way of life. This precludes the possibility of respecting people's rights while objecting to their political opinions and way of life.

Finally, the identico-political construction of people versus elite involves a valorization of the former that is denied to the latter. This precludes the requirement of mutual accountability and the idea that claims must be assessed on their merits. Moreover, the populist claim is difficult to understand and evaluate as a claim that any particular right (to free expression, to vote, to an adequate standard of living, etc.) of any particular person has been violated. And if a claim does not refer to any particular or clear violation of an obligation on someone else's part, it is difficult to assess whether the claim is valid or not. The populist claim lacks both a clear subject and a clear addressee.

The Kantian approach, which separates the issues of respect and esteem, and which regards the rights claims made by individual persons as constitutive of a just society, enables us to distinguish between what we owe to each other, what are reasonable disagreements, and which demands have no place in a community of free and equal persons. If we do not separate the person who makes a claim from their way of life, there is no way of differentiating between the many claims made in the name of or to protect that collective identity. If we do not distinguish between respect for individual persons and the collective people invoked by populism, there is no way to discriminate between and assess on their merits the many claims made on behalf of the "the people." If we do not distinguish between the respect we owe to everyone as persons and the appraisal of their views, we block the possibility of mutual critique and learning among citizens.

[71] The idea of populism as a way of constructing and articulating antagonistic identity groups is prominent in Laclau, *On Populist Reason.*

3.4   The Question of Anti-Populism

To my argument that we should regard a way of life as composed of different kinds of claim, some readers might object that it is foreign to how many people view their way of life. Most people do not distinguish between the various aspects of their way of life in the way I have suggested we must, this objection would say. People just want to be able to continue to live according to their own ideas of what constitutes a good life, and not to be prevented from or ridiculed for doing so by others. Consequently, the objector might suggest that to respect people's way of life requires others to respect *those people's* understanding of what a culture is, rather than imposing a different view of culture on them and requiring that they hold their culture in a more open-minded or "liberal" spirit. What I urge such an objector to consider is whether and how such a view is consistent with a society of equal and mutual respect. To be sure, the objector can reject the aim of establishing a society of equal and mutual respect, but then they have also relinquished the possibility of appealing to the latter principle. "A person's right to complain is limited to violations of principles he acknowledges himself," as Rawls says.[72] As a moral principle, democratic respect places demands on people, and it cannot simply be a question of uncritically accepting people's claims.

What we must remember is that among people who are living side by side, when one demands respect for one's way of life, one imposes duties on others to adjust *their* way of life. To say that we should recognize people's way of life or identity in its entirety and as they see it is tantamount to giving people a veto over how they should be treated. Such a veto is incompatible with the mutuality and equality of democratic respect. It is to demand respect from others without recognizing that others have a reciprocal and equal claim against one.[73]

This is not to deny that people's beliefs and their understanding of who they are, their identity, and their way of life are often so closely bound together that they are hard to separate.[74] When we discuss and criticize other people's beliefs, this often feels like an attack on them as persons. It feels like disrespect for their status as co-citizens rather than an expression of disagreement on norms that regulate our common

---

[72] Rawls, *Theory of Justice*, 190.
[73] Cf. Darwall, *Second-Person Standpoint*, 136.
[74] See in this connection Williams's ("Persons, Character and Morality," 12–14) discussion of "ground projects" and Hill's (*Respect, Pluralism, and Justice*, 73, 78–9) Kantian consideration of this point.

life.[75] Does this mean that citizens should refrain from discussing claims that are embedded in people's way of life, or should treat them as vetoes? I do not see how this could be possible.

First, all of our beliefs, including our political opinions, are in some way embedded in our way of life and connected to our identity. If we cannot discuss issues embedded in people's way of life, we cannot discuss politics with our fellow citizens. The totalizing populist framing of political conflict as one grand social conflict between the endangered way of life of common people and the threatening elite has the effect that we cannot have any common discussion of specific claims and their validity. Everything is reduced to whether you are for or against the people and want to protect or destroy their way of life.[76] This is not only harmful for the discussion of policy[77]; it is also detrimental to democratic respect. For, as I have emphasized, in accepting or rejecting a way of life as a whole, we may accept or reject too many or too few of the demands for recognition made by the people in question.

Second, one of the most common complaints of populists is that they are *not heard* by the surrounding society. While everyone being heard and listened to is an essential aspect of democratic respect, this obligation should not be confused with an uncritical acceptance of all the claims embedded in people's identity or way of life. To be listened to in a democratic way means having one's claims seriously considered in public deliberation. And to be respected in public deliberation means being met as "a voice that cannot properly be ignored, a voice which speaks to issues raised in common with others and which speaks with a certain authority [...,] to be taken as someone worth listening to."[78]

In Chapter 2, I argued that the Kantian notion of respect for persons entails regarding others as autonomous and mutually accountable persons that are capable of responding appropriately to reasons. Moreover, I said that we show one another respect by soliciting each other's participation in common political discussion. When we discuss people's opinions with them, we treat them as reason-responsive persons who can defend their claims and learn from the exchange of reasons, rather than passive beings who are inflexibly bound to and determined by their identity.[79] Not to consider the validity of other people's claims is to treat them as if their validity were irrelevant, which amounts to not taking those claims

---

[75] Elsewhere, I have discussed this point in more detail and in a different context: Rostbøll, "Autonomy, Respect, and Arrogance," 633–5.

[76] Moffitt, *Global Rise of Populism*, 148.

[77] Weale, *Will of the People*, 114.

[78] Pettit, *Republicanism*, 91.

[79] Cf. Hill, *Respect, Pluralism, and Justice*, 79.

seriously as beliefs about how people ought to live or be treated, or how we ought to organize our common affairs.[80] If we refrain from critically engaging with other people's views, we place them outside participatory relationships of mutual accountability and reason-giving. We respect others as autonomous beings and fellow participants in democracy not by accepting their claims as an expression of an unchangeable way of life to which people are bound, but by subjecting them to public discussion and critical assessment.

It might be that some people do not separate the different claims inherent in their way of life and that they experience criticism of their beliefs as a rejection of *them*. However, if we are to live together on terms of mutual respect and engage in democracy as more than an antagonistic struggle between different identity groups, we have to learn to think and act differently. Everyone has to learn, first, that ways of life are not something we should protect or reject as monolithic wholes, and second, that disagreement on and criticisms of the specific beliefs embedded in a way of life are not the same as disrespect for people as persons or fellow citizens. The trouble with the type of polarization created by populism is precisely that the parties confront one another as undifferentiated wholes, in which case you have to either accept or reject *everything* the other stands for.[81] It is not only right-wing populists that think this way; some liberals and progressives also relate to their opponent's way of life as something that has to be rejected entirely – because it has some intolerable aspects, or because it is historically privileged. My suggestion is that the only way we can go beyond that kind of confrontation is by engaging with the *specific* claims made by the other party as claims about our relationships, standing as citizens, and rights. In a democracy, it is crucial that opposition and criticism concern clear violations of obligations and rights, rather than being expressed as rejections of entire ways of life.

A different objection to my argument about regarding cultures as composed of multiple claims is that it is in the very nature of "the political" to pit group identities against one another. This is the view of Ernesto Laclau, who for this reason holds that all politics is populist. According to Laclau, the formation of collective identities through an antagonistic confrontation between different groups is part of "the ontological

---

[80] "On almost any view of what constitutes respecting a person, it is hard to take seriously the complaint that conducting a sober examination of the truth of another's beliefs amounts to not treating him, or his beliefs, with respect. Arguably, it is more insulting to have one's beliefs treated as though their truth or falsity were of no consequence; for that is to have one's beliefs not taken seriously as *beliefs*" (Jones, "Respecting Beliefs and Rebuking Rushdie," 429).

[81] Rostbøll, "Populism and Two Kinds."

constitution of the political as such."[82] While Laclau's theory provides valuable theoretical tools for understanding populist politics, I am not convinced that he succeeds in showing that politics *necessarily* has to follow the populistic logic of "us versus them." Collective identity formation might always be part of democratic politics, but I do not see why it has to take the extreme form of pitting undifferentiated and homogenized identity groups against one another. While Laclau accepts that the populism of different movements and parties is a matter of degree,[83] his theory leaves no space for understanding the value of a kind of politics where we consider the discrete claims that individual citizens make on one another. Moreover, if it were true that politics is necessarily and only about antagonistic confrontation between collective identity groups, then there would be no way to adjudicate between the claims made by different groups. Politics would just be a question of taking sides.

It might be argued that anti-populist discourse – including this book – also simply takes sides, and that it treats populism as an undifferentiated whole and fails to consider the specific claims made by parties labeled "populist."[84] Thus, Yannis Stavrakakis – a follower of Laclau – writes: "'Populism' often becomes the negative index through which European political, economic and intellectual elites attempt to identify, stigmatise and contain demands for dignity and recognition, wider participation, egalitarian justice and the radicalisation of democracy."[85] This is an important concern, and it partly explains why I think we should consider the specific demands made by everyone, including supporters of both left- and right-wing populism. However, I think this position is irreconcilable with Stavrakakis's own defense of populist discourse that sets up "an antagonistic representation of the socio-political field along an us/them dichotomy."[86] We cannot have it both ways: *either* politics is necessarily about antagonistic confrontation between "us" and "them," and then stereotyping, stigmatization, and so on is part of the game; *or* politics is not necessarily populist, and then we can consider the specific claims made by other groups and discuss their validity in common.

Stavrakakis asks us to consider the demands for dignity and recognition made by *left* populist parties such as the Greek Syriza, *and* he defends the latter's use of populist rhetoric. However, this form of discourse itself treats "the elite" and those who agree with it in a stereotypical

---

[82] Laclau, *On Populist Reason*, 67.
[83] Laclau, "Populism," 161.
[84] Stavrakakis, "Populism in Power"; Stavrakakis, "Populism and Hegemony," 540.
[85] Stavrakakis, "Populism in Power," 274.
[86] Stavrakakis, "Populism and Hegemony," 540.

and undiscriminating way. There is no room in this discourse either to consider the specific claims made by the other side or to respect the authority of the other side to make claims. In this connection, we should remember that right-wing populist parties often also make demands for dignity, recognition, and wider participation, and that they also direct their demands against "the elite." People on the left must think that supporters of right-wing populism are in some way mistaken in their demands; otherwise, it is difficult to understand why they would oppose them. But how do we *know* whose demands for dignity and recognition are valid and should be heeded? My point here has been that this requires that we actually consider people's specific demands, and that the logic of populism destroys this option. Populism is a denial of the very possibility that there can be any discussion of whose claims for recognition and justice are valid. The populist claim is that "the people" is right because it is the oppressed part. This articulation of political conflict not only denies those designated the elite the right to defend their opinions, but also obstructs the discussion of who actually suffers the greatest injustice in particular cases.

Here I am in agreement with Pierre Rosanvallon, who puts the point well in his criticism of populism:

Instead of stigmatizing *the* caste, *the* oligarchy, *the* establishment in a simple sociology of denunciation, one ought to focus on *situations* and *practices* of domination, stigmatization, and exploitation to combat these divisions .... The point is not to exalt an imaginary people, but rather to create a *democratic society* based on accepted principles of distributive and redistributive justice, a common vision of what it means to form a society of equals. This requires also that one move away from a mystical invocation of the people to a recognition of its internal tensions and diversity.[87]

In this chapter, I have argued that we should not reject and delegitimize groups as monolithic wholes, but rather should consider their specific claims individually and on their merits. However, some readers may wonder whether there are *political parties* that should be rejected as a whole. When citizens respectfully consider the demands of a party, when the media reports on it in a neutral manner, and when other parties cooperate with it, they normalize it and legitimize it. Does my analysis suggest that this is always the right approach? Notice that in this and the previous chapter, I have been discussing the recognition of ways of life and identities, rather than political parties. But, an objector might insist, sometimes people feel a strong connection between their way of life and

---

[87] Rosanvallon, *Le siècle du populisme*, 224–5, my translation.

a political party. They feel that an attack on their political party is an attack on them, on their identity.[88] Populist politicians are especially skillful in making people feel this way. My argument is exactly that we must counteract this feeling and resist the populist articulation of political conflict that exacerbates it.

Democratic respect requires that we be able to separate critique of or disagreement with specific political positions from attacks on an entire way of life. Disagreement with and even rejection of cooperation with a political party should not be seen as a rejection of the entire way of life of its supporters – it is a distortion of the spirit of democracy to look at it in this way. But should parties ever reject all cooperation with another political party? While the overall thrust of my argument in this book is in favor of cooperation and compromise, there are limits to this requirement. Parties that violate fundamental democratic norms of mutual respect have no claim to be legitimated through cooperation and compromise. It does not improve our democratic culture and our understanding of democratic obligations to so legitimize antidemocratic ideas and practices.[89]

---

[88] On partisanship as an identity, see the literature on affective polarization, for example, Iyengar et al., "Origins and Consequences"; Iyengar, Sood, and Lelkes, "Affect, Not Ideology"; Mason, *Uncivil Agreement*.

[89] Admittedly, this is too quick a treatment of a complex issue. I return to the question of the limits of cooperation and compromise in Chapter 5.

4   Procedures, Outcomes, or Identification?

In Chapters 2 and 3, we discussed feelings of disrespect and loss of status as general societal issues, and we concentrated on the question of respect for ways of life. In this chapter, our concern will be with feelings of disrespect and loss of status, esteem, and power in citizens' *political relations.* Commonly, supporters of populist parties do not just feel a lack of recognition for their way of life; they also feel ignored and powerless in their political relations with other citizens and the government. Thus, both qualitative and quantitative empirical studies have documented the connection between perceptions of political powerlessness and feelings of political disrespect on the one hand and support for populism on the other.[1]

What kind of recognition, status, and political power can people legitimately demand in their political relations with other citizens and the government, and what kind of recognition, status, and power are populist politicians supplying to the people? To answer the question of what kind of political recognition it is legitimate for people to demand, we must consider what the normatively best way to understand democracy is. The question of what kind of recognition populism supplies to the people connects to the question of how populists understand and practice "democracy." As mentioned in the Introduction, I see populism as promoting a distinctive conception of democracy, and I assume that part of the appeal of the populist conception of democracy lies in how it promises to recognize the people. One of the claims of populism, I suggested, is that politics should recognize and restore the privileged standing of the people. This chapter provides an elaboration, analysis, and discussion of this claim and of the populist conception of democracy.

In particular, I examine and dispute the idea that populism's promise to recognize the people is based on a commitment to a purely *procedural* understanding of democracy that rejects all substantive standards and

---

[1] Cramer, *Politics of Resentment*, 40, 52, 66, 105; Eribon, *Returning to Reims*, 119–34; Gest, Reny, and Mayer, "Roots of the Radical Right"; Gidron and Hall, "Populism as a Problem"; Spruyt, Keppens, and Van Droogenbroeck, "Who Supports Populism."

constraints on democratic decision-making. We cannot understand populism as essentially democratic and committed to the procedural aspect of democracy and as only against liberal or constitutional constraints, as influential researchers suggest.[2] The primary shortcoming of the populist understanding of democracy is not that it lacks substantive constraints on popular decision-making, but that it is not fully committed to the procedural aspect of democracy and the respect the latter expresses for individual citizens. Moreover, insofar as populists speak of democratic procedures, they have a very limited and minimalist understanding of these, focusing on aggregative mechanisms such as referendums and elections, with no concern for broader frameworks of free opinion formation and deliberation in civil and political society.

The issue of whether populism has a procedural or nonprocedural understanding of democracy is crucial if we are to understand and evaluate the kind of recognition populism claims the political system should provide for the people. This chapter distinguishes three different kinds of recognition: (1) *procedural respect*, which demands that every citizen has an equal standing in political processes and procedures; (2) *outcome respect*, which demands that political outcomes (policies) should correspond to the people's opinions; (3) *identification recognition*, which demands identification between the political leader and a homogenized people. I argue that the populist understanding of democracy fails to appreciate the importance of procedural respect, while it promotes outcome respect and identification recognition. The idea of securing respect for the people through a correspondence between public policy and people's opinions is incompatible with the circumstance of disagreement, which characterizes a free society, and the ideal of recognition through leader-people identification has equally anti-pluralistic implications.

4.1 Procedure and Substance in Populism

Contemporary democracies are liberal democracies, which in brief means that they combine free and fair elections with the protection of individual rights and the rule of law. Many writers on populism exploit the idea that liberal democracy can be divided into a democratic and a liberal pillar, and they suggest that populism is in favor of the democratic pillar and only rejects the liberal pillar.[3] Moreover, they suggest that this makes

---

[2] Mény and Surel, "Constitutive Ambiguity of Populism"; Mounk, *People vs. Democracy*, 29–52; Mudde and Rovira Kaltwasser, *Populism*, 80–6.

[3] Mény and Surel, "Constitutive Ambiguity of Populism"; Mounk, *People vs. Democracy*, 29–52; Mudde and Rovira Kaltwasser, *Populism*, 80–6. For a presentation and critique of the two-pillar model, see Abts and Rummens, "Populism versus Democracy."

populism "essentially democratic"[4] because it is a form of democracy without constraints.[5] This suggestion fits the self-depiction of populists such as Hungarian prime minister Viktor Orbán, who claims to advance a form of illiberal democracy.[6] The same idea is sometimes described as a matter of populism accepting the procedural aspect of democracy and only rejecting liberal and constitutional constraints on democratic decision-making. Thus, Cas Mudde insists that (right-wing) populism accepts democracy "*in a procedural sense* [while] core tenets of its ideology stand in fundamental tension with *liberal* democracy."[7]

In the following, I would like to analyze and discuss the idea that populism should be committed to and promote a procedural understanding of democracy and be against substantive constraints on majoritarian decision-making. Other theorists have argued against the division of democracy into two pillars – a democratic and a liberal one – and concluded that one cannot have democracy without rights.[8] I also present a version of that argument. However, in addition, I want to argue that populism in fact cannot be seen as truly committed to a procedural understanding of democracy. In populism, the notions of "the people" and "popular will" are substantive notions that trump respect for procedures. I connect this argument to different ways of understanding how democracy may recognize or respect the people.

Hence, I contend that it is a mistake to view populism as fully committed to the procedural aspect of democracy and as only rejecting liberal constraints on democratic outcomes. While it is true that populists are against liberal and constitutional constraints on existing majorities – constraints that protect individual rights and the rule of law – this does not mean that they are not committed to substantive values of their own. The substantive value that outcomes are judged against and constrained by in populism are just not respect for individual rights (as in liberal democracy), but the idea of popular will. Political theorists are so used to understanding both procedural and substantive values in liberal terms that they fail fully to understand populism. Therefore, I will have to

---

[4] Mudde and Rovira Kaltwasser, "Populism," 506.

[5] Mounk, *People vs. Democracy*, 8.

[6] The notion of "illiberal democracy" was introduced by Zakaria in *Future of Freedom* and taken up later by Orbán. For a discussion of illiberal democracy and populism, see Müller, *What Is Populism?*, 49–60. Mounk (*People vs. Democracy*, 29–52) uses the term "democracy without rights" as a description of illiberal democracy.

[7] Mudde, *Populist Radical Rights Parties*, 138, first emphasis added. Rosanvallon (*Le siècle du populisme*, 42) suggests that populism has a procedural understanding of democracy.

[8] Abts and Rummens, "Populism versus Democracy."

clarify exactly how I understand procedural and substantive understandings of democracy and consider how populism relates to these ideas.

4.1.1 Procedural versus Substantive Theories of Democracy

In what follows, I distinguish between procedural and substantive theories of democracy in terms of their distinctive ideas regarding what makes political outcomes (laws and statutes) democratically legitimate.

According to the *procedural view* of democracy, a political outcome is democratically legitimate if and only if it is (1) a product of and (2) consistent with the maintenance of a democratic procedure, such as majority rule for example. It might be thought that a proceduralist is someone who thinks it is sufficient for legitimacy that a decision be a product of a democratic procedure, and who does not consider the content of decisions at all. In other words, it might be thought that the question of the democratic legitimacy of a decision only requires that we make a retrospective judgment regarding how it was made. However, if we regard a procedural democrat as someone who is *committed to democratic procedures* such as universal suffrage and majority rule, this means that in order for an outcome to be democratic it must respect these procedures. Hence, the question of democratic legitimacy also has a prospective aspect. This is why I add (2) and suggest that in order to determine whether an outcome is legitimate, the procedural democrat must also ask whether it is consistent with upholding democratic procedures into the future.[9] Thus, it is possible on purely procedural grounds to call a decision that undermines democratic procedure – for example, a decision to arbitrarily disenfranchise a part of the adult population – undemocratic.

According to the *substantive view* of democracy, what determines the democratic legitimacy of political outcomes is not only the procedure through which they are made but also their content or substance. While there are theorists who claim to be pure proceduralists and only care about procedures, theorists of substantive democracy tend to hold that not only procedures but *also* substance matters.[10] There are different kinds of substantive theories of democracy. For our purposes, two kinds will be important. First, there are substantive theories that hold that political outcomes are legitimate if and only if they are *consistent* with certain substantive values (for example, if they do not violate individual rights or the rule law), but apart from that side constraint many different outcomes may be legitimate. Let us call these *side constraint theories* of

---

[9] Estlund, *Democratic Authority*, 86–7.
[10] See, for example, Cohen, "Procedure and Substance."

democratic legitimacy.[11] Second, there are substantive theories that hold
that outcomes are legitimate if and only if they are substantively correct
(for example, if they correctly identify the general will or justice). Let us
call these *correctness theories* of democratic legitimacy.[12]

The terminology of procedure versus substance might give the impres-
sion that only substantive theories of democracy are committed to moral
values, while pure proceduralism would somehow be value-neutral. However, if that were the case it would be difficult to explain why anyone
would be a committed procedural democrat (as opposed to just accepting democracy for strategic reasons). A procedural democrat, as I have
defined them, is someone who is committed to and favors democratic
procedures over nondemocratic procedures. If they are truly committed
to democratic procedures, they must have moral reasons for being so; for
example, they must be committed to some values that make them hold
that majority rule is better than minority rule.[13] Thus, what distinguishes
a proceduralist and a substantivist is not that only the latter is committed
to values or principles, but rather whether the principles are standards that
apply only to procedures or also apply to the content of outcomes, beyond
their consistency with procedural principles. Both proceduralists and substantivists have values, and both are concerned with the content of outcomes, but proceduralists limit their concern with the content of outcomes
to the question of whether they are consistent with upholding democratic
procedures, while substantivists are also concerned with the content of
outcomes beyond the question of whether they respect procedures.

The main appeal of procedural theories of democracy is that they seem
to respect the decisions of the people, whatever they may be (as long as
they do not undermine democratic procedures). The main objection to
pure proceduralism is that we should not regard as democratically legitimate decisions that violate basic rights, harm minorities, or are in other
ways grossly unjust. Conversely, the main appeal of substantive theories
of democracy is that they allow us to deem illegitimate and undemocratic
decisions that violate basic rights or are in other ways grossly unjust.[14]

---

[11] Constitutional democrats who hold that there must be constitutional limits on legislation take a side constraint view of democracy. For such a view of constitutional democracy, see Rawls, *Justice as Fairness*, 145.

[12] I take the notion of the correctness theory of democratic legitimacy from Estlund,
Democratic Authority, 99.

[13] Gutmann and Thompson, *Why Deliberative Democracy?*, 25.

[14] Whether or not we can call decisions that violate basic rights "undemocratic" or only
unjust is a matter of controversy among political theorists. Cohen ("Procedure and
Substance") argues that decisions that violate basic rights are not only unjust but also
"undemocratic," while Estlund (*Democratic Authority*, 90–2) argues that Cohen invokes

The main objection to substantive theories is that they do not respect but limit the will of the people.

4.1.2   Populism between Procedure and Substance

In their attack on liberal democracy and constitutionalism, populists sound like pure proceduralists. When they win elections and are in government, they demand that the will of the electoral majority be implemented without delay or constraint. This is required by their idea of respect for the people. This aspect of populism is exemplified by the hostility to courts that block or in other ways interfere with the decisions of popular majorities in referendums or general elections. An extreme example appeared during the aftermath of the Brexit referendum, when the British newspaper *Daily Mail* displayed a picture of three judges under the headline "Enemies of the People."[15] The background of the article was that the court had ruled that Brexit could not be triggered without an act of parliament.[16] Thus, on the one hand, the example shows a form of proceduralism insofar as it demands respect for the result of a democratic procedure (the Brexit referendum), but on the other hand, it was a rejection of the protection of the democratic procedures that the court sought to uphold.

Populists also often speak like substantivists. They do so when they demand that political outcomes be responsive to or correspond to the will of the people. Responsiveness and correspondence are substantive outcome principles, not procedural ones.[17] That is, to ascertain whether a political outcome corresponds to the will of the people, you do not just look at whether it was produced by and maintains democratic procedures, but you also consider the content or substance in a way that goes beyond these questions. When populists claim that political decisions must correspond to the will of the people, then, they are not pure procedural democrats. Rather, they invoke a procedure-independent standard – viz, the will of the people – which political outcomes must match in order to be legitimate. For populists there is only one possible legitimate outcome, and for this reason I think there is a tendency in populism toward what I called a correctness theory of democracy. We see this too when populist politicians lose an election and reject its legitimacy because it failed to get the result right.[18]

---

standards that go beyond democracy in order to reject outcomes that violate basic rights as illegitimate. See also Gutmann and Thompson, *Why Deliberative Democracy?*, 24.

[15] See Wikipedia contributors, "Enemies of the People (Headline)."

[16] Rozenberg, *Enemies of the People?*, vii.

[17] See Estlund, *Democratic Authority*, 74.

[18] Krastev, "Majoritarian Futures," 75; Müller, *What Is Populism?*, 27; Ochoa Espejo, "Power to Whom," 78–83.

4.2   Recognition through Procedures, Outcomes, or Identification

If populism were fully committed to a procedural (rather than substantive) understanding of democracy, then we should expect it to promise and deliver what we might call procedural respect. However, I shall argue that the main form of recognition promised by populism is not really procedural but rather substantive or outcome-based. That is, populists promise to implement the popular will understood as a substantive and procedure-independent standard, rather than respecting anything that goes on in or is produced by a democratic procedure. Moreover, populism also promises and expresses what I call identification recognition, that is, a leader who identifies with the people and with whom the people can identify. Thus, in terms of democratic respect, the problem with the populist conception of democracy is not that it is too procedural, but that it is not procedural enough.

In a democracy, citizens are involved in two different kinds of political relation. First, citizens have political relations with one another when they engage in – including listening to and watching – politics through communication (personal and mediated), activism (in the streets, online, in political parties and social movements, etc.), and formal decision-making (voting directly in elections and referendums, and indirectly through representatives). Second, citizens have political relations as subject to government decisions and coercive power, law, and public policy.[19] In a democracy, these two aspects of our political relations are in principle related in the way that citizens as subject to political power are also the source of political power.[20]

With regard to the first kind of relation, this section is concerned with citizens' role in informal and formal democratic processes and procedures, through which they as citizens detect problems, raise issues, discuss, and make law and public policy. Here the relevant notion of respect is what I call procedural respect. Outcome respect, by contrast, concerns citizens' relation to the government as subject to political power, and the connection between public policy and citizens' political opinions.

[19] On these two aspects of political relations, see Habermas, *Between Facts and Norms*, Chapter 3; Rawls, *Political Liberalism*, 135–6.

[20] This idea was first clearly formulated by Rousseau in *On the Social Contract*, Book I, Chapters VI–VIII. Contemporary formulations can be found, most famously in Habermas (*Between Facts and Norms*, 120), for whom ideally "those subject to law as its addressees can at the same time understand themselves as authors of law," and also in Rawls (*Political Liberalism*, 68), who states that "while political power is always coercive power, in a constitutional regime it is the power of the public, that is, the power of free and equal citizens as a collective body."

4.2.1   The Demand for Recognition in Politics

Feelings of a lack of recognition in political relations connect with perceptions of political powerlessness. Empirical studies suggest that people's perceptions of a lack of political influence and power in politics is part of the explanation for their support for populist parties.[21] Many people feel overlooked and ignored by traditional politicians and mainstream political parties, and therefore turn to populist parties that promise to speak for them and ensure a "return of power to the people."[22] A study from Belgium, for example, concludes: "Of all indicators in our model, a lack of external political efficacy was by far the single most important predictor for the support of populism, accounting for about half of the total explained variance."[23] Lack of external political efficacy "refers to the belief that institutions and politicians are unresponsive to citizens' demands."[24]

When we examine empirical studies of resentment and feelings of political mis- or nonrecognition among supporters of populist parties, the issue is not only whether those supporters are seeking esteem or respect, but also, when it is the latter, whether the respect in question is for their status *as political equals*. As explained in Chapter 2, respect is for status, standing, or position (not merits and character), and it can be for one's standing either as a superior (aristocratic "honor respect") or as an equal (democratic "dignity respect"). Thus, we should ask whether the issue that causes feelings of political disrespect is a perception of *unequal* political power and status, or rather, of the people in question having *lost* their former (superior) political power and status. A comparative study of right-wing populism in the United States and UK concludes that it is the latter: "Political deprivation [the idea that one has less power and say in the political process now than in the past] is the most consistent correlate of support for multiple Radical Right outcomes among Republicans and Conservatives."[25] Similarly, Diana Mutz explains the 2016 election of Donald Trump as a case of "support for the candidate who emphasized reestablishing status hierarchies of the past," which was "a result of anxiety about dominant groups' future status rather than a result of being overlooked in the past."[26]

---

[21] Berman, "Populism Is a Symptom"; Cramer, *Politics of Resentment*; Gest, Reny, and Mayer, "Roots of the Radical Right"; Gidron and Hall, "Populism as a Problem"; Spruyt, Keppens, and Van Droogenbroeck, "Who Supports Populism."

[22] Canovan, "Taking Politics to the People," 31; see also Mair, "Populist Democracy vs. Party Democracy."

[23] Spruyt, Keppens, and Van Droogenbroeck, "Who Supports Populism," 344.

[24] Spruyt, Keppens, and Van Droogenbroeck, "Who Supports Populism," 341.

[25] Gest, Reny, and Mayer, "Roots of the Radical Right," 1712.

[26] Mutz, "Status Threat," E4330, E4338.

There is an important normative difference between having less political power than in the past and having less than equal political power. The democratic ideal, of course, is equal political power, and whether loss of political power is a democratic wrong or not depends on the starting point. Sometimes losing power *feels* wrong even if one's former superior power was illegitimate. From the normative perspective, the issue is not how people feel, but what people have good democratic reasons to feel and can defend with reference to the ideal that "equal means to affect the collective conditions of their shared social life are available to each citizen."[27]

4.2.2   Three Kinds of Political Recognition

In addition to the question of whether supporters of populism are seeking to protect their former superior political power and status or whether they are struggling for political equality, we should ask whether their feelings of political deprivation and disrespect depend on their standing in the political process or on something else. I shall argue that what populism can provide is not procedural respect, which concerns how citizens stand and relate to one another in the political process, but another kind of recognition. The kind of recognition that populism provides is ambiguous and can be found in two similar but different claims of populist leaders: "I do what the people want" and "I am the people."[28] Against this background, I distinguish between three different ways in which people can feel recognized (respected and/or esteemed) in politics.

First, political relations might provide *procedural respect*, which concerns the standing one has in the political processes through which citizens propose, discuss, and produce authoritative decisions to which they are subject as addressees. It is expressed by formal rights, such as the equal right to vote and run for office, and freedom of speech, association, and assembly. Arguably, formal equality in the political process is not enough for procedural respect. The political liberties must have what Rawls calls "fair value," that is, all citizens must, independently of their social and economic position, have approximately equal opportunities to

---

[27] Brighouse, "Egalitarianism," 119.

[28] The populist Argentine president Juan Perón, for example, used to say, "the political leader is the one who does what the people want." Venezuela's Hugo Chávez famously claimed "I am the people," and during the 1995 French presidential election the Front National campaigned under the slogan "Le Pen, *le people*," referring to party leader Jean-Marie Le Pen as the people. Trump's "I am you" and "I will do what you say." For these and other examples, see Moffit, *Global Rise of Populism*, 51–63; Mounk, *People vs. Democracy*, 41–6; Müller, *What Is Populism?*, 31; Rosanvallon, *Le siècle du populisme*, 47–53.

gain public office and influence political decisions.[29] Finally, procedural respect is expressed in informal norms that require that citizens speak and listen to everyone and consider all claims equally. "Thus, what is fundamental is a political procedure which secures for all citizens a full and equally effective voice."[30]

Second, political relations might provide *outcome respect*, which concerns the extent to which the government is responsive to citizens' political preferences or opinions. Outcome respect and responsiveness can be understood in different ways, but I will concentrate on the idea that they require congruence between public policy and citizens' political opinions. This is the ideal expressed by populist leaders who claim to do what the people want. If political decisions correspond to your opinions about what constitutes a fair distribution of benefits and burdens in society, you enjoy outcome respect in this sense. Whether or not citizens are shown outcome respect depends on whether political decisions correspond to their view of what people are entitled to receive and required to contribute. If your concern is with outcome respect, you focus on political outcomes rather than on the process that produces them.

The third kind of recognition that political relations can provide is *identification recognition*, and it lies in the identification of those who govern with those who are governed, or the people.[31] It is the kind of recognition that is provided by the political leader who claims to *be* the people. "I am not an individual, I am the people," as Chávez used to say.[32] We might think of this type of recognition as happening through symbolic representation or embodiment.[33] People feel recognized by the political leader, in whom they somehow see or mirror themselves or their own aspirations. By speaking, acting, and looking a certain way, a political leader can somehow strengthen people's self-esteem (we are the *good* people) and/or self-respect (we are the group that has the *status* of the sovereign people).[34]

---

[29] Rawls, *Political Liberalism*, 327, 358. Rawls (*Political Liberalism*, 318–20) connects the fair value of political liberties to self-respect.

[30] Rawls, *Political Liberalism*, 361.

[31] I use "identification *recognition*" rather than "identification *respect*" because the former may be a case of either respect or esteem, or a combination of both.

[32] According to Rosanvallon (*Le siècle du populisme*, 48–50), the source of this kind of rhetoric is the Colombian leader Jorge Eliécer Gaitán in the 1930s.

[33] According to Pitkin (*Concept of Representation*, 102), "the crucial test of [symbolic] political representation will be the existential one: Is the representative believed in? ... Hence, political representation will not be an activity but a state of affairs, not an acting for others but a 'standing for'; as long as people accept or believe, the political leader represents them." On symbolic representation and embodiment in populism, see Arato, "Political Theology and Populism"; Urbinati, *Me the People*, 125–7.

[34] For a nuanced analysis of how populist leaders perform the people, see Moffitt, *Global Rise of Populism*, 51–69.

The distinctions between these three kinds of political recognition are highly pertinent to the analysis and evaluation both of the resentment and struggle for recognition among supporters of populism and the claims made by populist leaders. Thus, when we are told that some people turn to populist parties because they do not feel respected by the political establishment, or that they feel as if they are not heard and seen, then we should be careful to differentiate three different types of case. First, there is the type of case in which people actually have not been listened to, or where their views have not been equally considered, or where their political rights have been violated. This type of case raises issues of what I call procedural respect. Second, there is the type of case in which people cannot see their views reflected in political outcomes, or in the substance of political decisions and public policy. This type of case raises issues of outcome respect. Third, there is the type of case in which people cannot see themselves in or identify with the political establishment. Here people feel that their way of life or identity is not recognized because the political elite speaks in a way that is alien to them and implicitly or explicitly shows contempt for their way of life and political opinions.[35]

It is not my aim here to settle the empirical question of which of the three kinds of (lack of) political recognition draws people to populist parties. My concern, rather, is to analyze the question regarding which of the three kinds of recognition a democracy can and should provide, and which kind of recognition populism can provide. Some commentators regard populism as being only about identity and not at all about policy, but I think that is too strong. I agree that what defines populism is not a specific set of policies,[36] but this does not mean that populist parties do not have policy positions, or that they do not promise people what I have called outcome respect. It might be that the appeal and success of populism has more to do with the affirmation of supporters' identities than with the realization of any specific set of policies, but these issues cannot be sharply separated in practice. When a populist leader says, "I will do what you want," or "I am your voice," she is both saying that she is the people and promising to realize the people's political preferences. Moreover, and as mentioned above, empirical studies indicate that people are often drawn to populist parties because they feel other parties are unresponsive to their demands. Thus, I begin by analyzing the idea that recognition requires that political outcomes correspond to the people's wishes.

---

[35] Moffitt (*Global Rise of Populism*, 143) argues that it is a "democratic tendency" of populism when populist politicians speak and dress in ways that recognize previously excluded identities.

[36] Mudde, "Populism"; Müller, *What Is Populism?* See also the Introduction in this volume.

4.2.3 Procedural Respect versus Correspondence

Outcome respect understood as a correspondence between public policy and people's opinions is neither sufficient nor necessary to regard a system or decision as democratic. We can see that correspondence is not *sufficient* for a system or a decision to be democratic from the fact that a dictator might impose a policy that matches people's opinions.[37] The decision of the dictator might just happen to match people's opinions, or the dictator might choose to do what most people want. Obviously, neither of these choices makes dictatorship democratic. If we look only at outcomes – the content of political decisions and public policy – we cannot tell whether a decision was made *in a democratic way*. If a government chooses to implement policies that correspond to the people's opinions "out of respect" *for their preferences*, this is also not sufficient for it to be called a democratic government. Any type of government can choose to do so, no matter how it came to power, and no matter whether it can be removed from power (assuming that the leader can know what the people want[38]). To determine whether a decision is made in a democratic way, we must look at the processes and procedures of decision-making, and consider whether they involve and solicit participation by all citizens and afford them equal influence on outcomes. There is an important difference between respecting people's preferences and respecting their authority as equal co-rulers.

What I have just said indicates that a correspondence between public policy and citizens' views need not be a result or expression of respect at all, at least not respect in the Kantian sense explained in Chapter 2. As I stressed there, dignity respect concerns how people treat and relate to one another, rather than the presence of a certain state of the world.[39] Respect entails that people have the authority to demand certain treatment from others, not merely that they get certain things and are not ill-treated. Correspondence between policy outcomes and citizen preferences is a state of the world, which in itself says little about the existence of respectful relations among people and government. The reason why I still speak of outcome "respect" is that correspondence might create a feeling in people of being respected, and more importantly in relation to

---

[37] Kolodny, "Rule Over None I," 199.

[38] Mill (*Considerations on Representative Government*, Chapter 3) argues against the superiority of benevolent despotism partly on the grounds that a benevolent despot could not know the interests and preferences of everyone.

[39] Similarly, in Chapter 1, I argued that Strawson's understanding of reactive attitudes entails a relational view of morality that focuses on the relations in which people stand to one another and what they owe to each other, rather than on states of affairs.

populist resentment, noncorrespondence can create a feeling of being disrespected – even if in the end these feelings are misguided.

In order to see that correspondence is not *necessary* to regard a system or decision as democratic, we must look more closely at the idea of "the people's opinion." In a free and democratic society, "the people's opinion" is not one but many, and no government can secure a correspondence between all the diverse opinions in society and public policy. If correspondence between the people's opinion and public policy were a necessary condition for calling a society democratic, only a society with complete unanimity regarding public policy could be democratic.

In a democratic society in which people disagree on substantive issues of justice and in which everyone has an equal say, it is perfectly possible for there to be no violations of procedural respect even when some people cannot see a correspondence between public policy and their own view. A person who belongs to the minority will not be able to see their view of justice in political outcomes to the same degree as a person in the majority. In fact, this is a consequence of political equality, rather than a violation of it. Insofar as supporters of right-wing populist parties feel powerless because "people like them" have lost the political power they used to wield, then, this need not be a consequence of their being disrespected (not treated as equals) in the political process; it might simply be a consequence of their no longer being part of the political majority. To put the point in more deliberative terms, it might be a consequence of their having lost the ability to *convince* a majority of their fellow citizens to share their view.[40]

Being unable to garner a majority for one's position does not in itself demonstrate a violation of procedural respect. Of course, it might *feel* like that for people who used to be in the majority. However, you cannot complain about not belonging to the majority if due procedural respect has been shown through equal rights of participation, if these rights have fair value, and if informal norms of the equal consideration of claims have been respected. If the fact that a decision goes against you can be seen as tough luck, rather than as a result of a violation of a principle of equal availability of political influence, then you have no procedural reason to complain of disrespect.[41] As will be clear from my discussion later in this chapter and in Chapter 5, the fact that one must learn to accept losing an election as tough luck does not mean that majorities should not accommodate the views of the minority, or that majorities should not seek to justify their decisions in a way that is also acceptable to the minority.

---

[40] I discuss majority decision-making and deliberation more fully in Chapter 5.

[41] I borrow the idea of tough luck in democratic processes from Pettit, *On the People's Terms*, 177–8; see also Rostbøll, "Non-Domination and Democratic Legitimacy," 434.

Still, it is important to understand that under circumstances of disagreement, citizens in a democracy must learn that not getting one's preferred outcome need not be undemocratic or a case of lack of respect.[42]

Thus, when we consider whether populist politicians make valid claims on behalf of their supporters, we must ask both (1) whether they promote political equality or protect political privileges, and (2) whether they demand respect in political procedures or as a correspondence between policy and "the will of the people." The feelings of political powerlessness and resentment toward political elites reported in empirical studies oftentimes fail to tell us what is at play. From a principled democratic standpoint and as a general matter, it is clear that only the fight for political equality, and not the aim of protecting political privileges, can be justified.[43] Some people may feel resentment at losing their political privileges or superior standing, but this in and of itself does not generate any valid grievances.

None of what I have said implies that the political struggle for outcome respect as a kind of correspondence is illegitimate in the way that the struggle to maintain political privileges is illegitimate. Indeed, political disagreements and political struggles are supposed to be over which policies are for the common good or just.[44] We cannot determine whether a party's inability to see its own interpretation of the common good in political outcomes is a democratic problem by looking exclusively at the outcome; rather, it requires that we examine the process and procedure that produced the outcome. Did the procedure violate principles of political equality, and/or did the participants fail to show one another the required procedural respect? Democracy, as I see it, is first and foremost a procedure for discussing and deciding issues of common concern. However, as we shall see in the final section of this chapter, stressing the importance of the *procedural* aspect of democracy and political respect cannot be independent of a concern for the quality of outcomes and the respect these show for citizens. As mentioned above, if you are really committed to democratic procedures, you must also be committed to upholding them into the future.

Neither the distinction between losing political privileges and having less than equal political power nor the distinction between procedural and outcome respect can find a place in populism. In the populist understanding, when you as a member of the people do not get what you

---

[42] See also Müller, *Democracy Rules*, 58–71.
[43] To be sure, while the general principle is clear enough, its application to particular cases is by no means straightforward.
[44] Cf. White and Ypi, *Meaning of Partisanship*, 48–54.

want, this is *necessarily* because the political system is corrupt, rigged, or in some other way unfair to you. My point is not to deny that often-times the system is corrupt and unfair, or that political elites and political institutions routinely fail to provide everyone with procedural respect.[45] Rather, the reason to emphasize the distinction between procedures and outcomes is to demonstrate that the political system can be perfectly fair – everyone can adhere to norms of procedural respect and political equality – and yet some people still will not get what they want or think they deserve. This is the case when the citizenry disagrees on justice and public policy, and citizens or their representatives need to take a major-ity vote or make a compromise. To put it simply, if they take a majority vote, only the majority gets what it wants, while if they make a compro-mise, no one gets their preferred outcome.[46] This point is important to recognize if we are to avoid confusing avoidable and criticizable aspects of actually existing democracy (corruption and oligarchic tendencies, for example) on the one hand, and unavoidable and justifiable features of democratic decision-making in a free and pluralistic society (that not everyone's understanding of justice can be realized) on the other.

The underlying idea of populism is that democracy means that "the people" can and should get what they want. This view disregards the fact that the people are a plurality and disagree on which direction their society should take. Under circumstances of disagreement, procedural respect does not mean that everyone will see political outcomes as corresponding to their political opinions. Moreover, sometimes a group no longer gets what it wants because the system has become *fairer* and extended political equality and procedural respect to formerly marginalized groups in soci-ety. One danger of populism as an interpretation of democracy is that it blinds us to these possibilities. This is a danger because it entails a failure of respect for disagreement and for the norm of political equality. The idea of giving the people what they want and understanding responsive-ness as a correspondence between public policy and popular will make sense only on a homogenizing and exclusionary view of the people.

From empirical research, we learn about *feelings* of disrespect and *perceptions* of political powerlessness among supporters of populist par-ties. However, if our concern is not merely pragmatic but principled, we must ask both which principles can be associated with these feelings and

[45] Indeed, all current democratic systems might be corrupt, but this fact cannot be part of our conception of democracy. In order to understand corruption as a democratic prob-lem, we need a norm from which it can be criticized. Corruption is a form of decay and deviation from the norm, and we need to know what that norm is to identify corruption.
[46] Rostbøll, "Second-Order Political Thinking." See Chapter 5 for a further discussion of majority rule and compromise.

whether people's perceptions have any evidence to support them.[47] Is the feeling of being overlooked based on a principle of equal power and influence, and is it actually the case that, for example, conservative views are ignored? In fact, one study shows that conservative opinions have a disproportionally large influence on politicians in the United States. Candidates from both parties think voters are more conservative than in fact they are.[48] In many countries in Europe, the populist right keeps insisting that problems of immigration are silenced, even though no issue has been more discussed for the last two decades, and countless restrictions on asylum and immigration have been imposed.

It is a favorite trope of populist politicians to claim that the people are not heard and do not get what they want, and that it is they (the populists) alone that listen and deliver. However, it is essential to assess whether this claim has any basis in reality. Moreover, regarding cases where populists have a lack of success in getting their positions accepted, it is imperative to assess whether this is because they are treated unfairly and with a lack of procedural respect, or if it is simply because their positions have lost out in democratic deliberation, political compromises, and majority decision-making. This assessment requires that we understand the centrality of procedures in democracy.

Procedural respect is crucial for what I call democratic respect, and insofar as outcomes matter for democratic respect, we should not understand this in terms of a correspondence between public policy and the will of the people. Acknowledging the difference between procedural respect and correspondence is crucial under circumstances of political disagreement and pluralism. However, it is a difference that is difficult for a populist understanding of democracy to appreciate and accommodate. This is because populists understand democracy mainly as a matter of mutual identification between ruler and ruled, leader and people, which confuses and obscures the relationship between issues of lawgiving and policy on the one hand, and issues of identity on the other.[49] Consequently, people might be drawn to populism to gain procedural and/or outcome respect, while the kind of recognition that populism can supply is identification recognition.

4.2.4   Identification beyond Procedures

While populist leaders routinely promise to do what the people want, the most prominent form of recognition that they actually provide is what I

---

[47] See the section "Reactive Attitudes and Principle-Dependent Feelings" in Chapter 1.
[48] Broockman and Skovron, "Bias in Perceptions."
[49] The idea of democracy "as defined by identity of governed and governing" has a predecessor in Schmitt, *Crises of Parliamentary Democracy*, 14.

call identification recognition. As I said, this is the kind of recognition that is provided by the populist leader who claims to embody or *be* the people. You are seen and heard through me; your standing and value are affirmed through our mutual identification, the populist leader tells their followers. It is important to stress first that the mutual identification provided in populism requires an idea (or creation) of a *homogenous people,* and second that it happens through or in the person or name of *the leader.*[50] Populist identification recognition is not of citizens in their diversity, but of the people as a unified, homogenous whole. This also explains the tendency of populists in power to strengthen the executive branch, at the cost of the recognition of plurality and disagreement found both in parliaments and in the contestations and dissent of the informal public sphere of civil society.[51] Insofar as people feel that their political recognition depends on identification with the political leader, all forms of dispersion of power between government institutions, disagreements among political parties, and dissent in the public sphere will be seen as a threat to this mutual identification, and hence to people's identity and standing.

Populists leaders claim both to give people what they want (outcome respect) and to *be* the people (identification recognition). Both of these claims bypass the procedural aspect of democracy, and therefore fail to acknowledge the important kind of respect citizens can give one another as plural participants in democratic processes over time. The claim for outcome respect as correspondence ignores the fact that under circumstances of political disagreement, political decisions can never give all the people everything they want. The populist leader's claim to be the people homogenizes the people, and will always exclude some groups who cannot identify with the leader and see her as representing them. Identification recognition inevitably entails an aspect of esteem for a particular identity or way of life, which I have argued always involves drawing distinctions (Chapter 2). When populist leaders claim to be the people, they never just seek to lift up one group for inclusion in the people; they claim that the part of the people that they embody constitutes the only true, good, or worthy people. In short, populist identification recognition is inherently exclusionary.

---

[50] According to Laclau ("Populism," 157), the logic of populism is "to bring to equivalential homogeneity a highly heterogeneous reality .... At the limit, this process reaches a point where the homogenising function is carried out by a pure name: the name of the leader."

[51] Arato and Cohen, *Populism and Civil Society,* 153–84; Urbinati, *Me the People,* 24–7, 69, 109–10.

Many scholars have noted that populists are impatient with procedures and political institutions,[52] but we can be more precise regarding this issue. Populists might be distinguished from fascists by their acceptance of democratic elections, among other things, as the historian Federico Finchelstein argues,[53] but they do not have what I would call a *procedural* understanding of elections.[54]

Populists have an ambivalent relation to elections. On the one hand, the populist leader claims to know what the will of the people is independently of any vote, and they insist that they represent the will of the people even when they do not win a majority in an election.[55] Thus, populists claim that they do not need elections to tell them what the people want. Their understanding of the popular will cannot be falsified by a formal procedure. On the other hand, populists use electoral victories to justify their actions as democratically legitimate, including actions that limit the political power and rights of minorities. Hence, when populists are in power, they speak and act as strongly committed majoritarian proceduralists who think that the majority is the people and that there can be no limits to the will of the people.[56]

It is a central characteristic of populism that the people are not defined juridically, but are understood as *the part of the population* that has the particular identity that qualifies it to be the real or authentic people.[57] For populists, therefore, electoral competition is not just a matter of electing the best candidates, much less of securing diversity among representatives; it is rather a matter of validating a particular identity group as the true people who deserve to rule, to rule alone, and to do so indefinitely. Populist politicians do not only promise honor and esteem for a specific group; this esteem is seen as providing legitimacy to this group as the *only* legitimate ruler. In the eyes of victorious populists, the opponent has not just lost the competition for governmental power this time around; they have lost the esteem required to count as true representatives of the people. Oftentimes, populists utilize this idea to justify the curtailment

---

[52] Brubaker, "Why Populism," 365; Canovan, "Trust the People," 10; Crick, "Populism, Politics and Democracy," 626; Urbinati, "Populism," 575.

[53] Finchelstein, *From Fascism to Populism*, 4–5, 28–9, 99.

[54] Arato and Cohen (*Populism and Civil Society*, 11) also note that populism "does not abolish but decisively transforms elections."

[55] Krastev, "Majoritarian Futures," 75; Müller, *What Is Populism?*, 27; Ochoa Espejo, "Power to Whom," 78–83.

[56] Urbinati, "Populism."

[57] Arato, "Political Theology and Populism," 156–66; Laclau, *On Populist Reason*, 81; Müller, *What Is Populism?*, 25–32, 98.

of rights and the limitation of opposition groups' means to compete as equals in future elections.[58]

Political leaders who use politics to attain honor and esteem for the identity and way of life of a particular group of people risk turning political competition into a conflict over which groups have a legitimate place in society. Populists, who use politics as a means to bestow honor and esteem on one group as the true, good, or real people, transform political competition and elections into an existential conflict over who belongs to "the people" that in a democracy have the right to rule.[59] The danger posed to democratic respect and political equality by this kind of understanding is that those who are not valued as having the right identity or being part of the true people lose their standing as equal participants in democracy. Populists might accept elections, but when they win them, they see them as validating their understanding of who truly belongs to the people, and the losers are seen not just as losers of an election but also as having lost their *standing* as legitimate members of society and equal competitors in future elections.

Next, populists have difficulty accepting the unending and recursive character of democratic procedures, that is, the fact that the procedures can and must be applied repeatedly to their own results, with no final decision. The populist logic bypasses any procedures in which diverse people deliberate, reach consensus, compromise, or aggregate their diverse positions in a majority vote. Consequently, the only forms of recognition that a populist leader can articulate are the form that comes from a correspondence between their will and the collective, undifferentiated will of the people, and the form that is expressed in the leader's identification with the people. In the populist logic, citizens can see themselves as recognized only if political outcomes correspond to their own preferences or if they see themselves reflected in the populist leader. Anything less or different than that will be seen as a sign of disrespect. Hence, the respect that the populist leader shows for "the people" is not a form of procedural respect. It is not respect for something produced *by* a procedure, and it is not respect for something that happens *in* the temporal process that the procedure lays out.

---

[58] In Europe, the clearest examples of this are the populist governments of Viktor Orbán in Hungary and Jarosław Kaczyński and his successors in Poland. See Arato and Cohen, *Populism and Civil Society*, 168–9, 171–2; Applebaum, *Twilight of Democracy*; Wind, *Tribalization of Europe*, 41–53.

[59] An example of this, which I mentioned earlier, is Sarah Palin's description of small towns as "the real America." For a discussion of this and other examples, see Mounk, *People vs. Democracy*, 41–6.

In order to maintain procedural respect, a society must respect the procedures. Moreover, we need to understand that democratic procedures are recursive and expand over time, from one decision or election to the next. In addition, in order for people to display procedural respect for one another, and for political institutions to embody procedural respect, we need a differentiation between and separation of procedures and outcomes. Democratic institutions are procedures that aim to make people able to govern themselves as free and equal persons over time. As political procedures, they are populated by diverse people and parties that interact from one election to the next. There is plurality among people in the temporal process of interaction that produces democratic decisions, and there is plurality among those subject to law. Further, the in-principle perpetual aspect of democratic proceduralism means that no result is final. The application of democratic procedure is unending and recursive in the sense that no election is the final election, no majority the final majority, and no victory a final victory.

What we need as a democratic society, then, is an assessment of the fairness of democratic procedures and an ethos of procedural respect among people. In a society characterized by political disagreement and plural ideas of the good, we cannot assess procedural fairness in terms of whether people feel that they get what they substantively deserve; nor can we assess it with reference to a nonprocedural idea of what "the people" wants or authentically is. Populists use a nonprocedural idea of the popular will when they claim to represent the people without reference to any procedures and even against the results of democratic procedures such as elections.[60] But in the face of political disagreement, we need procedures to secure political equality and procedural respect, as well as a means to determine what counts as authoritative political decisions.

Some readers might object to the preceding argument that populists accept majoritarian elections and often promote referendums, and that these are procedures that treat people as equals. However, populists do not defend these procedures as ways of respecting the equal standing of *all* members of society, but rather as verifications that the populist party got its understanding of the popular will right.[61] In other words, in populism, procedures and political processes have no *independent or intrinsic value*, in terms of respect or otherwise. Populists are not against democratic procedures, but they treat them as mere means that

---

[60] Krastev, "Majoritarian Futures," 75; Müller, *What Is Populism?*, 25–32.

[61] An example of this, as already mentioned, is Nigel Farage's description of the 2016 Brexit referendum as "a victory for real people." See Williams, "Nigel Farage's Victory Speech."

can be exchanged at will according to an end that is given independently of them, namely the end of rule by the authentic will of the people.[62] Recognition is shown only in the outcome, or by identification: the (alleged) identity between the will of the people and the will of the leader. This means not only that there is no respect for the losers, but also that there is no process for discussing whether the populist leader actually expresses the will of the people. Thus, in populism there is no respect for opposing claims, that is, there is no acknowledgment of the authority of *other* people's claims – which, as we saw in Chapters 1 and 2, is key to the democratic participant attitude and mutual respect, and which we saw in Chapter 3 is what rights essentially demand.[63] In sum, the idea and possibility of procedural respect is ruled out by the very understanding of the people and democracy that we find in populism.

Some sympathetic writers on populism, most notably Ernesto Laclau, see populism as "a logic of articulation" in which "the people" is constructed.[64] As such, you might say that populism is a form of process. However, I would argue that populism is a process that has to hide its own processual character, or at least that it is an understanding of democracy where the process does not play a role in its appeal as a form of respect for the people. The way in which populist leaders appeal to the people, and the way in which they show "respect" for the people, is not by pointing to a process or procedure in which the people have been shown respect.[65] The populist leader recognizes the people by embodying – or claiming to embody – the will of the people.[66] This also means that you can only see yourself as respected and esteemed by a populist government if you can identify with its representation of the popular will. A populist government has nothing to say to those who disagree with it or cannot identify with it, except that they are not part of the real people.[67] I think this is a consequence of populism's lack of appreciation of procedures and institutions that, in the words of Canovan, contribute to *"bringing people into politics*

---

[62] Rostbøll, "Second-Order Political Thinking," 571; Müller, "Populism and Constitutionalism," 597–600.

[63] "The experience of the authority of another's claims is the feeling known as respect" (Anderson, "Democracy," 220).

[64] Laclau, *On Populist Reason*.

[65] As Valdivielso ("Outraged People," 304) argues, Laclau's "theory eludes the question whether there are more or less legitimate forms of articulating hegemony or populism in general."

[66] Arato ("Political Theology and Populism") finds this embodiment model in Laclau's populism.

[67] Ochoa Espejo, "Power to Whom," 74.

[by] providing avenues and mechanisms to allow their concerns to be fed into the political process."[68] In contrast to this, Laclau simply notes that democracy can take many different forms, and he is therefore "very proud" of the institutional deficit of his theory of populism.[69]

In Chapter 5, I discuss majority rule, consensus, and compromise as procedures, decision rules, or logics that in different ways may both display equal respect for citizens and help them to become in some sense self-ruling. Here I would like to stress that while free and fair democratic procedures produce authoritative decisions (binding rules), we need not say – indeed, we should not say – that the results of democratic procedures represent the will of the people. No procedures are perfect, and in actual politics unanimity is rarely achieved – and even when it is, it should not be regarded as final or eternal. Thus, while everyone must recognize the results of fair democratic procedures (whatever they may be) as binding, this does not mean that they must surrender their judgment to the majority, the winners of the argument, or the compromise solution.[70] In a democracy, no one can say with complete confidence that they represent "the will of the people." In this connection, we also see and should stress the need for a critical public sphere that challenges any claim of political leaders or individual formal institutions to represent or stand for "the people."[71]

4.3   Minimal versus Expansive Understandings of Democratic Procedures

So far, I have spoken of democratic procedures in a rather minimal way, mentioning only referendums, elections, and majority rule. I have done so because these are the type of procedures that most commentators see as accepted by populism, and because my aim has been to show that populism is not truly committed even to a minimalist procedural conception of democracy and the respect for citizen equality that it entails.[72] However, we might also understand the procedures of democracy in a more expansive way, and I think we should. This more expansive

---

[68] Canovan ("Taking Politics to the People," 26) argues that that there is a paradox in populism because on the one hand it succeeds in *"taking politics to the people,* by allowing them to form an intelligible and persuasive mental picture of it" while on the other hand it fails in *"bringing politics to the people* [by] providing avenues and mechanisms to allow their concerns to be fed into the political process."

[69] Laclau, "Interview with Ernesto Laclau," 268.

[70] Estlund, *Democratic Authority*, 104; Rawls, *Theory of Justice*, 313–14.

[71] Manin, *Principles of Representative Government*, 174; Richardson, *Democratic Authority*, 68–70; Rostbøll, *Deliberative Freedom*, 195–6.

[72] I do not mean that populism is not committed to holding elections, but only that it is not committed to the intrinsic procedural value of elections.

understanding of democratic procedures includes not only the aggregation that happens during elections or referendums but also the activism, deliberation, and opinion formation that happens in civil society.[73]

We should distinguish, then, between a minimal and an expansive understanding of democratic procedures. My way of understanding this distinction overlaps with the distinction between purely aggregative procedures and deliberative procedures, but the expansive understanding of democracy also includes different forms of activism.[74] Aggregative procedures of democracy are procedures that count the preferences or votes of citizens as they are – for example, referendums and elections. Deliberative procedures are procedures in which citizens learn about their own and society's needs, interests, and problems, exchange information, experiences, and arguments, and form their opinions and judgments about issues of common concern. Thus, whereas the minimal understanding of democratic procedures is concerned only with aggregating existing preferences, the expansive, deliberative understanding includes procedures in which political opinions are contested, debated, and formed. For the minimalist, the relevant democratic procedures are only the formal ones, that is, elections and referendums, whereas the broader deliberative and activist understanding also includes the informal public sphere of civil society among democratic processes or procedures.

I should make clear here that I understand the core of a *deliberative* conception of democracy as primarily expanding our purview of what constitutes democracy to include all the processes and relations that affect people's opinion and will formation, rather than a conception of democracy that seeks to mandate one form of communication at the cost of others.

It might seem odd to include in the *procedure* of democracy what goes on in the *informal* public sphere, that is, in social movements, the media, and so on. However, I use "democratic procedure" to refer to the way or manner of reaching democratically legitimate decisions. In the more expansive and deliberative understanding of democracy, the way a society should reach democratic decisions is not merely through aggregative mechanisms but includes processes of the public sharing of information, experiences, and arguments. As I describe it here, a deliberative democratic procedure is not a formal way of doing things with a clear order of steps of the kind we know from legal proceedings. Nor should it be. Part

---

[73] For a conception of democracy that gives pride of place to the public sphere and civil society, see Cohen and Arato, *Civil Society and Political Theory*; Habermas, *Between Facts and Norms*, especially Chapter 8.

[74] See Rostbøll "Dissent, Criticism."

of the added value of the informal aspects of democracy depends exactly on their spontaneous and "wild" character.[75] Only in societies where there is a public sphere of private citizens that is independent of the state can the people (1) show that they have a plurality of life forms, identities, and political persuasions; (2) be sufficiently sensitive to new problems in all corners of society; and (3) challenge and resist the routines and domination of ordinary politics without fear of reprisals.[76]

Notice, however, that the fact that the public-sphere and civil-society aspects of democracy cannot be formalized does not mean that they do not depend on formal and legal guarantees. An autonomous civil society and the public sphere depend on and are constituted by basic rights.[77] This means that a government that violates basic right also inhibits public discussion and civil-society action and, thereby, it is contravening democratic procedures. It undermines some of the elements that are essential to how democracy should be exercised, according to the more expansive and deliberative conception.

If we see the deliberative and public-sphere approach as a more expansive notion of democracy than the aggregative one, as I think we should, it is a mistake to regard populism as a form of democratic maximalism or extremism.[78] It is also a mistake to regard populism as a particularly participatory conception of democracy. It is true that populists often speak in favor of expanding the use of referendums, but this only adds further aggregative mechanisms to democracy. It does not by itself extend the options for citizens to engage in political activism, critical discussion, or other forms of deliberative and civil-society participation. If this is right, the critique of populism need not be based on a desire to limit democracy in favor of a more minimal conception, but can in fact be the opposite: a quest to expand democracy beyond its aggregative mechanisms to include free and equal participation in all the spheres that affect political opinion and will formation.[79]

There is a reason internal to populism as a distinctive set of claims not to include deliberation and the public sphere as core aspects of its understanding of democracy. As Simone Chambers notes, for populists in

---

[75] Habermas, *Between Facts and Norms*, 307.

[76] Habermas, *Between Facts and Norms*, Chapters 7 and 8.

[77] Cohen and Arato, *Civil Society and Political Theory*, 346; Habermas, *Between Facts and Norms*, 368.

[78] Rovira Kaltwasser ("Ambivalence of Populism," 195) describes populism as a kind of "democratic extremism" because it rejects constitutional limits on popular will.

[79] Defenders of populism often see critiques of it as expressions of ochlophobia and defenses of democratic minimalism or even technocracy. See Laclau, *On Populist Reason*, x, 1–64; McCormick, "New Ochlophobia?"

power, "the public sphere only holds dangers and impediments to the will of the people,"[80] because the public sphere by its nature includes a plurality of voices and the possibility of contesting the idea that the populist government or its leader is the people without remainder. Therefore, populist governments often take measures that shut down debate rather than promoting it. In this way, populists in government recognize the people that have voted them into power, but they fail to respect the opinions of everyone else. If there is no protection of the public sphere and civil society, there is no respect for the opinions and standing of citizens who want to protest and contest the claims and actions of the current government.

4.3.1   Proceduralizing Popular Sovereignty

Popular sovereignty – the notion that the people is the source of all political power – is central to populism and other conceptions of democracy. But again, populism has a distinct way of understanding the idea. In populism, popular sovereignty is a substance that exists independently of political institutions and procedures. Moreover, it is somehow connected to the specific way of life and identity of "the people." As an alternative to populism, one might entirely give up on the idea of popular sovereignty and the notion that the people can ever rule themselves, as some liberals do.[81] However, we can also retain the democratic promise of the idea of popular sovereignty but see the latter in procedural terms, as suggested by Habermas.[82]

Jan-Werner Müller argues that populism is partly the product of "democracy's broken promises." The promise of democracy that populism regards as unfilled is "that people can rule," implying the notion that "democracy is self-government, and who can rule ideally is not just a majority but the whole."[83] Similarly, Margaret Canovan suggests that the contradiction between "the shining ideal" of "government by the people" and democracy's actual practice "is a standing invitation to populists to raise the cry of democracy betrayal."[84]

A number of contemporary democratic theorists have argued against the idea that we can understand democracy as a matter of self-government by the people. They point out that unless there is unanimity among all citizens, democracy cannot ensure that every member of the people can get

[80] Chambers, "Democracy and Constitutional Reform," 1118.
[81] The classical text here is Riker, *Liberalism against Populism*. See also Weale, *Will of the People*.
[82] Habermas, *Between Facts and Norms*, 135–6, 298–302; Habermas, "Popular Sovereignty as Procedure," especially 485–7.
[83] Müller, *What Is Populism?*, 76.
[84] Canovan, "Taking Politics to the People," 26, 35, 43.

what they want from political decisions and in that way be self-governing.[85] While I agree that democracy cannot make every citizen self-governing in the sense that each citizen can dictate political decisions – this was also part of the reason for my critique of the idea of outcome respect as correspondence – I deny that this means we must give up on the ideal of popular sovereignty entirely.[86] Rather, the response must be to reinterpret popular sovereignty in a way that on the one hand does not make the unrealistic promise that democracy guarantees that all the wishes of each individual are realized, but on the other hand also does not undermine the democratic promise that each citizen can participate in co-ruling. It is for this purpose that I turn to Habermas's notion of popular sovereignty as procedure.

Habermas argues that we should "proceduralize" the notion of popular sovereignty, because he rejects the premise that democracy entails that "the people" simply takes over the vacated place of the sovereign monarch. This understanding of popular sovereignty is "too concrete" and does not fit the complex nature of modern democracies. The people cannot be seen as a unified "macrosocial" subject with one will. Rather, the people in a democracy exercise their sovereignty through communicative interactions in the informal public sphere of civil society (social movements, the media, and other forms of noninstitutionalized, nongovernmental, and extraparliamentary political action), legally institutionalized elections, and representative institutions. Thus, Habermas's notion of "popular sovereignty as procedure" uses the expanded, deliberative notion of procedures that I introduced above.

There are several issues at play in the notion of popular sovereignty as procedure. First, modern democracies are very large, normally encompassing millions of citizens. This means that the citizens can never all be physically gathered in one place, much less know each other's experiences, perspectives, and political opinions. Second, modern societies have an important dividing line between state and (civil) society.[87] This means

---

[85] In the words of Buchanan ("Democracy and Secession," 17–18): "It is simply false to say that an individual who participates in a democratic decision-making process is self-governing; he or she is governed by the majority [.... A]n individual can be self-governing only if he or she dictates political decisions." Similarly, Christiano (*Rule of the Many*, 25) writes: "Democracy is a system of decision-making where each is dependent on the assent or actions of many others to secure what they want"; thus, for Christiano, democracy is in fact incompatible with self-government.

[86] I have discussed these issues at length elsewhere: Rostbøll, "Democracy as Good in Itself"; "Kant, Freedom"; "Non-Domination and Democratic Legitimacy"; "Non-Instrumental Value of Democracy."

[87] For a good discussion of the importance of the separation of state, market, and civil society for democracy, see Cohen and Arato, *Civil Society and Political Theory*. See also Arato and Cohen, "Civil Society, Populism, and Religion."

that political participation can happen both in the informal public sphere of civil society and in formal publics such as parliaments. Third, modern societies are characterized by pluralism in life forms, conflicts of interest, and disagreements over policy. All of this means that the people never appear as one, but only as a dispersed and diverse plurality. They act together only through shared procedures that connect millions of diverse and dispersed citizens, their opinion formation in civil society, and their will formation in elections and formal representative institutions.

For Habermas, the key point is that a proceduralized popular sovereignty depends on robust forms of *communication* that circulate between civil society and formal institutions of government.[88] If the channels of free debate and dissent are shut down, if the legal, social, and cultural conditions of mutual respect and equal participation in the communication between the public sphere and government are destroyed, there is no way for citizens in their plurality to be part of the sovereign people.[89] Popular sovereignty as procedure therefore depends on both a system of rights that institutionalizes "the demanding communicative presuppositions of democratic opinion- and will-formation"[90] and a public culture of mutual respect for the equal deliberative authority of all citizens.[91] This form of proceduralized popular sovereignty involves "a two-track deliberative politics" that "lives off the interplay between democratically institutionalized will-formation and informal opinion-formation."[92]

To proceduralize the notion of popular sovereignty is not to abandon the idea that the people can and should rule themselves, but to provide a very different interpretation of the idea than we find in populism (as well as in other models of democracy[93]). Following Henry Richardson, we may understand "rule by the people" to be "distributed among government institutions, which extend from elections through legislative debate and voting to administrative elaboration, all within the context of an informal public sphere that enables and encourages free political discussion."[94]

---

[88] Habermas, *Between Facts and Norms*, 135–6, 298–302.
[89] See also Chambers, "Democracy and Constitutional Reform."
[90] Habermas, *Between Facts and Norms*, 298.
[91] In Chapters 1 and 2, I demonstrated the connection between the participant attitude, mutual accountability, and mutual claim-making on the one hand, and respect for others as authorities in common deliberation on the other hand. Chapter 3 connected these ideas to the meaning and value of individual rights.
[92] Habermas, *Between Facts and Norms*, 304, 308.
[93] Habermas (*Between Facts and Norms*, 295–302) contrasts his own discourse-theoretical understanding of popular sovereignty with what he calls liberal and republican models.
[94] Richardson, *Democratic Autonomy*, 67, 70.

Insofar as we hold on to the ideal of rule by the people, democracy should be seen as providing respect for citizens' status as joint participants in collective self-legislation – in short, as co-rulers. This is still a form of procedural respect, because being a co-ruler is a standing one has in democratic procedures of common discussion and decision-making. But to respect others as co-rulers points to the idea that democratic respect is about respecting citizens as equals in a specific sense, namely as equal parts of a people that jointly rule themselves.[95]

4.4   Outcomes Should Respect Procedures

I have argued for the importance of procedural respect – in expanded terms relating to both aggregation and deliberation – to a proper understanding of democracy, and I have indicated the neglect of this idea in the competing populist understanding. The value of procedural respect, however, does not mean that the quality of outcomes is irrelevant from the perspective of what I call democratic respect. If all we cared about were procedural respect, we would design democratic procedures and assess informal norms of political interaction with a view only to their inherent qualities. That is, we would be concerned exclusively with procedural norms, such as people having an equal say and being listened to. However, there are at least three reasons why this is insufficient.

First, democracy, as we normally understand it, is not only about people being seen and heard; citizens should also be able positively to *influence* political decisions. Citizens' votes and contributions to public deliberation and negotiation should be able to affect outcomes. We would have a skewed view of democracy if we were to ask only whether each citizen had an equal standing in the process, and ignored their ability to affect outcomes.[96] This is the reason why I emphasize that in a democracy, we should respect one another in our capacity not just as equals in some unspecified sense, but as equal co-rulers. I have rejected the idea that democracy is about correspondence between people's views and public policy, but the idea of influence is different. Political influence is secured "by a process that is positively sensitive" to citizens' opinions and choices.[97] Citizens can have influence in the political process without being able to dictate the result or ensure that it matches their own political opinions – and there can be correspondence between popular opinions and public policy without citizens having any influence in

---

[95] Rostbøll, "Democracy as Good in Itself"; "Democratic Respect and Compromise."
[96] Chambers, "Democracy, Popular Sovereignty," 158.
[97] Kolodny, "Rule Over None I," 199.

the decision-making process. Moreover, the populist understanding of correspondence that I have criticized is one that demands an immediate correspondence between the people's view and public policy, while the idea of influence allows that responsiveness to people's concerns and opinions is something that happens in processes that stretch over time.

Second, positive sensitivity to citizens' opinions is hardly the only quality that we would want political outcomes to have. There should also be a concern for the epistemic quality of political decisions, law, and public policy. The quality of democracy is not only measured by procedural fairness or the equal availability of political influence; political decisions should also be as wise and just as possible, and should reflect people's informed and reflective judgments rather than their immediate preferences. This is one of the points of deliberative models of democracy.[98]

The third reason to be concerned with the quality of political outcomes that I advance is based on our concern with procedural respect itself. To explain this, we need to stress first that procedural respect is a substantive norm, and second that democracy, properly understood, is not a one-off event or decision, but rather a perpetual system that involves never-ending discussion and recursive decision-making. As to the first point, remember that I have rejected the idea that procedures are normatively neutral and not committed to a moral substance. As I see it, there are moral reasons for choosing one set of procedures rather than another, and thus procedures do not take us to normatively neutral ground. Democracy is a moral proposition committed at a minimum to human equality, freedom, and nonviolent conflict resolution – or as I prefer to put it, to a norm of respect for all members as free and equal participants in society. If we are committed to democracy, political outcomes must be judged in terms of whether they respect this norm.

To the idea that democracy is committed to substantive moral norms of political freedom and equality, we should add the idea that democracy is a system of cooperation that extends into the infinite future. It is a standard point in democratic theory – even in the most minimalist conceptions – that we cannot call a society democratic just because its government at some time in the past was elected through free and fair political procedures; it must also be possible to get rid of the government and elect a new one in a democratic way.[99] This is why, in order to be democratic, elections must not just be free and fair; they must be frequent.

---

[98] Rostbøll, *Deliberative Freedom*, 176–99.

[99] In his minimalist understanding, Przeworski (*Crises of Democracy*, 5) makes it part of the very definition of democracy that people "have a reasonable possibility of removing

Now, the fact that a government, in order to be democratic, not only must be able to point back in time to a democratic procedure that put it in power but also must be replaceable in the near future by a democratic procedure entails that there are limits to the decisions a democratically elected government can make. In very general terms, a democratic government cannot, without ceasing to be a democratic government, make decisions that undermine the possibility of its own democratic replacement.[100] To put this in our previous vocabulary, democratic respect requires that political outcomes do not undermine the continued standing of citizens as free and equal participants in democracy. This argument is derived from the commitment to procedural respect, but it acknowledges that democratic procedures cannot be seen as providing final decisions but are recursive procedures that must be kept intact by political decisions (outcomes) that maintain procedural respect. Hence, understanding democracy as based on the mutuality of democratic respect entails seeing it as "a cooperative system of reciprocal constraint."[101] Democratic decision makers must limit themselves to making decisions that respect the conditions necessary for the continued free and equal participation of all citizens in the democratic process; otherwise, they cannot be seen as committed to democracy.[102]

In short, political outcomes should respect democratic procedures. The quality of political decisions is relevant for democratic respect, because only some decisions are compatible with maintaining – and some decisions are required for creating – the conditions of procedural respect. We might say that decisions that maintain or create the conditions for equal political participation and influence show a form of outcome respect. It is the outcome and not just the procedure that shows respect. However, outcomes that respect procedures do not display respect for people by securing correspondence between public policy and people's political opinions – a form of respect that I have argued cannot be shown to every last citizen under normal conditions of disagreement. Rather, outcomes that respect procedures express a form of respect in outcomes that allow and support the conditions for continued expressions of political disagreement, contestation, and the reversal of former decisions.

---

incumbent governments they do not like .... Democracy is simply a system in which incumbents lose elections and leave when they lose."
[100] Cf. Schmitter and Karl, "What Democracy Is," 80–3.
[101] Schedler, "Democratic Reciprocity," 255. See also Levitsky and Ziblatt (*How Democracies Die*, 107): "Think of democracy as a game that we want to keep playing indefinitely .... This means that although individuals play to win, they must do so with a degree of restraint."
[102] Cf. Dahl, *Democracy and Its Critics*, 171.

Populists often imply that – and act as if – it is undemocratic to place *any* limit on the will of the majority or "the real people." But that cannot be right if democracy is understood as a system committed not just to respecting the present majority, but also to respecting future majorities or free and equal participation *over time*. With populism, democracy is reduced to unconstrained rule by the last majority – those who won a majority in the last election. On the populist view, an illiberal democracy or "democracy without rights" is not only a meaningful idea; it is justified as *more* democratic than a liberal democracy, because it is without constraints. As already mentioned, some commentators accept that populism is "essentially democratic" and only at odds with *liberal* democracy.[103] I think this position fails to appreciate the extent to which individual rights are enabling necessary conditions of democracy.[104]

Without protection of individual rights, a democracy cannot secure the standing that is required for the free and equal participation of all citizens over time. Individual rights *constitute* the type of procedure that I have defended as essential to democracy in this chapter. Civil society, the public sphere, and electoral procedures are all legally constituted by rights. A society cannot have a free and vibrant public sphere, or free and fair elections, without the protection of basic rights. When the government denies protection to basic rights, this is not merely a denial of liberalism; it harms democracy as a procedure of free and equal participation in public discussion and decision-making among all citizens. An illiberal government might provide outcome respect and identification recognition to the homogenized last majority, but it cannot provide procedural respect to every citizen as a free and equal participant in co-ruling over time.

The more expansive – deliberative and civil-society – understanding of democratic procedures can explain the internal relationship between democracy and a broad range of basic rights, as can the idea that we must understand popular sovereignty in procedural terms. If democratic procedures are seen to include not merely elections but also an autonomous civil society, a democratic society must not only protect rights that enable people to criticize the government and organize to replace it, such

---

[103] Mudde and Rovira Kaltwasser, "Populism," 506; see also Mounk, *People vs. Democracy*, 27, 29–52.

[104] For a strong argument for the necessary connection – the "co-originality" – between individual rights (liberalism and constitutionalism) and democracy, see Habermas, *Between Facts and Norms*. For an application of Habermas's argument to populism, see Abts and Rummens, "Populism versus Democracy," 413.

as freedom of speech, association, and assembly. There must in addition be rights that protect different forms of life and identities, including freedom of conscience and privacy. Basic rights are necessary to protect the plural character of the people and their ability to form their own identities independently of state and government.[105]

What I am arguing here is not that there is *nothing* democratic about populism. Yascha Mounk is right to insist that we can explain part of the success of populist parties by the undeniable democratic idea that the people should rule.[106] Therefore, it can be misleading to flatly claim that populism is "undemocratic," both because to do so obscures its democratic aspects and because it entails a failure to understand its appeal. However, I deny that the fact that populists are committed to *some* democratic ideas (popular sovereignty) and even some democratic procedures (majoritarian elections) means that they are "deeply democratic."[107] Mounk suggests that we can distinguish between the *nature* of populism (which is democratic and illiberal) and its likely *effect*, which he accepts is to undermine liberal institutions that "in the long run are needed for democracy to survive."[108] I do not think this distinction holds. Rather, I would argue that lack of commitment to the institutions that uphold democracy over time is part of the very nature of populism. The disagreement over populism's democratic credentials concerns not just what contingently *maintains* a democracy but what *constitutes* a democracy. Thus, it is one of the core claims of populism that the will of the people has a reality that is independent of any and all political procedures and institutions. In a truly procedural view, by contrast, the will of the people depends on and is constituted through democratic procedures.

When other writers describe populism as proceduralist, this is because they see populists as being against constraints on popular will. However, I have argued that (1) a committed proceduralist must accept the constraint that outcomes should be consistent with the maintenance of democratic procedures over time, and (2) the populist notion of the popular will is not procedural. Thus, I see democratic proceduralism as committed to (moral) norms of procedural respect, freedom, and equality in aggregation and deliberation, and I have argued that we can derive a justification for limits on democratic decision-making from this very commitment. Populists do not share this commitment to respect for

---

[105] Arato, "Political Theology and Populism," 153–5; Cohen and Arato, *Civil Society and Political Theory*, 366; Habermas, *Between Facts and Norms*, 366–73.
[106] Mounk, *People vs. Democracy*, 8, 35, 50–2.
[107] Mounk, *People vs. Democracy*, 8.
[108] Mounk, *People vs. Democracy*, 35, cf. 52.

procedural norms, not even the norms entailed by aggregative procedures such as majority rule.[109] Moreover, when populists claim that "the
will of the people" should be unconstrained, this is not out of respect for
a specific set of democratic institutions or procedures, but is based on
their noninstitutional and nonprocedural understanding of the people.[110]
Populism can give no authority to political institutions and procedures,
because it operates with a notion of democratic legitimacy – based on the
will of the authentic people – whose connection to any institutions and
procedures remains, and must remain, unexplained.[111]

[109] See Chapter 5.
[110] Müller, *What Is Populism?*, 25–32.
[111] Rostbøll, "Second-Order Political Thinking."

5   Respecting Disagreement

In Chapter 4, I argued that populism fails to appreciate the processual character of democracy and the intrinsic value of its procedures. In this chapter, I expand this argument in relation to specific democratic procedures: voting, majority rule, compromise, consensus, and public deliberation. The focus will be on how these different ways of reaching and making decisions connect to claims for recognition and democratic respect. Deliberation, compromise, voting, and majority decision-making are all part of any existing democracy, but I argue that how we understand the meaning and value of these ways of relating to and deciding with – or against – our fellow citizens is essential for democratic practice. Populism as an interpretation of democracy brings an alternative view to the assessment of the meaning and value of majority rule, compromise, consensus, and deliberation. Thus, populism challenges us to explain and defend our own view of these democratic processes. As democratic citizens, we need to determine how to engage with one another other and how to make decisions together, which includes the questions of how we understand and how (or to what extent) we value majority rule, compromise, consensus, and public deliberation. These questions require that we clarify what we owe to each other when we respond to our disagreements and make decisions that are binding for everyone.

It is common to regard populism as fully committed to democratic principles of popular sovereignty and majority rule and less committed to liberal principles of the rule of law, constitutionalism, and protection of individual rights.[1] At the end of Chapter 4, I questioned the coherence of the idea of illiberal democracy or democracy without rights – and other writers have similarly argued that we cannot separate the democratic and liberal parts of democracy as two pillars that can stand, be understood, and be exercised independently of

---

[1] Canovan, "Taking Politics to the People"; Mény and Surel, "Constitutive Ambiguity of Populism"; Mounk, *People vs. Democracy*, 29–52; Mudde and Rovira Kaltwasser, *Populism*, 80–6.

149

each other.[2] What has been less discussed is that populism also cannot be said to be truly committed to majority rule as an institutional principle that guides political practice *over time*. Populism does not simply accept majority rule, as this decision rule is usually understood and practiced; it reinterprets the idea and transforms its practice.[3] Additionally, populism does not simply reject (liberal) constitutionalism and protection of individual rights; it also rejects the intrinsic value of a central democratic practice, namely political compromise.[4] The populist rejection of the idea that compromise is a valuable part of the democratic process is not best understood, I think, by drawing a dichotomy between democratic and liberal principles, and insisting that populism is committed to the first but not the second. Thus, by analyzing the populist view of majority rule and compromise, as well as contrasting it with alternative interpretations of these processes, we will see that populism is not just an attempt to get rid of something it regards as an external constraint on democracy, but is also a reinterpretation of the democratic process itself.[5]

This chapter is divided into two main sections, one on majority rule and one on compromise. Public deliberation and consensus will be discussed in relation to these two notions. Populist politicians often invoke the idea of the majority and claim to speak on its behalf. I argue that populism is committed to an acclamatory interpretation of majority rule and understands majority decision-making as a form of consensus, not of everyone but of the real or relevant people. Populists do not reject the ideal of consensus – they just want their own consensus to prevail. What populists despise is compromise. Populist politicians might engage in political compromises for strategic reasons, but they reject the notion that compromise is something they owe their opponents as a matter of democratic respect. In contrast to populism, I defend a complex view of democratic respect that highlights the intrinsic value of both majority

---

[2] Abts and Rummens, "Populism versus Democracy"; Müller, *What Is Populism?*, 49–60.

[3] This point is not lost on all commentators and is emphasized by Urbinati (*Me the People*, 77–112).

[4] Some writers have noted that populism contrasts with party democracy, but without going into the issue of compromise as much as I do below. See Arato and Cohen, *Populism and Civil Society*, 53–106; Bickerton and Accetti, "Populism and Technocracy"; Caramani, "Will vs. Reason"; Mair, "Populist Democracy vs. Party Democracy."

[5] Of course, while populists regard individual rights as external to democracy, I have rejected this idea. My point here is that populism does not maintain the democratic process as we know it, with compromises and majority rule, but has a different view of the democratic process altogether. My own preferred understanding of compromise and majority rule entails that one cannot understand the meaning and value of these processes independently of respect for individual rights.

decision-making and compromise, as well as the intrinsic and epistemic value of public deliberation. Democratic respect can take many forms, and our understanding of democratic practices and institutions should allow all of them to be realized and appreciated.

5.1   Majority Rule between Acclamation, Aggregation, and Deliberation

As a claim, the populist division of society into "the people" and "the elite" is simultaneously a division between the many and the few. By demanding that society follow the many rather than the few, populism appeals to a commonly accepted understanding of the essence of democracy. Among most people in the contemporary world, majority rule is an idea that wins immediate acceptance as an obviously democratic decision procedure. Normally, when someone says, "let's decide this democratically," they mean, "let's take a vote and let the majority decide." The alternative – decision by a minority – is obviously undemocratic. Among political theorists, there is more disagreement regarding the democratic credentials of majority rule, but no one denies that majority decision-making should play *some* role in democracy. The challenge posed by the rise of populism is what kinds of political practice and what institutions the appeal to the majority can respectively justify and discredit. From the perspective taken in this book, the question is what kind of recognition majority rule entails. What does the principle of majority rule mean for how citizens should regard one another and what they owe to each other? The question is not for or against majority rule, but what we mean by the majority principle and the reasons we have for supporting it. Which ideals we see realized by majority rule matters for how politicians and citizens engage in democracy, how they relate to one another, and which institutions they support.

5.1.1   Rousseau versus Populism

From prominent scholars, we learn both that populism is strongly committed to popular sovereignty understood as rule by the people,[6] and that populism (in power) is a form of "extreme majoritarianism."[7] In Mudde's influential definition, the populist commitment to rule by the people is expressed in Rousseauian terms, as the requirement "*that politics should be an expression of the* volonté générale *(general will) of the people.*"[8]

---

[6] Canovan, "Taking Politics to the People," 33–8.
[7] Urbinati, "Populism," 572.
[8] Mudde, "Populist Zeitgeist," 543, emphasis in original

This double commitment to popular sovereignty and majority rule raises the question of how we can combine the ideal of rule by the people (all) and rule by the majority (a part). This thorny question goes back to the foundation of modern democracies in the eighteenth century. It preoccupied the French revolutionaries, most prominently Emmanuel-Joseph Sieyès, who discussed how one could combine the principle of consent by the governed, which seems to require unanimity, and the practical necessity of making decisions using majority rule.[9] Before that, it had troubled Rousseau himself, and it did so in a way and to an extent that demonstrate an important, and for our purposes instructive, difference between Rousseau and populism.[10]

In order to understand the challenge that the need for majority decision-making in actual politics creates for Rousseau, we must begin with his fundamental normative commitment to individual autonomy. Rousseau's aim in *On the Social Contract* is to find a form of political association in which "each one, while uniting with all, nevertheless obeys only himself and remains as free as before."[11] For Rousseau, individual freedom means that one obeys only "the law one has prescribed for oneself."[12] Thus, it seems that only if everyone agrees to the law can they be free and the law legitimate; that is, it seems that freedom and political legitimacy depend on unanimity. Nevertheless, Rousseau accepts that a political association must make use of majority rule in decision-making, and he honestly accepts that this creates a challenge to his theory. He writes: "It is asked how can a man be both free and forced to conform to wills that are not his own. How can the opponents be both free and be placed in subjection to laws to which they have not consented?"[13] Before we turn to Rousseau's answer, note first that Rousseau's theory of political legitimacy is individualist in the sense that it based on the autonomy of each individual person, and second that he thinks it incumbent on him to give a justification of political coercion to the dissenting minority.

In his response to the challenge, Rousseau invokes the idea of the general will (*la volonté générale*). He argues that majority decision-making can be justified to those who end up in the minority by insisting that

---

[9] For a discussion of Sieyès's attempt to reconcile individual consent and majority rule, see Manin, "On Legitimacy and Political Deliberation," 341–4; Rosanvallon, *Democratic Legitimacy*, 23–9.

[10] Note that I present Rousseau's view not because I endorse it, but in order to get a better grasp of the distinctiveness of the populist understanding and justification of majority rule.

[11] Rousseau, *On the Social Contract*, Book I, Chapter VI, 148.

[12] Rousseau, *On the Social Contract*, Book I, Chapter VIII, 151.

[13] Rousseau, *On the Social Contract*, Book IV, Chapter II, 206.

they were "in error" and failed to understand what the general will was. If their mistaken view had prevailed, they "would not have been free."[14] For our purposes, it is not necessary to go into exactly what the general will is for Rousseau, except to say that it is an ideal or principle for citizens' common decision-making – what they *ought* to decide. What is important for our contrast to populism is that for Rousseau, as Bernard Manin explains, "the general will is, in principle, the will of all the members of society; otherwise, it would be impossible to understand how they could remain free, and obey only themselves, while still submitting to it."[15] In other words, in his justification of majority decision-making, Rousseau seeks to show that what the majority decides is not only good for every member of society but also what they actually want. Majority decisions are legitimate and consistent with individual freedom because (or when) they correctly identify what is good for and the "constant will of *all the members* of the state,"[16] including the dissenting minority.

Now compare Rousseau's justification of majority rule with that found in populism. Populists' invocation of "the majority" varies, depending on whether they are looking forward to the next election or looking back at an election they have won. Populists who are competing for political power claim that they represent the majority, whether it be vocal or silent; when they actually win the majority in an election or a referendum, they claim that this majority *is* the people.[17] The core concept in populism is, of course, the people,[18] but insofar as populists invoke the idea of majority rule, they treat the majority, in Margaret Canovan's words, as an "oracle who declares the will of the sovereign people."[19] There are two remarkable aspects to the populist understanding of majority rule. First, it treats the "majority – actual or imagined – as if it were the whole people."[20] Second, it regards the majority as being in possession of and expressing some kind

---

[14] Rousseau, *On the Social Contract*, Book IV, Chapter II, 206. It is true, Rousseau adds, that this argument presupposes "that all the characteristics of the general will are still in the majority" (p. 206).

[15] Manin, "On Legitimacy and Political Deliberation," 343.

[16] Rousseau, *On the Social Contract*, Book IV, Chapter II, 206, emphasis added.

[17] The idea of "the silent majority" was popularized by Richard Nixon and has since been used by Donald Trump, among others. On the populist use of "the silent majority," see Müller (*What Is Populism?*, 27): "If the majority were not silent, it would already have a government that truly represented it. If the populist politician fails at the polls, it is not because he or she does not represent the people, but because the majority has not yet dared to speak." Müller takes this as evidence that populists see "the people" as "a fictional entity outside existing democratic procedures."

[18] Canovan, "Taking Politics to the People," 33; Mudde, "Populism," 31–2.

[19] Canovan, "Taking Politics to the People," 34.

[20] Rosenblum (*On the Side*, 48) sees this view as characteristic of what she calls "shadow holism," while Urbinati ("Populism," 579) sees it as characteristic of populism.

of truth. For the populist, therefore, following the majority (silent or vocal) expresses respect and esteem for the people as a collective, unified body, as well as for their insight into justice or the common good.

On the face of it, it seems as if populism shares Rousseau's theory of political legitimacy and majority rule. They both suggest that the will of the majority for the purposes of political legitimacy can be treated as the will of the people: What the majority wills is what the people wills. Either we can understand this idea in voluntarist terms, focusing on the fact of willing itself, or we can understand it in epistemic terms, focusing on the object of the will. In the latter case, we might speak of a correctness theory of majority rule and its legitimacy.[21] There are two aspects to such a correctness theory of majority rule. First, what makes a decision legitimate is its correctness: A decision is legitimate if and only if it is correct (correctly identifies the best outcome, the common good, or the general will). Second, what the majority pronounces is correct. Populists adhere to such a correctness theory of majority rule and legitimacy when they treat the majority as an oracle that pronounces the true will of the people.

Despite these similarities between Rousseau and populism, there is a crucial difference in their understanding of the relationship between the majority and the people. The difference is this: Rousseau does not suggest that the majority *is* the people, but that the majority's will is also the true will of the minority. In populism, the will of the majority is simply the will of the people, because the minority is not part of the people. Populism does not need and does not try to argue that what the majority wants is also what the minority wants. In contrast to Rousseau, populism does not even attempt to show that what the (actual or imagined) majority wants or decides is compatible with the freedom of the minority, in the latter's interest, or what they want. All that matters in populism is the part of the voters that populists call "the people." The rest does not count. So when we say that in populism the people is a part that stands for the whole – that it follows a *pars pro toto* logic[22] – this should not be understood as if populism suggested that the majority will is also the will of the members of the minority. Rather, the populist majority is only a part of the citizenry, but for the populist it is the "whole" and "right" people.[23] In populism, the will that is expressed and identified by the majority – or

---

[21] I introduced the idea of a correctness theory of democratic legitimacy in Chapter 4. Here I am indebted to Estlund, "Beyond Fairness and Deliberation," 174–5, 181–6. See also Rostbøll, *Deliberative Freedom*, 69, 188, 195.

[22] On the *pars pro toto* logic of populism, see Arato, "Political Theology and Populism," 156–66; Müller, "People Must Be Extracted," 485, 490; Müller, *What Is Populism?*, 25–32, 98.

[23] Urbinati, *Me the People*, 101, 107.

what the populist leader claims to be the majority – is not the true will of everyone, but the true will of the real people.

5.1.2 Fair Proceduralism and Equal Respect

I have argued that despite some similarities between Rousseau's and populists' justifications of majority rule as identical to rule by the people, it is crucial to see that in contrast to populism, Rousseau's people include all the members of society, and that his justification is addressed to all citizens as free and equal persons. I now contrast the populist defense of majority rule with one that rejects the idea that majority rule can secure self-government and instead justifies it as a fair procedure.

What I will call the *fair proceduralist* justification of majority rule holds that the value of the majority principle can be explained by the fact that it treats the participants with *equal (epistemic) respect*. By counting everyone equally, majority decision procedures treat the judgment of each citizen as of equal merit and importance. No one is treated by the decision procedure as better, more insightful, or more important than anyone else. Decision procedures that require more than a majority, from supermajorities to unanimity, all entail rule by a dissenting minority or that some votes and judgments count more than others.[24] The fair proceduralist justification of majority rule is often connected to disagreement as a fundamental circumstance of politics. Jeremy Waldron expresses the idea well: "Majority-decision respects the individuals whose votes it aggregates. It does so in two ways. First, it respects the differences of opinion about justice and the common good .... Second, it embodies a principle of respect for each person in the processes by which we settle on a view to be adopted as *ours* even in the face of disagreement."[25] This fair proceduralist justification of majority rule, then, emphasizes respect for *individual* judgments and for their impact in the political process that defines the *common* view.

On the fair proceduralist justification of majority rule, the latter is justified not only because it gives every last individual a say in the process, but also because it ensures an *equal* say. Following an article by the mathematician Kenneth May, three features of majority rule in particular make it a uniquely egalitarian procedure.[26] First, majority rule ensures

---

[24] Dahl, *Democracy and Its Critics*, 137; Schwartzberg, *Counting the Many*, 7; Shapiro, *Politics against Domination*, 40–2.

[25] Waldron, *Law and Disagreement*, 109.

[26] May, "Set." We should note that this justification for majority rule assumes that the vote concerns two alternatives, and that there are complications when more alternatives are introduced. For a discussion, see Dahl, *Democracy and Its Critics*, 139–48; Christiano, "Political Equality," 154–7, 174.

procedural equality by being *anonymous* in the sense of not favoring any individuals or groups in advance. The outcome of the majority procedure does not depend on which specific group or individual favors or opposes an alternative. Thus, each individual is treated in the same way. Second, majority rule is *neutral* among the alternatives that are being voted on. The procedure is not biased in favor of any outcome. In particular, it is important to recognize that majority rule does not favor the status quo, as do decision rules that require more than a majority, especially a unanimity rule. Finally, majority rule ensures *positive responsiveness*, which means that the procedure responds to changes in individual preferences in a positive way. That is, if enough individuals change their vote, the outcome will be different. At the margin, the change of one vote can break a tie and change the result.

If we contrast the populist practice and defense of majority rule with the focus on equal respect in fair proceduralism, the first thing that springs to light is the individualist character of the latter. In populism, the value of majority rule lies in its (alleged) ability to identify and declare the will of the authentic people, where the latter is conceived as a unified identity group with one will.[27] The populist understanding of majority rule is concerned neither with respect for individual judgments under circumstances of disagreement, nor with ideals of anonymity and neutrality. Indeed, we may say that populism praises majority rule for its opposite qualities, namely that it favors a particular identity group, "the people," and that it favors a particular outcome, "the will of the people." This might sound puzzling, and it might be said that to favor the people is not to favor anyone in particular, and that favoring the outcome the people want is not a bias toward any particular outcome but the purpose of a democratic procedure. Here again it is important to highlight two core characteristics of populism. First, "the people" does not refer to all citizens but to a part of the people, a particular identity group.[28] Second, this group is identified prior to and independently of any decision procedure. My point is that in populism, the value of majority rule lies exactly in the idea that it expresses the will of this pregiven group. Populists always have a particular group – less than the total population – in whose name they claim to speak and that they want democratic outcomes to favor. For the populist, it is not a worry that persons who do not belong to the group in whose name they speak cannot see the decision procedure as anonymous and neutral. Bias is

---

[27] Canovan, "Taking Politics to the People," 34; Urbinati, "Populism."
[28] Arato, "Political Theology and Populism"; Müller, *What Is Populism?*, 3, 20–3, 29.

only a problem if it goes against the will of what the populist has identified as the real people.[29]

Consider now the ideal of positive responsiveness, which for May is
the third feature that makes majority rule a uniquely egalitarian procedure. For the fair proceduralist, the value involved in this feature of
majority rule is that it shows this procedure to be respectful of *changes*
in individual judgments of voters. It should be emphasized that this feature of majority rule requires its continuous and repeated application
over time. Majority rule is valuable for the fair proceduralist not just as
a one-off decision procedure, but also because the outcome of applying the procedure will change as the preferences or judgments of those
who use the procedure (citizens or their representatives) change. If we
accept majority rule because it is positively responsive to changes in the
judgments of individual voters over time (as well as changes in the com-
position of the voting population), we must also accept that no majority
is "the last majority."[30] By contrast, the aim of populists is precisely to
become the last majority, which finally gives power back to the people
and puts an end to the self-interested and corrupt politics of the establishment. This aim, of course, precludes positive responsiveness to any
future changes in individual citizens' judgments.

The populist idea that when the populist party or leader has won political power they can legitimately rule as "the last majority" entails that
the current majority expresses not only the true but also the *permanent
and unchangeable* will of the people. Moreover, we can say that populists
use a majority victory to show the minority that they ("the people" as
understood by and embodied in the populist leader) are everything, and
that members of the minority are nothing and "don't mean anything,"
as Trump once said.[31] For the fair proceduralist, by contrast, majority
rule does not identify any true will of "the people," much less a permanent one. To be justified, therefore, majority rule must not be a one-off
event but must be reapplied periodically and recursively.[32] Members of
the dissenting minority on this view are also part of the people and must
be free to try to change majority decisions. Hence, on the proceduralist

---

[29] As Urbinati (*Me the People*, 107) writes, in populism "only one majority is the right one
[and it] must rule."

[30] On the idea of "the last majority," see Urbinati (*Me the People*, 91–2). See also Muirhead's
(*Promise of Party*, 38–9, 105–10) discussion of good partisanship as requiring that one
does not see one's own party as "the last party."

[31] "'The only important thing,' [Trump] declared at a rally in May [2016], 'is the unifica-
tion of the people, because the other people don't mean anything.' Trump defines who
belongs to the people; no one else counts, even if they happen to be American citizens"
(Müller, "Capitalism in One Family").

[32] Cf. Chapter 4.

view, any majority must be seen as temporary, fallible, and changeable.[33] Democracy is the rule of successive majorities, not of *the* majority. Only by understanding democracy in this way can majority rule be justified as a way of expressing respect for each and every citizen as an equal member of the people and as an equal participant in democratic processes.

When democratic theorists justify majority rule due to its procedural quality of respecting the equal standing of citizens, this justification is independent of any claim to the correctness of the outcome of majority decisions. In other words, when they see majority rule as justified, and when they grant the majority the right to make law, this is not because they think that what the majority wills is just. This also means that on the proceduralist understanding and justification of majority rule, while all citizens under certain conditions must obey majority decisions as authoritative, there is no question that they must submit their judgment to it.[34] On this account, the minority voter "can hold both that the process was properly carried out and that the outcome, while morally binding on citizens for procedural reasons, is morally mistaken."[35] In the populist understanding of majority rule and democratic legitimacy, this possibility is rejected, because populism allows no distinction to be drawn between just and legitimacy-generating procedures on the one hand, and correct outcomes on the other. For the populist, a decision supported by the (real) majority and a just outcome are one and the same thing. Populism regards the majority *qua* the people as infallible, and everyone must submit their judgment to it. This is why populists see it as disrespectful of the people to criticize majority decisions.[36] The politically dangerous implication of this view is that it can be and is used to curtail the rights of minorities to criticize populists in power. By contrast, when we separate majority decision-making as a way of making binding decisions from the question of the justice of outcomes, we can explain why democratic citizens must be free to criticize majority decisions as well as to seek their revision.

5.1.3   Acclamation versus Aggregation

In order better to understand the difference between fair proceduralism and populism, we can distinguish between an aggregative and an acclamatory understanding of majority rule. On the aggregative view, majority

---

[33] Rummens, "Populism as a Threat," 558. Rummens is not a fair proceduralist but a deliberative democrat, but on this point the two agree.

[34] Rawls, *Theory of Justice*, 313–14. See also Chapter 4 in this volume.

[35] Estlund, *Democratic Authority*, 104.

[36] Of course, populists who lose elections do criticize actual majority decisions, but they always do so with reference the idea that it is not the true majority.

decision-making derives its value "from the veneration of independent and individual judgments and the importance of granting them equal weight," while majority decision-making as acclamation seeks "only to discern the view of the mass as a whole."[37] On the aggregative view, there is value in actually counting the votes and establishing how many were for the decision, and just as importantly, how many were against it. On the acclamatory interpretation, by contrast, what matters is not to count or make visible individual judgments by enumerating individual votes, but simply to affirm that a certain decision is what the people want.

In the ancient world, acclamation happened through shouts, the raising of lances, and other symbolic gestures, but without actually counting anything. In democratic Athens, earlier forms of acclamation – determined by the intensity of the shout in the assembly – were rejected, and the first steps toward actual voting were taken. Only later did democracies start *counting* the votes.[38] Melissa Schwartzberg suggests that the justification for the latter was that enumeration is more impartial and respectful of individual judgments; counting the vote confers dignity on those rendering decisions.[39] In this light, what is special about contemporary populism is that it applies an acclamatory understanding of majority rule to a political system where the votes are counted.

Populism regards majority decision-making as a form of acclamation insofar as it shows interest neither in the circumstance that a majority vote is needed only because there is disagreement among people's judgments, nor in the fact that counting the vote also enumerates the votes of the minority. The populist understanding of majority rule as a form of acclamation also differs from its ancient use in the way that the former regards it as elevating the standing of the people, whereas the ancient use of acclamation was reserved for the masses because they were seen as lacking the necessary political judgment to actually vote and take active part in decision-making.[40] Or perhaps populism's acclamatory

---

[37] Schwartzberg, *Counting the Many*, 106–7.

[38] Hansen, *Athenian Democracy*, 147–8; Rosanvallon, *Democratic Legitimacy*, 18–21; Schwartzberg, *Counting the Many*, 19–48; Thucydides, *History of the Peloponnesian War*, 87–8.

[39] Schwartzberg, *Counting the Many*, 6, 19–20, 106–7, 139; see also Urbinati, *Me the People*, 99–100.

[40] As Schwartzberg (*Counting the Many*, 19–20) explains: "The assignment of a 'counted' or 'aggregated' vote conferred dignity on those rendering decisions: it was originally an 'aristocratic' institution, designed to assess the independent votes of those, and only of those, who possessed a special and superior faculty of political judgment. In contrast, acclamation was a mechanism for the masses, lacking such developed faculties and not worthy of having their judgments counted discretely. Only with the rise of democracy in Athens did the view emerge that ordinary citizens merited a counted vote."

interpretation of majority rule is an indication that it is not in fact an ideology that is interested in active political participation by the people.[41]

There are two implications, then, of the populist interpretation of majority rule as a form of acclamation. First, majority voting is seen as recognition of a collective will, rather than as a way of expressing respect for the judgments of individual persons. Second, members of the minority are not seen as having a standing that needs to be positively recognized (respected). In this way, populism treats a majority vote – as well as an unexpressed silent majority – as if it were an expression of consensus. This notion follows logically from the idea that only the majority is the people, while minorities do not actually belong to the people.

A key difference between the populist-acclamatory and proceduralist-aggregative justifications of majority rule is that only the latter implies that it is morally important that majority decisions can be justified *to the dissenting minority*. For the fair proceduralist, the whole point of asking about the justification and authority of majority decisions is that "we are interested in why the minority ought to regard themselves as bound" by the majority decision.[42] Since the minority voter does not agree with the outcome of the vote, the authority of the decision cannot, for them, be based on the rightness of the decision, or on the idea that it represents the will of (all) the people. One way a majority decision can be justified to the dissenting minority is based on the intrinsic qualities – the fairness – of the process leading up to the vote and the majority decision procedure itself. The proceduralist can say to the person who ends up in the minority that their voice was heard, that they had equal opportunities to influence the outcome, that their votes were equally counted, and that they are free to criticize the decision and try to change it in the future. All of these conditions fall under what I referred to in Chapter 4 as procedural respect.

Notice here that everything the proceduralist says to the dissenting minority can be assessed and, if warranted, challenged on empirical grounds. The outvoted minority can complain if they were not heard or

---

[41] Arato and Cohen (*Populism and Civil Society*, 169) conclude on the basis of a comparison of several cases of populist constitutional change in Europe and Latin America that left populists "on paper at least" introduced different elements of popular participation, while cases on the right did not; "nevertheless, with populist governments in power, the differences between left and right versions could be and was reduced if not entirely eliminated." All their cases include the strengthening of the executive. For a similar conclusion regarding the political consequences of populist rule in Latin America, see Houle and Kenny, "Political and Economic Consequences." Müller (*What Is Populism?*, 29) argues that populists might want people to vote in referendums, but they do not aim for continuous and active participation by the people: "Populism without participation is an entirely coherent proposition."

[42] Waldron, *Dignity of Legislation*, 135; see also Richardson, *Democratic Autonomy*, 212–13.

listened to, if their opportunity for influence was not equal, if their votes were not equally counted, and/or if they are not free to criticize or change the decision in the future. Thus, from the perspective of fair proceduralism, one can ask whether or to what extent actual social conditions and institutions live up to the ideal of procedural respect, and one can criticize any shortcomings in that regard. And criticize we should, for no country fully realizes the ideal. The populist understanding of majority rule, by contrast, provides no corresponding possibility of critique and discussion of how the majority was actually formed and ascertained. Insofar as populists claim that the majority pronounces the true will of the people, they can say nothing to justify their interpretation of the majority will – or when in power, their rule – to those people who do not see themselves reflected in the populist party and who disagree with its policies.[43]

5.1.4 Aggregation and Deliberation

I have contrasted the populist-acclamatory interpretation of majority rule with a proceduralist-aggregative interpretation in order to show that only the latter expresses respect for individual judgments and highlights the importance of enumerating and making visible the minority. I now want to argue that majority decision-making as a way of aggregating individual judgments does not rule out a deliberative interpretation of democracy, while the populist-acclamatory interpretation does. In contemporary democratic theory, we often contrast an aggregative with a deliberative view of democracy.[44] However, while it is true that deliberative democrats emphasize that democracy is not only about counting votes, most of us acknowledge that aggregative mechanisms and majority rule are not only a pragmatically necessary but also an intrinsically valuable aspect of democracy.[45] From the vantage point of the deliberative interpretation of democracy that includes majority decision-making, we can give a different interpretation of how the principle of majority rule makes the dissenting judgments of the minority visible.[46] Manin explains this well:

The final tabulation lets the people know which solution prevailed, that is, which solution has won the approval of the largest number. The approval of the greatest number reflects, in that context [of common deliberation], the greater strength of one set of arguments compared to others. The process nevertheless

---

[43] Ochoa Espejo, "Power to Whom," 74; Rostbøll, "Populism, Democracy."
[44] Cohen, "Democracy and Liberty," 185–7; Rostbøll, Deliberative Freedom, 19–31; Young, Inclusion and Democracy, 18–26.
[45] Bohman, Public Deliberation, 182–7; Mansbridge et al., "Place of Self-Interest," 68–9.
[46] Chambers, "How Can the People Rule?"

institutionalizes the admission that there were also reasons not to desire the solution finally adopted. The minority (or minorities) also had reasons, but these reasons were less convincing.[47]

Bringing in the deliberative interpretation of democracy makes apparent an important omission in our discussion of majority rule so far. We have spoken as if the application of the majority decision procedure were sufficient as a (democratic) justification for the decision. However, it is important to stress that majority decision-making by necessity is something that comes at the end of a process and is merely a closure device.[48] Before a vote can be taken, the problem must be identified, the alternative solutions must be found and formulated, the voters must be informed about their options, and so on. Thus, there is a long and democratically significant process before the majority procedure can be applied. Whether or not the majority vote is legitimate depends on whether the process leading up to the vote met certain standards of fairness, free and equal participation, and deliberation.[49] If people cannot express their problems and get solutions to them onto the agenda, or if they have no real opportunities to be informed about their options, the value of voting is lost or at least severely limited.

Populism provides no justification of its (aspirations to) rule to the minority: It speaks only to the many. In contrast to this, we have seen that both Rousseau and the fair proceduralist justify majority rule to the minority. Rousseau does so on the grounds that the will of the majority is actually the will of everyone, and the fair proceduralist does so on the grounds that the members of the minority are shown the same kind of respect as members of the majority. Both of these positions give a justification for the majority principle as such, one based on correctness and the other based on equal procedural respect. Deliberative democrats share Rousseau's idea that the content of majority decisions must be justified to everyone, and this goes beyond the fair proceduralist idea that it is sufficient justification for a decision that all views are equally counted. However, deliberative democrats reject the Rousseauian idea that majority decisions are necessarily right, and they therefore think procedural respect is a core part of the justification for majority rule.[50] In contrast to fair proceduralists, deliberative democrats do not think it is sufficient that everyone is equally heard and counted in the decision-making process and that the majority can decide whatever they want. They maintain

[47] Manin, "On Legitimacy and Political Deliberation," 359.
[48] Richardson, *Democratic Autonomy*, 204–13.
[49] Dewey, *Public and Its Problems*, 207–8; Richardson, *Democratic Autonomy*, 204.
[50] Rostbøll, *Deliberative Freedom*, 188–9, 195–6.

in addition that the content of each majority decision must be justified to the minority, the existence of which was made visible by the majority vote. For deliberative democrats, everyone is part of the people, including the minority, and political decisions must be justified as good for everyone, even if the majority has the authority to elect the government and make the decisions.[51]

Populists, fair proceduralists, and deliberative democrats would all seem to agree on the general point that the process matters. After all, populists often discredit majority decisions that go against them with reference to the contention that the process was "rigged," and fair proceduralists and deliberative democrats have proposed many different conditions regarding what is required for a fair or deliberative democratic process. The important difference between populists on the one hand and fair proceduralists and deliberative democrats on the other is in how they respectively think we can know whether the process is legitimate or not, that is, what we should examine to attain this knowledge. Populists tend to look at the outcome, and if the latter does not fit their own understanding of the popular will, they claim that the process is rigged.[52] Fair proceduralists and deliberative democrats concerned with political equality, fairness, and the deliberative quality of the process, by contrast, consider both conditions that are internal to a fair political process (such as freedom of speech and association) and external conditions that are necessary means for equal participation in the process (economic resources, education, and information, for example).[53]

It might be objected here that I am being unfair to populism. We have seen that many supporters of right-wing populism are resentful at not being seen and heard by mainstream politicians. This is a problem of an unfair political process and not just about outcomes. And left populists clearly see current political processes as unfair because they favor the rich.[54] Thus, left populists share the view of liberal egalitarians who think politically relevant resources should be distributed equally, or in Rawls's terminology, that political liberties should have "fair value."[55]

---

[51] Chambers, "How Can the People Rule?"; Rummens, "Populism as a Threat," 558.

[52] This is why I argued in Chapter 4 that there is a substantive dimension to the populist view of democratic legitimacy.

[53] Christiano, "Political Equality," 170–8; Dahl, *Democracy and Its Critics*, 167. On the social conditions of deliberative equality, see Bohman, *Public Deliberation*, 107–49; Knight and Johnson, "What Sort of Equality."

[54] Left populists therefore speak of contemporary democracy as oligarchic (Mouffe, *For a Left Populism*). McCormick's (*Machiavellian Democracy*; "Machiavellian Democracy") work is also relevant here, but despite his endorsement of the populism label, his Machiavellian republicanism does not fit my understanding of populism.

[55] Rawls, *Theory of Justice*, 313; Rawls, *Political Liberalism*, 327, 358. See also Chapter 4 in this volume.

Yet, my point is that populists reason from the quality of outcomes to the fairness of procedures. That is, populists claim that we can see and know that the political system is rigged or corrupt *because* outcomes favor the elite or the rich – and that we can know the system is rigged *when* populist candidates lose an election.[56] While liberal egalitarians will agree that outcomes that favor the rich are *unjust*, if they are also committed to the norm of respect for disagreement and the procedural values of political equality, they cannot say that this *in itself* makes the outcome *illegitimate*. If people disagree about justice, the democratic process leading up to the majority vote need not be unfair just because another view of substantive justice than one's own prevails. This difference is important because it says something about our commitment to democratic procedures. If we make our commitment to democratic procedures contingent on their producing the right outcomes (as populists do), our commitment is weaker than if we can show that democratic procedures have intrinsic value.[57]

From a fair proceduralist perspective, the worry about populism is that it does not show sufficient respect for disagreements among people and thus is unconcerned about the ideal of equal epistemic respect for all citizens. In populism, only the people as a unified collective actor is recognized. From the deliberative perspective, the worry about populism is that it fails to understand the importance of the learning processes that precede (and succeed) voting. Populists do not see political processes as processes in which citizens can learn from one another and form their opinions and wills in a way that reflects insights gained in common deliberation, but only as a means to verify a predetermined will. Both fair proceduralists and deliberative democrats have ideas about what counts as a legitimate political process. They both should worry that populists do not.

Populists may speak of processes being rigged or corrupt, but it is unclear what their ideal democratic process would look like, except that it would produce the result they desire. The problem with this outcome-based, substantive correctness theory of legitimacy is twofold. First, it

[56] Ochoa Espejo ("Power to Whom," 78–83) gives the current (since 2018) Mexican president, Andrés Manuel López Obrador, as an example of a candidate who thought it "morally impossible" that the people could lose an election to the elite.

[57] McCormick is an example of a defender of populism who gives up procedural equality for the sake of outcomes that are more favorable to the poor. In response to Urbinati's criticism of populism, he argues that we have to "slacken ... unreasonable rigid standards of formal equality" in order to avoid the rich dominating the political process (McCormick, "New Ochlophobia?" 151). While McCormick makes some interesting institutional proposals that might counter the influence of wealth on politics and which deserve serious consideration, I worry that his model fails to respect disagreement among the poor, as well as dividing lines in society other than that between rich and poor.

assumes that there is some procedure-independent way of determining the right result. This creates an epistemic problem: How do we know who has the will of the people right? How do populists know that it is the populist leader who has rightly discerned the popular will? Second, the outcome-based view neglects the kind of respect for individual views that processes of deliberation and aggregation express.[58]

5.1.5   The Principle of Majority Rule over Time

We have seen that the value of majority rule in populism lies in the way it recognizes the standing of a section of the voters, the real people, as the true rulers. This justification of majority rule differs from justifications that suggest that it expresses respect for the judgments of individual voters, whether these judgments are seen as given (as in purely aggregative models) or as the results of deliberative processes (as in deliberative majorities[59]). In terms of respect, an important difference between the populist and the two other justifications of majority rule is that the populist defends it because of its respectful result, while the others justify it as a respectful procedure. Populists seem less concerned about the respect that is shown to individuals by providing them with an equal say in the process than with the respect that the result shows to the people as a collective identity group.

In the terminology introduced in Chapter 4, populists see majority rule as providing outcome respect and identification recognition, while fair proceduralists and deliberative democrats see it as providing procedural respect. For aggregative and deliberative proceduralists, there is something intrinsically right about majority rule as a decision procedure, namely that it shows respect for the equal standing and judgments of the participants. For the populist, by contrast, the value of majority rule is not part of the procedure but lies in its ability to identify or declare the true or authentic will of the people. As such, we might also say that for the proceduralist majority rule has intrinsic value, while for the populist it has at best instrumental value. Or perhaps it is too empirical to say that populists grant the procedure of majority rule instrumental value. The latter would suggest that majority voting is needed to verify something, but populist politicians claim that they do not actually need any

---

[58] In this way, the populist justification of majority rule resembles the utilitarian one, which justifies majority rule as a means to discover what is of greatest benefit to society as a collective rather than because of anything that is going on *in* the process of aggregating individual votes (Waldron, *Dignity of Legislation*, 148). But in contrast to utilitarianism, in populism there is no clear idea of what kind of results majority rule offers, except the vague idea of "what the people want."

[59] I take the term "deliberative majorities" from Bohman(*Public Deliberation*, 182–7).

empirical procedures to verify their interpretation of the will of the people.[60] In populism, recognition through the leader's identification with "the majority as the people" overshadows any concrete outcomes.

In Chapter 4, I argued that a fundamental normative commitment to procedural respect entails that political outcomes should respect the procedures that are necessary for relations of equal respect among citizens. I connected this argument to the idea that democratic procedures are recursive and in principle stretch over infinite time. I now want to contend that a commitment to majority rule as a constitutive principle of democracy as a political system that stretches over time does not preclude limits on the current majority. As Stephen Holmes pointedly puts it, "to grant power to all future majorities ... a constitution must limit the power of any given majority."[61] Thus, limits to majority rule can be derived from a commitment to the principle of majority rule and not only to some substantive theory of justice. This position should be seen in contrast to populism, which rejects any limits on its ("the real") majority as inherently undemocratic.

My aim here is not to defend a particular institutional design – limits on majority rule can also take the form of self-limitation[62] and be a matter of political culture[63] – but to make a more general point about our understanding and justification of majority rule. Indeed, it is part of my argument in this book that our current democratic troubles have more to do with how we understand and use our institutions – with our political culture – than with the institutions themselves. Let me put my claim about the populist understanding of majority rule like this: There is something limited in a defense of majority rule that says there should be no limits on majority rule. It is a limited defense because it entails a commitment only to the rule of the current or last majority, rather than to the rule of

---

[60] According to Urbinati (*Me the People*, 93), "populists claim to *embody* the 'right' people's will, and they stake this claim on a form of legitimacy that they believe exists before, and apart from, any voting." It might be objected that populists often promote greater use of referendums and that this demonstrates their commitment to a procedure that shows respect for individual votes and equal standing. But as Müller (*What Is Populism?*, 29) rightly notes, for the populist, "the referendum serves to ratify what the populist leader has already discerned to be the genuine popular interest as a matter of identity, not as a matter of aggregating empirically verifiable interests."

[61] Holmes, *Passions and Constraint*, 162.

[62] Ochoa Espejo ("Power to Whom," 75) clearly shows that the criterion of self-limitation can be used to distinguish populists from liberal democrats: "Thus, whereas populists claims [*sic*] to speak in the name of the people, and hold that this justifies refusing any limits on their claims, liberal democrats, *in the name of the people*, place limits on their claims." The liberal democratic appeal to the people must be self-limiting because liberal democrats see the people as unbounded, plural, and open to change.

[63] Indeed, institutional limits are not worth much in the absence of a political culture that supports them. See Dahl, *Democracy and Its Critics*, 172, 178, 186, 192; Levitsky and Ziblatt, *How Democracies Die*, 97–117.

all possible future majorities. In other words, it is limited because it is committed only to rule by one's own majority rather than to the *principle* of majority rule over time.[64] If we want to sustain democracy, it is crucial that we understand the difference between rule by the current majority and commitment to the principle of majority rule *over time*, and that the latter commitment should become embedded in our habits, practices, and political culture. This requires that we reject the populist equation of the actual or imagined majority with the people as a whole, and insist that the minority is also part of the people who should rule.

5.2   Compromise, Rooted Reciprocity, and Solidarity

We have seen that while populism claims to accept majority rule, it has its own interpretation of what this means for political practice. When it comes to another central feature of democratic decision-making, namely compromise, populism does not just reinterpret its meaning: It entirely rejects its intrinsic value. While majority rule is a technical decision procedure that states how big a part of a group must agree to a decision in order for it to be legitimate and have authority, this is not the case with compromise. "Compromise" can refer both to the process leading to a decision (give and take by all) and to the character of the decision (the end result of all gaining and losing something).[65] Compromise as a process and an end can aim for acceptance by a minority, a majority, or a supermajority, as well by all. In what follows, I am mainly interested in compromise as an *attitude or disposition* one can display and act on when one makes decisions with one's fellow citizens – "the spirit of compromise"[66] – not as a question of the numbers needed to make a decision. Moreover, it is essential that the spirit of compromise be used to accommodate the claims of minorities, not to mute them. Thus, the disposition to compromise, as a principled reluctance to press home advantages, is especially important among the majority, governments, and/or the most advantaged members of society.

Scholars have often noted that populism is an ideology that rejects compromise.[67] To begin our discussion, let me mention three main

---

[64] See also Urbinati, *Me the People*, 92–3.
[65] Benjamin, *Splitting the Difference*, 5; Kuflik, "Morality and Compromise," 39–41. In principle, compromise as an end state can be imposed on the parties involved and need not be the result of any process of compromise in which they have engaged themselves. However, I will focus on the standard case where the parties involved go through a process of compromise to reach the end of compromise.
[66] Gutmann and Thompson, *Spirit of Compromise*.
[67] Canovan ("Taking Politics to the People," 34) writes: "The emphasis on sovereignty [in populism] reinforces the implication that democracy is a politics of will and decision

reasons why political compromise is antithetical to populism. First, to accept compromise among different parties is to recognize that the people is divided, which goes against the core populist idea of the unified people. Second, to accept compromise is to acknowledge that no one can get their preferred outcome, which goes against the populist claim that the people should get what they want. Third, the spirit of compromise entails that the logic of politics is that victories and losses are never total, which goes against the all-or-nothing logic of populism.

In the literature, there is a tendency to focus on the bad *consequences* of the rejection of compromise, mainly in terms of gridlock, instability, and inefficiency,[68] while I shall argue that the rejection of compromise can also be wrong *in itself*, independently of the consequences. In this section, then, I argue that to accept democracy is to accept (among other things) that compromise can have intrinsic – and not only pragmatic or strategic – value. Under certain conditions, compromise can be an important expression of democratic respect. I do not argue that compromise is the master value of democratic politics, or that democratic respect requires that citizens seek compromise under all conditions. Rather, my contention is that the failure to appreciate that the spirit of accommodation involved in good compromises expresses an important form of respect and concern for one's fellow citizens is a failure to appreciate an important form that democratic respect can and sometimes should take. Populism's principled rejection of compromise indicates why our defense of compromise must be principled. The problem with the anti-compromise politics of populism is not just that it has bad consequences, but that it fails to respect political opponents. Political theorists have discussed whether the value of compromise is merely pragmatic, or whether there can be also principled reasons for compromise.[69] My suggestion is that if we think the reasons for compromise can only be pragmatic, we have not

---

rather than accommodation and compromise." Mudde ("Populism," 34–5) regards "the pure people" as the core idea of the "thin ideology" of populism and suggests that it therefore "discards societal divisions, denounces social groups as 'special interests,' and rejects compromise as defeat." Finally, Urbinati (*Democracy Disfigured*, 151) writes that populism is "the exaltation of the purity of the people as a condition for politics of sincerity against the quotidian practice of compromise and bargaining that politicians pursue." Cf. Rostbøll, "Second-Order Political Thinking."

[68] Gutmann and Thompson, *Spirit of Compromise*. For this consequentialist focus, see also the literature on polarization as an obstacle to compromise: For the United States, see McCarty, *Polarization*, 134–40; for a comparative perspective, see McCoy, Rahman, and Somer, "Polarization."

[69] May ("Principled Compromise") argues that there are only pragmatic reasons for compromise, while Beerbohm ("Problem of Clean Hands," 37), Rostbøll ("Democratic Respect and Compromise"), and Weinstock ("On the Possibility") argue that there can be also principled reasons for compromise.

fully understood the democratic threat of the populist rejection of compromise. At the end of the section, I connect the spirit of compromise to the notion of solidarity that I sketched in Chapter 2. I argue that good compromises are valuable forms of solidaristic inclusion of people with whom one profoundly disagrees.

5.2.1 Compromise versus Consensus

Earlier I argued that in populism, majority rule is understood as a kind of consensual rule – because the majority is seen as the whole people. What populists reject is not consensus – indeed, that is what populists seek to establish – but compromise. In order to make sense of this suggestion, we must distinguish between compromise and consensus, two concepts that are often conflated.[70] By compromise, I mean a form of collective agreement in which all sides make concessions in order to be able to act together, and in which the concessions are motivated by the presence of disagreement.[71] By consensus, I mean a form of collective agreement in which everyone accepts and is motivated by the result as the best one on its merits, and consequently no one needs to make any concessions.[72]

Three points clarify the difference between compromise and consensus. First, in a compromise, no one gets their preferred outcome, while when there is consensus, everyone believes the outcome is the best one on its merits. Thus, in a compromise, disagreement on what in itself is the best course of action persists, while in a consensus there is convergence regarding what is the best course of action on its own merits. Second, in a compromise, the parties are motivated to accept an inferior result because it is the best they can achieve *given the fact of disagreement*, while in a consensus they agree to the result for its own sake. Third, when people compromise, the outcome will embody their disagreements, whereas when people reach a consensus or already agree, there are no disagreements to embody.[73]

---

[70] In political science, the term "consensus" is often used synonymously with what I call "compromise" – for example, in Lijphart's (*Democracies*, Chapter 2) influential notion of consensus democracies.

[71] Rostbøll, "Compromise and Toleration," 19–20; "Democratic Respect and Compromise," 621–2. Cf. Gutmann and Thompson, *Spirit of Compromise*, 10; Margalit, *On Compromise and Rotten Compromises*, 20; May, "Moral Compromise," 583.

[72] Habermas speaks of rationally motivated consensus as one that people accept because of the strengths of the merits of the case. My definition of consensus here does not require that acceptance is rationally motivated, only that people accept the outcome as their preferred one. Habermas (*Between Facts and Norms*, 140–1, 165–6, 338–9) distinguishes rationally motivated agreement (consensus) from compromise.

[73] Gutmann and Thompson, *Spirit of Compromise*, 12; Rostbøll, "Compromise and Toleration," 20.

This characterization of compromise also distinguishes it from bargaining. In processes of compromise as opposed to bargaining, one will not press for the maximum satisfaction of one's own interests or for one's own view. Rather, in a compromise, as I understand it, the parties accept that they have moral reasons to concede something to the other party or parties. Moreover, in bargaining, one is motivated by the differential force of the parties involved, while compromise is a voluntary agreement.[74] In compromise, we concede something to others because they disagree with us, and not because we are forced to do so by their superior strength. Finally, in a compromise we give legitimacy to the other side by recognizing them as co-participants, which is not necessarily the case with bargaining. Thus, when I speak of "compromise" in what follows, it is important to remember that I am referring to what has been called sanguine, deep, or moral compromise, rather than an anemic, bare, or bargained compromise.[75]

For proponents of the politics of compromise, the point of democratic politics is to express and negotiate our disagreements, and to find ways of acting together while acknowledging and incorporating these disagreements. The aim of compromise is to accommodate citizens with different opinions and interests in a way that ensures that no one takes all and no one loses completely.[76] To compromise means to accept that one cannot get everything one wants. Thus, proponents of compromise do not view politics as an all-or-nothing game in which one can gain a complete victory. Rather than being a matter of making decisions that can defeat an enemy, the spirit of compromise is to deliberate with and accommodate opponents. This does not mean there is no room for partisan conflict or the quest for electoral victory, but it means that any party must accept that victories are always partial.[77]

For populists, by contrast, democratic politics involves a confrontation between two antagonistic camps with qualitatively different identities. The key difference between the politics of compromise and populism is that the former regards disagreement as natural, while the latter always regards divisions as signs of self-interest and corruption.[78] Moreover,

---

[74] Bellamy, "Democracy," 448–9.

[75] For the distinction between sanguine and anemic compromise, see Margalit, *On Compromise and Rotten Compromises*, 39–54. On deep and moral compromise, see Bohman, *Public Deliberation*, 83–105; Lister, "Public Reason and Moral Compromise," 18; May, "Principled Compromise," 318–23; Richardson, *Democratic Autonomy*, 144–9; Rostbøll and Scavenius, "Introduction," 6–7.

[76] Weinstock, "Compromise, Pluralism, and Deliberation," 638, 643; "On the Possibility," 551–2.

[77] According to Levitsky and Ziblatt (*How Democracies Die*, 77), accepting that victories are partial is essential for the survival of democracy.

[78] Crick, "Populism, Politics and Democracy."

proponents of compromise regard politics as a matter of conflicting interests and values, while populism is a form of identity politics.[79] The consequence of these differences is that for populists, politics is a game with total winners and total losers, while for proponents of compromise, democratic politics is about avoiding a complete loss by anyone. According to populism, democratic politics is about winning power back for the people from an untrustworthy elite.[80] Even when in power, populists will continue to claim this. It is part of the populist narrative – as well as what in Chapter 3 I called the populist claim for recognition – that in the past the elite took everything and the people got nothing. The promise is that in the future, the people will get everything they want and deserve, while the elite will get nothing.[81] In this narrative, there is no room for the possibility that past decisions could be products of compromise, nor for the idea that future decisions could or should be compromises. Both populism's diagnosis and its idea of what politics should be exclude the very possibility of principled moral compromise.

While in populism the fact that "the people" cannot get what they want is blamed on the elite, according to the compromise view this is simply a consequence of the fundamental circumstance of politics, that is, the fact that the people as a plurality of individuals do not agree on what policy to pursue. To the populist, who claims that the reason why the people do not get what they want is that the elite is corrupt and self-serving, the theorist of compromise will reply that the fact of disagreement and the need for compromise in politics point to the reality that in democratic politics no one gets their preferred outcome. Even if political representatives are not corrupt or self-serving, when political decisions are compromises among parties who disagree, no one will get exactly what they want.

It is true that populist parties and politicians often create conflict and polarization.[82] Moreover, some political theorists defend populism exactly for this reason – that is, as a means of politicization and breaking up the existing consensus.[83] However, the fact that populist politicians create polarization and conflict through their antagonistic "us versus them" rhetoric by no means shows that populism is against consensus. To be sure, when in opposition, populist parties often aim to shatter what they regard as the existing consensus, but their goal is the establishment

---

[79] Fukuyama, *Identity*; Müller, *What Is Populism?*, 3
[80] Canovan, "Taking Politics to the People," 31.
[81] Müller, *What Is Populism?*, 41–4; Urbinati, "Political Theory of Populism," 120–1.
[82] Pappas, *Populism and Liberal Democracy*, 212; Roberts, "Populism and Polarization"; Rostbøll, "Populism and Two Kinds."
[83] The most prominent exponent of that view is Mouffe in *For a Left Populism*, which I discuss in Chapter 6.

of a new consensus. When in power, populists fail to respect dissent and routinely limit the opportunities for contestation.[84] Populists either claim that existing politics does not mirror the true or authentic will of the people – that it in some sense represents a "false consensus" – or they decry existing politics as a corrupt politics of compromise between competing self-interested groups. In the first case, the alleged problem is that it is the wrong consensus that governs, while in the second case the problem is that politics is a mere compromise rather than an expression of the true, unified will of the people. The aim of populist parties, then, is to eradicate divisions and disagreements, not to find a way to respect and include them. Their way of doing so may require polarization and conflict as a temporary means, but the goal is always a new consensus.

The populist ideal of consensus differs profoundly from the one we find in deliberative democracy. There has been much discussion of the role of consensus in deliberative democracy, but today you will be hard pressed to find a deliberative democrat who thinks that consensus should be a *decision rule* in democratic politics. Rather, consensus works as a *regulative ideal of argumentation* in deliberative democracy. This means that citizens should seek "to find reasons that are persuasive to all who are committed to acting on results of a free and reasoned assessment of alternatives by equals."[85] Finding reasons that are convincing to all (democratically committed) citizens, rather than only to a few or the majority, can be seen as fulfilling two ideal aims: public justification and learning. To borrow a phrase from Rainer Forst, people have "a right to justification,"[86] and this right entails that when we impose coercive rules on others (as we do in politics), we have to justify this to them. As I said in my discussion of majority rule, the minority is also part of the people, and the ruling majority owes everyone – not just those who voted for it – justification for its exercise of power. In addition, the regulative ideal of consensus may be a way of improving the epistemic quality of political decisions. By being required to find reasons that are convincing to all democratically committed citizens, the participants are engaged in a learning process that aims to discover the common good.[87]

The idea of consensus that we find in populism is committed neither to public justification nor to politics as a learning process. Populism

---

[84] Levitsky and Loxton, "Populism and Competitive Authoritarianism"; Mudde and Rovira Kaltwasser, *Populism*, 82–8; Rovira Kaltwasser, "Ambivalence of Populism," 196–9; Weyland, "Populism and Authoritarianism."

[85] Cohen, "Deliberation and Democratic Legitimacy," 75.

[86] Forst, *Right to Justification.*

[87] Lafont, *Democracy without Shortcuts*, 35–45.

shows no interest in the idea that political decisions should be justified to all citizens as individual persons with a right to justification. Populism regards the reference to the will of the majority *qua* the people as sufficient justification for the exercise of political power. Moreover, in populism, "consensus" is not an ideal that regulates politics as a deliberative process in which citizens try to learn from one another and discover what is good for everyone. Rather, in populism, consensus is somehow always already there – it is something simply waiting to be expressed. According to the perspective of populism, the general will automatically shows itself as soon as the enemies of the people have been defeated.[88] Students of populism often mention the importance of the idea of common sense among populists.[89] Common sense is understood here as something ordinary people have, and as something that it does not require common deliberation to discover.[90] Indeed, populists often suggest that long debates and "theories" are distorting influences that move us away from the true will of the people and their common sense.[91]

Despite its anti-deliberative view, populism still presupposes that some results are better than others – otherwise populists could not speak as they do of the distorting influence of corruption and self-interest. Populists want to *correct* our politics so that it expresses the true will of the people. This, I suggest, is a consensus view of politics. However, the new consensus that populists are aiming for cannot be achieved by *convincing* the opponent, but only by *excluding* them and their views as not part of the real people and as distorting influences on common sense and the general will.

5.2.2   Including Interests and Including Opinions

Above I said that compromise entails accommodating citizens with different interests and opinions in a way that ensures that no one takes all and no one loses completely. However, it is important to stress that

---

[88] Rosanvallon, *Le siècle du populisme*, 43.

[89] Mudde, "Populism," 33.

[90] Habermas (*Structural Transformation*, 97–9) finds a similar idea of consensus based on common sense in Rousseau. He calls this "consensus of hearts" and speaks of "Rousseau's democracy of unpublic opinion," which he contrasts with his own idea of consensus "of arguments" and democracy of public opinion. Rousseau's general will expresses unpublic opinion because it exists without public debate. See also Manin, "On Legitimacy and Political Deliberation," 345–7. Rousseau (*On the Social Contract*, Book II, Chapter III, 156) suggests that it would be better if "the citizens were to have no communication among themselves."

[91] Müller (*What Is Populism?*, 26) provides the following quote from Viktor Orbán (who has refused to participate in election debates since 2006): "No policy-specific debates are needed now, the alternatives in front of us are obvious .... [W]e need to understand

accommodating people's interests and accommodating their opinions are not necessarily the same thing. Political compromises are compromises between participants' views – including but not limited to their views of their interests – and not directly between the participants' interests.[92] This means that people's interests are not necessarily equally accommodated and advanced through procedurally fair compromises; rather, in political compromises, opinions or judgments are respected and allowed to have an effect on the outcome. Of course, people may be the best judges of their own interests, as democratic theorists since Mill have emphasized,[93] but it is still important to note that what people bring to the process of compromise is opinions and judgments, not interests. What people bring to politics, moreover, is not just opinions about what their respective interests are, but also opinions about what is a fair resolution to conflicts of interests. Conflict between different people's (judgments of) interests is not yet political disagreement.[94] The kind of disagreement that motivates compromise is disagreement about what is just and what we should decide to do together.

The distinctions drawn in the previous paragraph are important for two reasons. First, if compromises were directly between people's interests, rather than their judgments of these, the natural thing would be to evaluate a compromise only in terms of how well or equally it advances people's interests. But when we appreciate that what people bring to the process of compromise is their judgments, the natural concern becomes whether or not these judgments are respected. Second, when people disagree about justice and do not just have conflicting interests, *they* cannot say of any particular compromise agreement that it is a fair solution to their conflict of interest. For it is precisely the issue of what constitutes a fair solution to their conflict that is in dispute. These points put into question the idea that compromises can be defended by their fair *results*, but leave open the possibility that they can be defended as respectful *processes*.[95] (The above points also leave open the possibility that compromises can be pragmatically defended, as creating or maintaining peace, stability, and the like.[96])

---

that for rebuilding the economy it is not theories that are needed but rather thirty robust lads who start working to implement what we all know needs to be done."

[92] As Christiano (*Rule of the Many*, 74) notes: "Citizens do not advance their interests directly; they advance what they believe to be their interests. So when there are conflicts of interests, they are conflicts between what citizens judge to be their interests."

[93] Mill, *Considerations on Representative Government*, 245–6; Dahl, *Democracy and Its Critics*, 97–105.

[94] Christiano, *Rule of the Many*, 49.

[95] For a discussion of the last issue, see Jones and O'Flynn, "Can a Compromise Be Fair?"

[96] Wendt, *Compromise, Peace, and Public Justification*.

5.2.3   Rooted Reciprocity

The reflections that I have advanced here point to the nonideal and situated character of theorizing about and defending compromise.[97] When we see compromise as respecting people's opinions and judgments, we see it as responding to their actual beliefs about justice and not to some ideally constructed claims or interests. Compromise, therefore, can be regarded as realizing what Steven Wall has called "rooted reciprocity."[98] The core of reciprocity is the idea that parties with conflicting claims must "mutually recognize one another as entitled to press their claims and seek concessions from one another."[99] Moreover, reciprocity requires that everyone must somehow benefit from the accommodation. But it makes a big difference whether we understand people's claims as their ideally constructed interests or as their *actual beliefs* about what they deserve or are due (their opinions). Political compromises, as we have seen, are between people's actual beliefs and not about idealized claims. The value of compromise is that it respects actual people's actual beliefs and judgments. In other words, it realizes rooted reciprocity. The flip side of the rooted reciprocity of compromise is that there is no guarantee that the outcome will be consistent with justice, because mutually accommodating people's actual beliefs means including beliefs that are the product of prejudice, ignorance, and other forms of unreason.

Now, refusal to compromise can be based on pure egoism and might: I want everything for myself, and I do not have to concede anything to you. However, theoretically this is not a particularly interesting idea, as egoism and might are generally agreed to be incapable of providing moral justification. The interesting case of refusal to compromise is based on convictions regarding what is truly good and just: I refuse to compromise because I know that my position is better or closer to the true and right than yours. To compromise with you is to compromise my (true) principles and deepest convictions. How can it be a moral requirement to do that? Populism might be seen as a form of egoism and pure power politics. However, the more interesting possibility is the idea that populists refuse to compromise with the elite because they see the latter as corrupt, immoral, and self-interested. Of course, many anti-populists take the same view of populists, whom they see as unreasonable and ignorant. As already mentioned, I do not think the value of compromise is unconditional, or that we owe everyone concessions no matter their views.

---

[97] Margalit (*On Compromise and Rotten Compromises*, 5–6) notes that the near absence of discussion of compromise in political philosophy is due to its bias in favor of ideal theory.
[98] Wall, "Rooted Reciprocity."
[99] Wall, "Rooted Reciprocity," 464.

Nevertheless, if compromise is to have any meaning and value as a way to respond to people's actual beliefs and opinions, and as an instantiation of rooted reciprocity, we cannot draw the limits of compromise too narrowly. We have to show that there can be principled reasons to compromise even when it entails a departure from ideal reciprocity and justice.

As T. M. Scanlon has emphasized, we all want society to conform to our own views of what constitutes a good society. And it seems legitimate to have and in some way pursue that interest.[100] Some might want their society to be more religious, more traditional, and with a clear national identity, while others might want it to be more secular, less traditional, and more cosmopolitan. It is unlikely that there is any neutral ground between these visions for society. Society has to be something or other. To be sure, the arguments for equal respect and equal rights that I gave in earlier chapters mean that no one should be forced to live one kind of life rather than another. But, as Scanlon argues, treating others as equals goes beyond equal rights and requires that "all members of society are equally entitled to be taken into account in defining what our society is and equally entitled to participate in determining what it will become in the future."[101] For Scanlon, this is a requirement of tolerance – and what shows its difficulty. The implication of tolerance is not just that other people should be recognized as having the right to live lives that we (in Mill's memorable phrase) find "foolish, perverse, or wrong,"[102] but also that our society will be *defined* by such ways of life. It is the latter that Scanlon calls the difficulty of tolerance. This is also the difficulty of compromise – indeed, of democracy. When we make political compromises with people whom we find mistaken and irrational, our laws and our society will be partly defined by foolishness, irrationality, and some degree of injustice.

There is no question that there are costs to compromise, as there are to tolerance. By engaging in compromise, the parties must accept decisions that they consider worse than those they would make on their own. They must accept that their society is shaped in a different way than they think it should be. The fact that compromise has costs for everyone is part of the very meaning of compromise and does not entail that there are not reasons to engage in it. If we accept that people have mutual obligations not just to treat one another as ideal reciprocity requires but also to respect one another's opinions about what they are owed, then we have (principled) reasons for compromise. These principled reasons for compromise are

[100] Scanlon, "Difficulty of Tolerance," 191.
[101] Scanlon, "Difficulty of Tolerance," 190.
[102] Mill, *On Liberty*, 15.

grounded in the respect we owe one another "as rooted co-participants in our shared political life," as Wall puts it.[103] "We manifest respect by treating others, including our political opponents, as partners in the governance of our society. By extending reciprocal concern to them, we acknowledge that they have a stake in the shape of our society and that they are entitled to participate fully in the process of determining it."[104]

5.2.4   Intrinsic Reasons for Compromise and Their Limits

I have submitted that we can have principled (intrinsic) reasons for compromise. On these grounds, populism can be criticized not merely for its detrimental effects, as is often done, but also because it fails to acknowledge that under some conditions political compromise can express democratic respect. The important question for our purposes is not whether populist parties sometimes enter political compromises (some of them do), but whether populism as an interpretation of democracy allows the possibility that compromise can have intrinsic value. Populist parties might enter into compromises for strategic reasons, but this does not show whether populism is committed to the intrinsic value of compromise.[105] In what follows, I explain the difference between intrinsic and pragmatic reasons for compromise, and I develop the argument that there can be intrinsic reasons for compromise.[106]

When we give pragmatic reasons for compromise, we refer to the valuable consequences of compromising. A party can be said to compromise for pragmatic reasons when it does so for the sake of some end that is external to the act of compromise itself. Pragmatic reasons can play a role both from the partisan perspective, as when a party compromises to get some of its program realized, and from an impartial perspective, as when a compromise is made in order to secure peace or stability. When we give intrinsic reasons for compromise, by contrast, we refer to the value of the very act of compromising, rather than to its external consequences. That is, we argue that the very fact of entering a compromise expresses something that is of value in itself. If compromise is justified pragmatically or instrumentally, the consequences rather than the compromise are doing

---

[103] Wall, "Rooted Reciprocity," 484.

[104] Wall, "Rooted Reciprocity," 484.

[105] Arato and Cohen (*Populism and Civil Society*, 53–106) show that populism's blurring of the logic of movement politics and the logic of party politics – that is, the creation of a movement party or anti-party party – can explain why populists only cooperate with political opponents for strategic reasons.

[106] This section draws on Rostbøll, "Democratic Respect and Compromise," 623–5.

the normative work. Intrinsic reasons for compromise give value to the fact of compromise itself.[107]

In the previous subsection, I said that compromises respect people's actual beliefs and treat them as partners in shaping our common life. Majority rule also respects people's actual judgments, but it does not respect others as partners in shaping and governing society in the same way as compromise does. Remember in this connection that "compromise" might refer both to an outcome and to a process, but in the standard sense, "an outcome characterized as a compromise is reached as a result of the contending parties' participating in a procedure, also called a compromise."[108] It is this standard sense that interests me. Whereas a procedure based on the equal vote and majority rule only represents each person's opinion equally in the political process, a compromise also represents people's views in the outcome.[109] Thus, when people reach a compromise in a procedurally fair way (everyone gives and takes something), the parties' opinions are respected equally not only in the process, but also in the outcome. However, this does not amount to a situation where the parties see their conception of justice or political preferences as realized in the political outcome. For a compromise to embody mutual respect, everyone must make concessions, and this means that no one gets what they want.

The respect displayed in compromise also differs from the respect displayed in deliberation that aims at consensus. It is not that compromise does not require deliberation; nor is it the point that the substitution of compromise for consensus excludes the possibility of deliberation as a learning process. The politics of compromise is fully compatible with deliberation and learning, as has been shown well by James Bohman and Henry Richardson.[110] My point is that the ideal of deliberation aimed at consensus assumes that everyone will be convinced by the same reasons, and that we respect one another precisely by assuming this convergence around shared reasons.[111] The idea of compromise, by contrast, is that people will not be convinced by the same reasons, and that we (under some conditions) should respect the judgments that people actually arrive at after deliberation, even if we do not share those judgments.

---

[107] Rossi, "Consensus, Compromise, Justice, and Legitimacy," 562.

[108] Benjamin, *Splitting the Difference*, 5.

[109] Rostbøll, "Democratic Respect and Compromise," 626, 629–30; Weinstock, "On the Possibility," 543.

[110] Bohman, *Public Deliberation*, 95–104; Richardson, *Democratic Autonomy*, 143–61.

[111] Habermas (*Between Facts and Norms*, 166) distinguishes rationally motivated consensus from compromise by saying that in the first kind of agreement the parties are motivated by the same reasons, while in the second kind of agreement they are motivated by different reasons.

My aim here is not to argue that the kind of respect shown in political compromises is a better or more genuine form of respect than that shown in majority rule or deliberation aimed at consensus. My aim is to show that political compromises under some conditions can also manifest democratic respect, that this is an intrinsic reason for compromise, and that our understanding of democracy should make room for this dimension of respect. Simon May has contended that there are only pragmatic reasons for compromise, using the argument (among others) that "there are many ways to express respect without resorting to compromise" – for example, by listening and responding to others in public deliberation.[112] But the fact that we can respect our fellow citizens in many different ways does not show that compromise does not *also* express mutual respect. Moreover, when we discuss *democratic* respect, it is crucial that we tie the notion of respect to the types of relationship that should exist between citizens as partners and co-participants in the rule of society. For example, the kind of respect that I show other political theorists by listening and responding to their arguments does not amount to a form of *democratic* respect. Political theorists as political theorists are not fellow participants in co-ruling, and we do not need to respect one another in a way that makes us so. But fellow citizens must show respect for one another in a way that brings about or sustains their mutual relations *as co-rulers*. Sometimes, these relations require the kind of respect involved in making compromises with one's political opponents.[113]

At the end of Chapter 4, I argued that political decisions should respect democratic procedures. Democratic respect requires that citizens ensure that political outcomes be consistent with the rights required for the continued free and equal participation of citizens in democratic processes over time. The same limit applies to political compromise. The intrinsic value of compromise is conditional on its not violating the status of all citizens as co-participants in democracy. Notice that I am speaking here of *a moral limit or side constraint on the intrinsic value of compromise*. This means, first, that the intrinsic value of compromise does not require that the compromise as an outcome be substantively just.[114] Above the moral minimum of democratic respect, there is ample room for disagreement, and hence many different compromises can be intrinsically valuable. Second, the notion that when compromises violate a minimum of mutual respect they lose their intrinsic value does not rule

---

[112] May, "Principled Compromise," 342.

[113] Rostbøll, "Democratic Respect and Compromise."

[114] Thus, what I propose here fits with what in Chapter 4 I called a side constraint theory of democratic legitimacy, while it rejects correctness theory.

out the possibility that under some (extraordinary) circumstances there can be pragmatic reasons for violating this moral minimum. In the latter case, we simply need very strong instrumental reasons for compromise.

It is the question of whether compromise can have intrinsic democratic value – not whether compromises can be pragmatically justified or strategically advantageous – that separates populism from the view of democracy that I defend. The main difference between populism and my view of the meaning and value of compromise is that in the populist ideology and logic, there is no differentiation between fundamental principles of political morality that everyone must accept and positions that can be negotiated and compromised. Populists regard *all* their positions, everything that "the people" allegedly want, as nonnegotiable.[115] In populism, there are no disagreeing others whose standing "the people" must respect, and no dissenting opinions they must accommodate. If recognizing the people means recognizing the unified will of a particular group, how could there be reasons of respect to compromise with others?

Now, it might be said that my position also does not accommodate all views, which is true. However, there is a significant difference between the populist view, according to which the (real or imagined) majority *qua* the people owes no concessions to *any* of the values and interests of the excluded other, and the view that the majority should seek to accommodate many of the positions of the minority, even if some positions are excluded as below the moral threshold of intrinsically valuable compromise.

To summarize, I have argued that there are intrinsic reasons for compromise and that these can be explained by a notion of democratic respect. Making political comprises is one of the ways in which citizens can express respect for one another as co-participants in democracy. I have also emphasized that compromises are only intrinsically good under some conditions and when they respect some limits or side constraints. My argument, then, is that the value of compromise has conditions, and under these conditions, compromise carries a normative weight that is independent of its consequences. Thus, my argument does not entail that all political compromises are democratically valuable, or that the norm of democratic respect requires us to compromise with everybody and on everything. But sometimes, under some conditions, compromise is called for because it is intrinsically good, and our understanding of democracy should allow for this. Hence, my objection to the populist understanding of recognition and democracy is that it cannot entertain

---

[115] Rostbøll, "Second-Order Political Thinking," 569.

even the possibility that a compromise with one's opponents might be intrinsically valuable or a requirement of democratic respect.

5.2.5 The Solidarity of Compromise

I want now to connect our discussion of compromise to the idea of solidarity developed in Chapter 2. In particular, I would like to show how compromise, like solidarity, under some conditions could be a necessary and valuable response to real-world difficulties in establishing and maintaining relations of mutual respect among diverse and disagreeing citizens. In the face of intractable political disagreement, compromise can be a way for citizens to demonstrate that even if they do not regard their opponents' views as valid, they accept them as legitimate positions that should be allowed to have some influence on the shape of their society. In this way, compromise can provide a form of respect that is absent from both majority voting and deliberation aimed at finding shared reasons.

In Chapter 2, I suggested that it is inevitable that any society will be more conducive to some forms of life than others, and I argued that this can be a reason for acts of solidarity. When we fail to achieve the ideal society that is equally hospitable to all legitimate ways of life – and thus meets a requirement of equal respect – then there are reasons to show solidarity with those who struggle to find a valuable place in the social recognition order. We might also describe this predicament of inevitable bias as a predicament of the impossibility of finding a unique solution of neutrality between different ways of life. This absence of a unique solution calls for a spirit of accommodation and compromise.[116] If there is no solution to the problem of enabling everyone equally to live and enjoy the life they have chosen, there are often reasons of solidarity to make a compromise that accommodates everyone's (democratically legitimate) political opinions as well as possible.

Treating others as equals goes beyond equal rights and includes *the manner* in which we exercise our rights. To treat others as equals requires that we exercise our rights in ways that allow everyone to participate in shaping our society. In a democracy, our most directly democratically relevant rights concern freedom of expression, association, assembly, the equal vote, and the right to run for public office. These rights do not require that we compromise with anybody and can be used in

---

[116] For the argument that the absence of a unique solution of neutrality between different conceptions of the good society calls for a spirit of accommodation, see Scanlon, "Difficulty of Tolerance," 189, 196.

unaccommodating and uncompromising ways. Moreover, as argued in Chapter 3, rights make for respect and self-respect. However, the right of the majority to rule can also be used in a manner that shows no concern for the plight of the minority. This is the case if members of the majority maximize their own advantage as forcefully as they can and show no inclination to moderate their claims for the sake of the interests, values, and opinions of the minority. While a majority might formally have the right to act in this way, and while the system might be said to respect everyone through the equal vote, this form of rule shows a lack of concern for and solidarity with the position of the loser of the election. The minority is given no influence on the shape of the policies that they must submit to.

As discussed in Chapter 1, many people turn to populism as a reaction to their difficulty in finding a valuable place in a new and changing recognition order. Populism provides a response to people's feelings that their way of life and their opinions are not recognized as legitimate options within their society. People cannot demand that others esteem their way of life or agree with their political opinions, as I argued in Chapter 2. However, under some conditions it is insufficient to tell people that they have a right to their opinions and that the surrounding society respects them by recognizing their equal rights to live and vote as they please. Sometimes we need actively to act in ways that demonstrate that even if we do not share each other's conceptions of the good, and even if we find each other's political opinions mistaken, we still recognize them as legitimate options. I have termed this kind of active inclusion a form of solidarity. One way to show other people that their opinions are legitimate options without affirming their validity is to engage in political compromises with them. By engaging in compromise with others, we show both that we disagree with them and that we accept that their opinions can legitimately influence the shape of our society. (When we publicly state that the intrinsic value of political compromise also has limits, we also demarcate some options as illegitimate.)

Solidarity as I understand it is a response to real-world obstacles to the realization of a society of equal respect. In Chapter 2, I focused on how solidarity is needed when inequality of esteem turns into inequality of respect. Compromise can be a response to this problem insofar as the act of compromising with others can show that one respects their status as equals even if one does not share their views. Sometimes citizens should compromise to prevent disesteem and disagreement from turning into disrespect. But compromise can also be a response to other imperfections in a political system that in principle is based on equal respect. Thus, Daniel Weinstock has argued – with reference to the fact that no possible voting system treats everyone equally – that the inevitable imperfection of democratic institutions can provide principled reasons for compromise.[117] Compromise, then, can be defended on remedial grounds, as a way to mitigate the imperfections of formal systems of equal respect. Moderating one's claims to accommodate a losing minority can be an expression of solidarity that aims to minimize the gap between actual democratic institutions and the ideal of equal respect. By contrast, a winning majority that is unwilling to concede anything to the minority can not only be seen as unconcerned with the values and judgments of the minority; it can also be seen as blind to the contingencies and imperfections that allowed it to win its majority. Thus, an uncompromising majority can be criticized for lacking the kind of solidarity that is needed to remedy the imperfections of social circumstances and political institutions.

Connect this point to the norm that Steven Levitsky and Daniel Ziblatt call *institutional forbearance*: "Avoiding actions that, while respecting the letter of the law, obviously violate its spirit."[118] The two political scientists argue that this informal norm is required to safeguard democracy because any constitutional system is incomplete, subject to competing interpretations, and "may be followed to the letter in ways that undermine the spirit of the law."[119] My suggestion is that if the spirit of the law – the spirit of a democratic constitution – is mutual respect and co-participation, this means that citizens and especially governments must exercise their rights in ways that are true to that spirit, even if legally they can press their claims without concern for the values of the minority.[120]

Michele Moody-Adams has argued that the kind of solidarity involved in some forms of compromise creates relationships that allow "a people [to] collectively constitute a democratic sovereign, and not simply exist individually as political subjects."[121] I think there is something to the idea that compromise can create ties among people that make them see themselves as more of a unity than is realized in the mere aggregation of individual votes. However, it is also important to remember that compromise does not create a people that is unified around one position. The meaning and value of compromise are predicated on the premise that

[117] Weinstock, "On the Possibility," 548–51.
[118] Levitsky and Ziblatt, *How Democracies Die*, 106.
[119] Levitsky and Ziblatt, *How Democracies Die*, 99.
[120] On the importance of the spirit that sustains democratic institutions, see also Näsström, *Spirit of Democracy*.
[121] Moody-Adams, "Democratic Conflict," 191.

people will remain diverse and continue to disagree – that they cannot be unified around one substantive identity, position, or general will.[122] The kind of solidarity expressed in political compromise is not one that requires a common identity or unified will, but one that gets its value from recognizing the oppressiveness of these constructs or illusions. Political compromise does not provide what in Chapter 4 I called identification recognition of a homogenous people, but respects and shows solidarity with people in all their diversity and disagreements.

Compromise means concessions and entails costs compared with what you could get if you could dictate political decisions. When we engage in compromise, we must accept something we would not choose on our own, and in this sense compromise entails making sacrifices. This is the case not only in terms of ends but also in terms of process. Political negotiations take time and require patience. If we see these as learning processes that make us wiser about the subject matter, we might accept them as worthwhile for that reason. But in processes of compromise in which the aim is not learning, it seems like a very big sacrifice indeed to go through lengthy debates.[123] Writers on populism often note its impatience with endless debates and institutional subtleties.[124] However, the question is not whether we like or enjoy long processes of negotiation and compromise; the question is whether we owe it to others to spend time with them deliberating and making compromises. My contention is that sometimes we do.

5.2.6   Making Disagreement Visible

When rightly understood and practiced, majority rule can help to make the dissenting minority visible. An objection often raised against the politics of compromise is that it discourages and/or obscures dissent.[125] In order to make a compromise, the parties must moderate their claims, while expressions of radical disagreement seem to block the possibility

---

[122] The rejection of the idea of a unified popular will was central to Kelsen (*Essence and Value of Democracy*, 35–6, 40), one of the few classical democratic theorists to give compromise a central place in their understanding of democracy.

[123] Moody-Adams gives the example of an organization called the Public Conversation Project, which convened meetings between representatives of the two sides in the American abortion controversy after a deadly incident of violence at a Planned Parenthood clinic in Massachusetts in 1994. As Moody-Adams ("Democratic Conflict," 212) wryly notes, "it was surely a sacrifice to spend nearly 150 hours of time over five years, talking and listening" with people they regarded as the enemy.

[124] Canovan, "Taking Politics to the People"; Crick, "Populism, Politics and Democracy"; Przeworski, *Crisis of Democracy*, 87–8.

[125] Ruser and Machin, *Against Political Compromise*, 29–44.

of compromise. When everyone seeks and makes compromises, the idea that democracy is about choosing between competing alternatives seem to vanish.[126] Hence, the spirit of compromise might seem to encourage centrist politics, and to discourage forms of politics that challenge the status quo and provide radical alternatives. This double danger of obscurity and the suppression of expressions of disagreement can be bad for democratic politics for three different reasons: (1) It is demotivating for citizen participation; (2) it creates problems of accountability; (3) it inhibits necessary change. Indeed, populism can be seen as a response to a form of politics where there appear to be no disagreements among political elites, and where current policies are presented as without alternatives.[127]

In order to respond to the above objections, we must distinguish between the disposition to compromise and centrism. The willingness to compromise is what I call a second-order disposition, while centrism belongs to the first-order level of policy commitments.[128] The meaning and value of compromise relies on the idea that political moral evaluation does not just take place on the first level of policy alternatives, but also on the second-order level of how a plurality of agents who disagree on policy should reach decisions and act together.[129] The spirit of compromise requires that we respect and accommodate other people's views, not that we give up our own views or move to the center. One can be a political radical at the first level while being willing to compromise at the second level. And one can be an uncompromising centrist, refusing to accommodate "extremist views."[130] Compromise only makes sense and attains value if people disagree on the first-order level of policy preferences. It is imperative, therefore, to stress that compromise gains its relevance and value only against the background of a "vigorous and sometimes contentious politics in which citizens press strongly held principles and mobilize in support of bold causes. Social movements, protest struggles, and electoral campaigns are among the significant sites of this kind of politics."[131] Thus, from the perspective of the spirit of

---

[126] See Shapiro, *State of Democratic Theory*, 60–1.

[127] Mouffe, *For a Left Populism*; Roberts, "Populism and Polarization."

[128] Rostbøll, "Second-Order Political Thinking."

[129] Kuflik, "Morality and Compromise," 51; May, "Principled Compromise," 318–19; Weinstock, "On the Possibility," 552; Wendt, *Compromise, Peace and Public Justification*, 23–30.

[130] For empirical examples, see Gutmann and Thompson, "Mindsets of Political Compromise," 1134–8; Levitsky and Ziblatt, *How Democracies Die*, 113. See also May, "No Compromise on Racial Equality," 37.

[131] Gutmann and Thompson, "Mindsets of Political Compromise," 1125–6.

186 Respecting Disagreement

compromise, disagreement at the first level of policy preference is not a democratic problem, as long as it is combined with willingness to compromise at the second level. All too often, the two levels are not properly distinguished, leading to the mistaken view that the spirit of compromise demands that one does not express dissent or promote radical alternatives to existing policies.[132]

Yet, while the distinction between the two levels is analytically clear, and while I think it is part of a democratic political culture to acknowledge its importance, there is still the danger that it is obscured in the way we organize the political process. In order for the political process to make disagreements visible, the politics of compromise must not overshadow the oppositional and competitive aspects of representative politics. It is crucial that the politics of compromise not hide the fact that some alternatives were excluded and some routes not taken. For citizens to be motivated to participate in politics, and for the sake of their ability to hold politicians accountable, they must be able to see that policy alternatives exist, who holds which views, and who has decided what.[133] In this connection, compromise has the advantage over consensus-oriented politics that it does not claim to be able to deliver decisions that can satisfy everyone's first-order preferences or transcend disagreement. Still, we should be careful not to apply the imperative to compromise too broadly. The spirit of compromise is not the only democratically valuable democratic attitude, and it must be weighed against other fundamental democratic values. There are times and domains in which one should dissent and oppose, rather than concede and accommodate. The politics of compromise is at best a supplement to and not a substitute for political competition and the politics of the informal public sphere of civil society.[134] The two tracks of deliberative politics mentioned in Chapter 4 should be kept separate and allowed to follow their respective logics.

Some readers might think that the last point vindicates the need for a populistic element as essential to the democratic process. They might think so because populists often criticize the obscurity of current representative politics, and because populists' antagonistic stance makes disagreement

---

[132] This mistake is made in the argument against compromise by Ruser and Machin, *Against Political Compromise*, 41–4. Of course, this does not mean that it is wrong to warn against the danger of silencing dissent in actual compromises. My point is only that this is not a necessary element in compromising.

[133] Rummens, "Staging Deliberation," 31–7.

[134] As Arato and Cohen ("Civil Society, Populism, and Religion," 285) argue, there is a difference between acting as a social movement in civil society and exercising political power: "Social movements may be ... uncompromising regarding their values in civil society, but must be self-limiting ... in the exercise of political power."

visible. However, the question is whether populism itself promotes the visibility of disagreement and the expression of dissent that are required for motivation, accountability, and change. The answer is that the populist notions of the homogenous people and antagonism themselves suppress disagreement and delegitimize dissent. In many places, democracy arguably needs reinvigoration and the encouragement of displays of dissent. However, populist politics is not the best way to achieve this, because when it succeeds, it threatens contestation rather than promoting it.[135] This is not just a contingent matter of how populists behave in power; it is part of the populist ideology, which promotes the idea of a unified people rather than valuing disagreements among the people as a diverse plurality. Moreover, the populist notion of representation as embodiment has no room or need for accountability, since the alleged identity between leader and people makes it nonsensical to hold the ruler accountable.[136] The idea of accountability makes sense only when there is distance and difference between the representative and the represented.

5.3   Democracy's Multiple Forms of Respect

Through the analysis of the meaning and value of majority rule and compromise, I have demonstrated that it is misleading to see populism as fully committed to democratic principles and only against liberal principles that constrain the will of the people. Populism has its own unique interpretation of what the democratic principles of popular sovereignty and majority rule mean and require in political practice. If we accept the populist understanding of democracy, we will not maintain the same democratic processes but without constitutional constraints. Rather, the very meaning and practice of democratic processes will change radically. Of course, my own understanding of majority rule, compromise, and deliberation is committed to and inspired by liberal principles. But this is part of my argument: We cannot cut off the liberal part of liberal democracy and uphold the same understanding of democracy. The "democracy parts" of liberal and illiberal democracy respectively do not constitute the same idea of democracy and democratic processes. In my view, liberal principles are not just external constraints on democratic processes. Nor are they merely enabling conditions of democracy, as many have argued liberal constitutionalism is. According to my democratic respect

---

[135] See Chapter 6.
[136] Arato and Cohen, *Populism and Civil Society*, 9; Caramani, "Will vs. Reason," 63; Urbinati, "Political Theory of Populism," 122.

view, liberal principles are part of the very meaning and interpretation of democratic processes such as majority rule, compromise, and deliberation. If liberal principles are discarded, as they are in populism, these processes will have a very different meaning and will be employed in fundamentally different ways.

Under nonideal circumstances, people and institutions must manifest respect in a number of different ways, and our understanding of democracy must be open to the value of all of them. Interpretations of democracy that entail that respect can take only one form fail to meet the challenges of a pluralistic and complicated reality plagued by inequality. Democracy is a complex way of making decisions, and it includes multiple ways for citizens to display respect for one another. Voting, majority rule, public deliberation, and compromise are all part of the democratic process, and they can all, in different ways, manifest respect for citizens as free and equal participants. To be sure, taking a majority vote, compromising, and deliberating will sometimes compete with one another as ways of reaching a decision or displaying the appropriate form of respect. I shall not seek to adjudicate here when one or another is the best way to proceed. This is a contextual question and cannot be determined at the abstract level of our discussion. However, I do want to suggest that we as a political community have failed in terms of respect for one other as fellow participants in democracy if we use only one of the three means of including and respecting one another. Majority decision-making and compromise without deliberation fail to respect others as fellow reasoners from whom we may learn. Majority rule without compromise leads to a form of "winner-take-all society" in which the values and concerns of the minority tend to be ignored. Deliberation without majority decision-making and/or compromise fails to acknowledge that "when an issue is in dispute there is more to be considered than the issue itself,"[137] or to tell us how to respect other citizens as equals when consensus is not forthcoming and disagreement persists – as it usually does in real politics.

---

[137] Kuflik, "Morality and Compromise," 51.

6   Publicity and Correcting Democracy

Populist struggles for recognition can often be connected to the real and deep deficiencies of contemporary democracies.[1] By this, I do not mean that all the grievances that motivate support for populism are legitimate. Indeed, it has been a central argument of the earlier chapters of this book that struggles for recognition are not always democratic, and that we need to be more careful in our assessment of their validity with regard to both factual circumstances and democratic principles. We have seen that many of the recognition demands intertwined with the rise of populism are either demands for public esteem of a particular way of life, which is irreconcilable with democratic pluralism, or demands to protect former status privileges, which is inconsistent with political equality. Still, this does not mean that existing democracies work reasonably – or even tolerably – well in terms of political equality, mutual respect, and responsiveness to the legitimate concerns of all corners of society. As institutionalized recognition orders that include sociocultural, economic, and political dimensions, contemporary democracies are far from fulfilling the demanding presuppositions of free and equal participation in co-ruling. Democratic respect is everywhere an unfulfilled ideal.

Given the severe flaws of actually existing democracies, the latter are in need of some kind of correction. Some scholars believe that populism can serve as a means for this correction of democracy. Among these scholars, there are two positions, which I will call the ambivalent position and the radical position. The ambivalent position holds that populism can correct democracy in some respects, but that it simultaneously threatens democracy in other respects.[2] The radical position holds that populism can deepen democracy, without being much concerned with

---

[1] Parts of this chapter draw on Rostbøll, "Populism, Democracy, and the Publicity Requirement."

[2] The most influential proponents of this position are Mudde and Rovira Kaltwasser. See Rovira Kaltwasser, "Ambivalence of Populism"; Mudde and Kaltwasser, "Populism: Corrective *and* Threat"; Mudde and Rovira Kaltwasser, *Populism*, 79–96.

the anti-pluralist, leader-centric, and authoritarian threats other writers believe populism poses.[3] Both positions share the idea that populism can correct democracy by motivating political participation, including otherwise marginalized groups, and bringing new items and alternative programs to the political agenda.

The question of whether populism is good or bad for democracy is, as Benjamin Moffitt notes, "*the* key question to which authors on the topic keep returning."[4] In a way, this question has motivated all the preceding chapters of this book. In this chapter, I take a different tack on the issue. So far, I have analyzed and discussed to what extent populist demands for recognition and populist ideas of democracy can be justified in light of our best democratic standards. Now I want to discuss the possibility that even if populism is not the best conception of democracy, it might nevertheless correct the deficiencies of actually existing democracies. This seems to be the view of both the ambivalent and the radical positions – even if the ambivalent position is, of course, ambivalent. Neither of the two positions endorses populism as such, that is, as an end and a political regime, but they both believe that populist politics can have good effects on democracy, as they (the proponents of the two positions) understand the latter idea.

My question is not whether populist parties can correct democracy, as this question might be posed by an external observer. My question is rather whether we, or anyone, *as fellow participants in democracy* can endorse and promote populism because it has positive effects on a non-populist understanding of democracy. Applying the publicity condition first suggested by Kant and later expounded by Rawls, I argue that we cannot. We cannot *publicly* both endorse populism and say we do so because it improves democracy understood in non-populist terms. The publicity condition, as we shall see, rules out the possibility of promoting one set of ideas (populism) for the sake of another set of ideas (non-populist democracy). The argument for promoting populism for the sake of a non-populist end cannot be made public without frustrating that very end. In addition, publicity is not only a matter of being honest, non-manipulative, and consistent – all virtues of democratic respect – but also a question of the *educative effects* of the political discourses of political actors and elites (which populist leaders cannot avoid becoming) on our common political culture. It is from their shared political culture that

---

[3] The most important proponent of this position is Mouffe in *For a Left Populism*. To be clear, Mouffe is by no means unconcerned with authoritarianism and anti-pluralism, but she does not see populism as entailing these threats. Regarding the leader-centrism of populism, she says: "There is no reason to equate strong leadership with authoritarianism" (Mouffe, *For a Left Populism*, 70).

[4] Moffitt, *Global Rise of Populism*, 133.

citizens learn about the nature of politics and democracy, about their democratic rights and obligations, and so on.

This chapter begins by specifying three respects in which current democracies are often said to need correction and in relation to which some writers regard populism as a remedy. This is followed by a presentation of the publicity condition in Kant and Rawls, where I explain which parts of the idea I find useful for my purposes. I go on to clarify how the publicity condition connects to the notion of democratic respect developed in this book. In addition to being an expression of democratic respect, I suggest, publicity matters because of the importance of the public political culture for the functioning of democracy. In order to show how the publicity condition can be applied, I explicate Rawls's use of it in his criticism of utilitarianism. Against this background, I subject to the publicity condition the view that populism can correct democracy according to non-populist democratic standards. Specifically, I consider Chantal Mouffe's argument that populism can deepen democracy. I demonstrate that her position is publicly self-frustrating. In this connection, the question of the value of political conflict is central, and I argue that its value depends on its type. Finally, the chapter turns to the educative and public culture-shaping effects of the ideas we promote in public. Here I argue that populism is a bad school of democracy and that this is something everyone must take very seriously in our current democratic malaise.

6.1   Populism as a "Corrective"

Populism might be said to have positive effects on the functioning of democracy because it *reveals* the dysfunction of contemporary democratic systems and/or because it *corrects* these dysfunctions.[5] While revealing deficits may help to correct democracy, there is clearly a gap between revealing something and correcting it. Even if it is accepted that populism can reveal that actually existing democracies "often do not live up to their full potential,"[6] this leaves open the question of whether populism or populist politics[7] can correct the deficiencies or just makes things worse. The ensuing analysis and discussion concern not the revealing but the democracy-correcting potential of populism.

When we examine whether populism can correct "democracy," we need to clarify which conception of democracy is being applied as a

---

[5] Moffitt (*Global Rise of Populism*, 144) lists populism's ability to reveal the dysfunctions of contemporary democracies as one of "the democratic tendencies of populism."

[6] Moffitt, *Global Rise of Populism*, 144.

[7] While I see "populism" as a set of claims and ideas, "populist politics" is politics based on these ideas.

standard for the correction. Correction requires not only an impetus but also a standard. To correct something means to make it conform to some standard, norm, or ideal. The scholars who suggest that populism can correct democracy may invoke different conceptions of democracy, but this is not always sufficiently clear. It is important to stress that the argument I consider in the following uses a *non-populist conception of democracy* as a standard. Our question, therefore, is not whether populism can make democracy more populistic, but rather, whether it can have positive effects given a non-populist conception of democracy. Hence, we should distinguish between the question of whether populism or non-populism has the best conception of democracy and the question of whether populism can have positive effects on our preferred non-populist conception of democracy. It is the latter question we consider in this chapter. To be sure, this dichotomist framing excludes a third possibility, namely, that populism can correct our conception of democracy by making it *more* populist without accepting a fully populist conception of democracy. However, this is not what the scholars I discuss suggest.[8]

The academic literature suggests three main ways in which populism is able to correct democracy (where the latter is understood in non-populist terms). First, populist parties are said to bring new issues to the political agenda and provide programmatic alternatives for the electorate to choose between. Populism shatters the existing rigidity, conformity, and consensus by politicizing hitherto unpoliticized issues and introducing more conflict into the political arena.[9] The diagnosis that animates this suggestion is that politics has long been too consensual and has not offered real alternatives to the voters. The argument is that mainstream political parties and political elites act as if there were no alternatives to the existing order, and that populism is beneficial because it challenges the existing order and politics as usual. For our purposes, it is important to emphasize that we do not need a populist understanding of democracy in order to see the value of this possible correction of actually existing democracy. Most, if not all, conceptions of democracy regard political competition, contestation, and real alternatives for the voters to choose

---

[8] Some readers might object that Mouffe wants to make democracy more populistic, even if she does not promote (left) populism for the sake of establishing a populist regime (Mouffe, *For a Left Populism*, 11, 80). However, as we shall see, her aim of agonistic pluralism cannot be understood as a more populist democracy.

[9] Mansbridge and Macedo, "Populism and Democratic Theory," 72–3; Moffitt, *Global Rise of Populism*, 144; Mouffe, *For a Left Populism*, 12–24; Roberts, "Populism and Polarization," 2, 5.

between as valuable features of politics, even if they understand these ideas in somewhat different ways.[10]

Whereas the first correction concerns bringing in new issues, the second potential correction concerns the inclusion of previously excluded people or identities.[11] The contention is that populist politicians both legitimize groups that are often excluded from the public sphere and mobilize them to participate in politics. In this way, populism makes democracy more inclusive and less elite-dominated, especially in terms of legitimizing and mobilizing "ordinary people." There is a connection between the first correction and the second insofar as a political landscape with more options is more motivating for political participation, because the people will see the point and value of voting more clearly. Again, I want to stress that the value of political inclusion is not a distinctively populist value (if it is a populist value at all), but one that is shared by many non-populist conceptions of democracy (excluding perhaps the most elitist). Thus, Rovira Kaltwasser uses Robert Dahl's democratic theory and its notion of inclusiveness to argue "that in societies where there are significant problems in the dimension of inclusiveness, populism might well represent a sort of democratic corrective."[12]

A third way in which populism is said to be capable of correcting contemporary democracies is by making the political system more responsive to the preferences of ordinary people.[13] One of the key problems of many contemporary democratic systems, pointed out by some defenders of populism, is that these political systems are much more responsive to the interests and preferences of the elite, especially the rich, than they are to the interests and policy preferences of the lower classes.[14] By challenging oligarchy, and by promoting or implementing policies desired by the lower classes, populism can secure responsiveness to a larger share of the

---

[10] Note that whereas the radical position of Mouffe sees populism as enhancing conflict and alternative voter choices, the ambivalent position of Mudde and Rovira Kaltwasser (*Populism*, 82) lists the restriction of political contestation as one of the *threats* of populism to democracy.

[11] Moffitt, *Global Rise of Populism*, 143; Mudde and Rovira Kaltwasser, *Populism*, 82–3; Rovira Kaltwasser, "Ambivalence of Populism," 196–9; Roberts, "Populism and Democracy," 147–53.

[12] Rovira Kaltwasser, "Ambivalence of Populism," 198.

[13] Kazin, *Populist Persuasion*, xv; Moffitt, *Global Rise of Populism*, 144; Mudde and Rovira Kaltwasser, *Populism*, 83.

[14] See McCormick, *Machiavellian Democracy*, 181, 279. There is much empirical research, especially on the United States, which supports McCormick's claim that contemporary democracies are not equally responsive to the preferences of all, but rather favor the wealthy. See Gilens, *Affluence and Influence*; Inglehart and Norris, "Trump," 450. While McCormick ("Machiavellian Democracy") explicitly defends "populism," his notion of "Machiavellian democracy" does not fit my understanding of populism, as mentioned in Chapter 5.

population than current democracies do. In Chapter 4, I expressed some reservations about the populist notion of responsiveness (as correspondence), but even non-populist conceptions of democracy will agree that we have a deep democratic problem if the political system is responsive to the interests and preferences of only a small segment of the population. If the rich can use their economic resources to attain more than equal influence on political outcomes, this violates a commonly accepted democratic ideal of equal opportunity for political influence.[15]

Promoting contestation, inclusion, and responsiveness to all sectors of society should be central concerns for all democrats. To be sure, different conceptions of democracy disagree on (1) the exact meaning of these standards or criteria, (2) when they can be said to be realized, and (3) how important each is compared with the others as well as with other democratic criteria. There are many detailed issues to analyze and discuss in relation to each of the three democratic criteria. I considered some of these issues earlier in the book (for example, regarding responsiveness), and I will consider others below (especially regarding contestation and conflict), but I cannot cover them all. The important point to repeat is that this chapter is concerned with whether populism can correct democracy in relation to these standards while denying that a populist understanding of democracy is superior to a non-populist understanding of democracy. Or to put it differently, can one publicly promote both populism and the end of realizing non-populist understandings of contestation, inclusion, and responsiveness? This is the question raised when we invoke the publicity condition.

6.2   The Publicity Condition

Kant introduces the publicity condition in the second appendix to "Toward Perpetual Peace."[16] Its object is "every claim to a right," which Kant says must have the "capacity for publicity." Hence, "all actions relating to the rights of others are wrong if their maxim is incompatible with publicity."[17] The core of the Kantian publicity condition is the idea that our political positions – our reason or justification for political action – should be capable of being made public without this resulting in their self-frustration. The "capacity for publicity" that Kant speaks of is a question of whether our *reason for action* (our "maxim"[18]) can be

---

[15] Brighouse, "Egalitarianism"; Dahl, *Democracy and Its Critics*, 114–15.
[16] Kant, "Toward Perpetual Peace," 347–51 (AK 8: 381–6).
[17] Kant, "Toward Perpetual Peace," 347 (AK 8: 381).
[18] Korsgaard (*Creating the Kingdom of Ends*, 13) explains Kant's notion of "maxim" as "the principle that you give yourself, that you act on .... Your maxim must contain your

communicated publicly without this frustrating the end that justifies the action in the first place. A maxim (a reason for action) "that I cannot *divulge* without thereby defeating my purpose, one that must absolutely *be kept secret* if it is to succeed" violates the publicity condition and is therefore "*not right* toward others."[19]

In *A Theory of Justice*, Rawls presents publicity as one of the formal constraints of right.[20] Rawls's understanding of publicity requires that the principles and rules one promotes for common affairs should be capable of being publicly recognized and accepted. The ideas behind political principles and the demands that they impose on us should be capable of being known and applied by everyone. Whereas Kant formulates the publicity condition in hypothetical terms – as a question of whether a maxim *could* be made public – it is also important for Rawls that political doctrines actually be made public. Only with *actual publicity* of political rules and their justification can citizens know their rights and duties, the principles that support them, and the arguments for them. Thus, part of Rawls's argument for the publicity condition is that insofar as a political doctrine aims to be the basis of political power, those subject to it should be able to publicly scrutinize it. A political doctrine or position should offer itself to public discussion and justification.[21] Political power should not be based on delusions or deceptions.[22]

For Rawls, the ideas of publicity and especially public reason and public justification are related to the aim of creating agreement on and stability around a shared conception of justice.[23] I do not see the aim of creating consensus, or "overlapping consensus," as a necessary part of the publicity condition, and it is not entailed by the way in which I shall use it. Thus, I do not invoke the publicity condition in a way that presupposes that reducing conflict or disagreement is an aim in itself.[24] On the contrary, I see publicity as a requirement for conflict to be democratic,

---

reason for action: it must say what you are going to do, and why." On Kant's use of "maxim," see also O'Neill, *Acting on Principle*, 13–16.

[19] Kant, "Toward Perpetual Peace," 347–8 (AK 8: 381–2).

[20] Rawls, *Theory of Justice*, 115.

[21] In this chapter, I speak of the publicity condition in relation to political doctrines, political positions, political views, political projects, and political arguments. I use these different terms as I think appropriate to the context. What is crucial is that the publicity condition applies to views that relate to the exercise of political power and, as Kant puts it, to the rights of others. Below I explain why I think it appropriate to apply the publicity condition to arguments for the corrective value of populism.

[22] Rawls, *Political Liberalism*, 68.

[23] Rawls, *Political Liberalism*, 66–71; Rawls, *Justice as Fairness*, 26–9, 89–95, 120–2.

[24] To be precise, my appeal to the publicity condition does not presuppose that the reduction of all kinds of conflict and disagreement is a good thing. However, I acknowledge

because it enables people to understand and scrutinize the alternatives, and because it promotes respectful interaction.[25] Still, it is important to stress that the publicity condition requires of citizens – when making political arguments for action that affect other people's rights – that they address everyone and consider the effects that their reasons for (recommending) action will have if they become common knowledge. The publicity condition, as I understand it, asks whether you could communicate your position – your reason for recommending a political action – openly, clearly, and in its entirety to all those who would be affected by it and who would have to realize its promise. Could your political position become common knowledge, generally accepted and acted upon, and still achieve its promised end?

The idea that political doctrines and reasons for political action should adhere to the publicity condition connects to the idea of democratic respect developed in this book. As Samuel Freeman notes, publicity has *the social function* of making possible mutually respectful public discussion.[26] If one hides the true ends of one's recommended course of political action because this is required for its success, one fails to treat other people as free, equal, and reason-responsive beings. Democratic respect therefore excludes esoteric doctrines, which are doctrines that (1) are communicable only to part of the public and (2) can only achieve their aims by not being publicly communicated. In contrast to esotericism, the application of the publicity condition to our political projects is grounded in respect for and trust in ordinary people's understanding of political affairs.[27]

The publicity condition is based on respect for the equal capacity for reason of everyone. With publicity, no one is treated as having privileged insight into the true and right, and political positions are made subject to the scrutiny and discussion of everyone. Moreover, the publicity condition entails respecting everyone as ends in themselves. It rules out the possibility of making some the means for ends that they cannot know and may not endorse. Finally, publicity is required for political power to be "the power of the public."[28] This is because publicity is

that acceptance of the publicity condition entails agreement on substantive norms of freedom, equality, and mutual respect. But this does not distinguish my position from that of Mouffe (*For a Left Populism*, 93), who also accepts that "democracy cannot survive without certain forms of consensus relating to allegiance to ethico-political values that constitute its principles of legitimacy, and the institutions in which these are inscribed."

[25] As we shall see below, there are different kinds of conflict and disagreement, and the aim of the publicity condition can be seen as limiting some forms of conflict and disagreement in order to enable other (more democratic) forms.

[26] Freeman, "Burdens of Public Justification," 6, 12, 16.

[27] Luban, "Publicity Principle," 154–6, 192–6.

[28] Rawls, *Political Liberalism*, 68.

a precondition for a plurality of citizens to discuss and act together *as
a public*, and thus *to form a public*.[29] Thus, by adhering to the publicity
condition and actually making their political positions public, citizens
respect and include one another as members of the same public and as
having the status of co-rulers.

The publicity condition requires that citizens adopt what I have called
the participant attitude in their interactions. This entails that when we propose political ideas and principles, we do so as participants involved in relationships with other human beings to whom these principles should apply.
The publicity condition and the participant attitude mean that we think of
our principles and reasons as things it is right for us to communicate to others and act on, and for our society to be regulated by. Promoting a political doctrine or political project entails establishing a certain relationship to
both our followers and our political opponents. It does so because political principles are addressed *to* others and entail making demands *on them*.
The publicity condition concerns the character of these relationships and
is grounded in the norm that such relationships should exhibit respect for
everyone as engaged in a common practice. Publicity matters because of its
potential to make all those affected into participants in a joint enterprise. It
is a precondition of "democratic social cooperation on a footing of mutual
respect between citizens regarded as free and equal."[30]

The preceding points should make it clear that lack of publicity is
a *democratic* shortcoming. Publicity is not only a liberal principle that
protects individuals against the abuse of power; it is just as importantly a
condition for citizens to participate as free and equal in democratic opinion and will formation. Arguably, publicity is what unites liberalism and
democracy.[31] Without a commitment to publicity, citizens cannot form
a public sphere where they can discuss their different political positions.
Without publicity, citizens cannot compare and scrutinize the positions
of political parties and form a judgment about how to vote. Without
publicity, citizens cannot form an enlightened opinion about whether to
assent to or dissent from government policies.

A further aspect of the publicity condition (emphasized by Rawls) is
the educative function of political conceptions and the public political
culture. While Rawls is concerned with how a political conception of
justice that regulates a society's basic structure affects the public political

---

[29] Dewey, *Public and Its Problems*; Habermas, *Between Facts and Norms*, 171, 183, 368.
[30] Rawls, *Justice as Fairness*, 28. Here Rawls actually refers to his own idea of "public justification" rather than to the publicity condition, but I think it is true of the latter, less demanding idea as well.
[31] Habermas, *Between Facts and Norms*, 359–87.

culture, and how this culture educates citizens about political justice,[32] I apply it more broadly to the effects of political projects on the shared political culture of society. Accordingly, my contention is that what citizens and politicians say and do in public will shape our public political culture, which in turn shapes people's views of what democracy means, what citizens owe to each other, what rights and obligations they have, and so on. Against this background, if you cannot want other citizens to learn from and be educated by the political doctrine or set of ideas you promote, then you have failed to adhere to the publicity condition. Thus, the reason for the publicity condition also concerns the consequences for the political culture and citizens' education of the ideas that politicians and theorists promote.

It is instructive for the application of the publicity condition to populism to consider how Rawls employs it in his criticism of utilitarianism. Rawls argues that adopting the principle of utility as a public conception of justice would undermine some citizens' self-respect, because this principle "requires some who are less fortunate to accept even lower life prospects for the sake of others."[33] If a citizen knows that she is worse off for the sake of others, and if she knows that everyone knows this, this will harm her self-respect. She will rightly feel that she is being used as a means to the end of others, and this feeling will be even worse because she knows that everyone knows this. Rawls therefore considers the *strategy* of increasing average utility by choosing another set of principles – such as his own two principles of justice – as the *public* principles. But in that case, what is being chosen is Rawls's principles and not the principle of utility. "If ... the public recognition of utilitarianism entails some loss of self-esteem, there is no way around this drawback."[34] Thus, the publicity condition forbids one to "choose" one set of principles (for example, Rawls's two principles of justice) and then use *another* principle (here, the principle of utility) to assess justice in society.

The core of Rawls's publicity argument against utilitarianism, then, is that we cannot publicly choose and share one set of principles as "the fundamental charter" of society and then have another set of principles as the standards we use to assess whether our society is just or not. We cannot proclaim that we have chosen to have our society regulated by conception A and then use conception B to assess whether our society is just. For then we have actually chosen B to regulate our society. If we believe B to be the right doctrine, then B must be both the publicly

---

[32] Rawls, *Justice as Fairness*, 56, 121–2, 146–8; Rawls, *Political Liberalism*, 71.

[33] Rawls, *Theory of Justice*, 157.

[34] Rawls, *Theory of Justice*, 158.

recognized charter of society and the theory used to assess the justice of society. If choosing B as the public conception of justice undermines B's end, then B has failed the publicity condition and should not be chosen. In short, the publicly proclaimed doctrine and the actually applied doctrine must be the same.

In sum, the publicity condition asks us to ensure that the public recognition of the doctrine we promote does not frustrate its end. If a doctrine cannot be publicly recognized without effacing its value, it has failed the publicity condition. An implication of this requirement is that the doctrine we promote and the principles we use to assess its effects must be the same.

6.2.1   Publicity and Populism

The question I ask in this chapter – whether we, or anyone, as fellow participants in democracy can endorse and promote populism because it has positive effects on a non-populist understanding of democracy – is already inspired by the publicity condition. As we have just seen, applying the publicity condition to one's position or reason for (recommending) action entails viewing oneself as a participant in a public enterprise shared by others. The publicity condition asks whether you could communicate your maxim, position, or argument openly, clearly, and in its entirety to all those who would be affected by it and who would have to realize its promise. In relation to our concern, the question is whether one can communicate the argument for the corrective value of populism for non-populist democratic ends to those who would be subjected to populism and who would have to realize the promise of this argument.

Before I apply the publicity condition to the view that we should promote populism because it can correct democracy according to a non-populist standard, let me consider the objection that the publicity condition is foreign to populism and therefore its application would amount to no more than an external critique. But what reasons could a populist have for rejecting the publicity condition? Historically, from Plato to Sidgwick, the justification for esotericism has been that ordinary people lack understanding and that the wise few or political leaders are therefore justified in keeping the true grounds of their actions secret.[35] It is difficult to see how a populist could reject publicity *because* the elite knows better and one cannot trust the people. It is a key claim of populism that we should trust the people.[36] Moreover, insofar as the

[35] Luban, "Publicity Principle," 179–80, 189–95.
[36] Canovan, "Trust the People!"

attraction of populism is that it "promises to make politics transparent,"[37] it can hardly reject the value of publicity. Perhaps the populist could consistently reject publicity in relation to the corrupt elite, but the lack of publicity that I shall highlight concerns lack of publicity in relation to the very people that populists claim to respect.

Nonetheless, whether or not people truly committed to populism could accept the publicity condition is not the most important issue for the question we are investigating in this chapter. Remember, we are concerned with the possibility that even if we do not accept populism as the best conception of democracy – that is, even if we do not share the core claims of populism – we should nevertheless promote populism because of its ability to correct the deficiencies of actually existing democracies. What I want to subject to the publicity condition is the argument that we can and should promote populism because it has positive effects on a non-populist understanding of democracy. Those theorists who suggest that populism can correct democracy do not normally use "populist democracy" as a standard, but invoke some other, non-populist conception of democracy. At the beginning of this chapter, I mentioned that there are both ambivalent and radical positions on the question of whether populism can correct democracy. For the sake of simplicity, and because she unambivalently speaks in favor of *promoting* populism – that is, she provides a reason for populist action – in the following I shall concentrate on the radical position of Chantal Mouffe. However, I believe that the main thrust of my argument also applies to other defenses of the democracy-correcting effects of populism. Mouffe is also relevant because of her influence on and cooperation with (left) populist politicians, such as Pablo Iglesias and Íñigio Errejón from *Podemos* in Spain and Jean-Luc Mélonchon from *La France insoumise.*[38]

In her recent book, Mouffe argues "for a left populism."[39] While she regards populism as a discursive strategy that can take different ideological forms, the book promotes a form of *left* populism. What differentiates left from right populism for Mouffe is not that left populism offers a different type of politics, but that it advances a more egalitarian and eco-friendly policy agenda. Hence, she recommends that the left use the same kind of discursive strategy with which the right has been so successful. She justifies the populist strategy as necessary to break the "consensus in the centre" and the "post-politics" of neoliberalism.[40] Thus,

---

[37] Canovan, "Taking Politics to the People," 34.
[38] Valdivielso, "Outraged People."
[39] Mouffe, *For a Left Populism.*
[40] Mouffe, *For a Left Populism*, 12–24.

the political analysis that is the basis of her promotion of populism is that contemporary democracies are too centrist and consensus-oriented, and that they therefore have failed to offer "real alternatives" to the electorate.[41] Through the populist strategy of "construction of the political frontier between 'the people' and 'the oligarchy,'" she holds that it is possible to "recover and deepen democracy."[42]

When Mouffe speaks of "populism," then, she accepts that its key characteristic is to divide society into two antagonistically opposed camps. Specifically, she explicitly endorses Laclau's understanding of populism.[43] Thus, she agrees that populism sees "the people" as a part that stands for the whole. Laclau is blatant about this: "The 'people' ... is something less than the totality of the members of the community: it is a partial component which nevertheless aspires to be conceived as the only legitimate totality."[44] This populist construction entails the idea that the views of the opponent cannot be legitimate. In populism, those who differ from or disagree with "the people" must be corrupt and self-serving and "cannot be a legitimate part of the community."[45]

Mouffe emphasizes that she is not in favor of a revolutionary break with liberal democracy. The deepening of democracy that she favors, and which left populism should deliver, is a radicalization of the principles of a liberal democratic regime, "liberty and equality for all."[46] Mouffe continues: "The objective of a left populist strategy is not the establishment of a 'populist regime' but the construction of a collective subject apt to launch a political offensive in order to establish a new hegemonic formation *within the liberal democratic framework.*"[47] Thus, Mouffe does not promote populism in order to reject liberal democracy and replace it with "populist democracy."[48] She believes that one can promote populism as a means to bring liberal democracy back to its own commitments (recovery) or to more fully realize its principles (radicalization and deepening). This is why I take her to be advancing the idea that it is possible to promote populism for the sake of a non-populist understanding of

---

[41] Mouffe, *For a Left Populism*, 17.
[42] Mouffe, *For a Left Populism*, 5.
[43] Mouffe, *For a Left Populism*, 10–11.
[44] Laclau, *On Populist Reason*, 81.
[45] Laclau, *On Populist Reason*, 86.
[46] Mouffe, *For a Left Populism*, 36–40, 48–9.
[47] Mouffe, *For a Left Populism*, 80, emphasis added.
[48] Mouffe (*For a Left Populism*, 11) denies that there is any such thing as a populist understanding of democracy or that populism designates "a political regime." However, throughout this book I have tried to show that populism does supply an alternative understanding of democracy, and I do not think that either Mouffe or Laclau succeed in

democracy. In other words, Mouffe's maxim, or her reason for recommending populist action, is that this will advance the end of more fully realizing the principles of liberal democracy.

The key reason for Mouffe to praise populism is that it introduces conflict into society and thereby shatters the existing consensus and enables opposition to the status quo. Importantly, the end that Mouffe aims for and to which she believes populism can contribute is a specific kind of conflict. Her problem with "the post-politics" of contemporary democracies is that it "eliminates the possibility of *an agonistic struggle between different projects of society* which is the very condition for the exercise of popular sovereignty."[49] Thus, Mouffe endorses a view of democracy that involves competition and choice between different programs, and she believes that democratic conflict should take a specific form that she calls "agonistic pluralism." She contrasts the latter with antagonistic conflict: "The agonistic confrontation is different from the antagonistic one, not because it allows for a possible consensus, but because the opponent is not considered an enemy to be destroyed but an adversary whose existence is perceived as legitimate."[50] Again, the maxim behind Mouffe's recommendation of populism is that it would realize the end of agonistic pluralism within a liberal democratic framework.

The question raised with the publicity condition is whether in public one can simultaneously proclaim populist ideas and a commitment to the end of agonistic pluralism. The publicity condition requires that one makes one's end public and that doing so does not frustrate that very end. Hence, when promoting populism, Mouffe must make it public that her end is agonistic pluralism. However, Mouffe's expressed end, her reason for promoting populism, comes into conflict with two aspects of populism, namely antagonism and the aim of establishing a new consensus. Notice that antagonism and the aim of creating a new consensus are part not just of populism as *I* understand it, but also of how *Mouffe and Laclau* understand it.

It is generally agreed that populism works by postulating or creating antagonism between two camps in society, the people and the elite. In Laclau's view too (which Mouffe says she accepts), populism works

showing that populism is "just a strategy" with no normative content. Here I agree with Canovan ("Taking Politics to the People," 33): "Populism also has a characteristic core of *concepts* that it asserts, prioritises and decontests – democracy, popular sovereignty, the people understood as a collectivity with a common will, and majority rule. These cannot be dismissed as empty rhetorical flourishes."

[49] Mouffe, *For a Left Populism*, 17, emphasis added.
[50] Mouffe, *For a Left Populism*, 91. For an elaboration of Mouffe's view of agonism, see Mouffe, *Democratic Paradox*, 101–5.

through the hostile conflict between these two camps. Populist conflict takes the form of a Schmittian friend-enemy relation, where the opponent is not seen as a legitimate adversary but rather as an enemy to be eradicated.[51] As we have seen, Mouffe herself sees the drawing of a frontier between two camps as part of what makes populism a useful strategy for the left. She advocates this antagonistic frontier-drawing because she thinks it will be motivating for participation and will shatter the existing consensus. The question raised by the publicity condition is whether one can publicly promote both the populist friend-enemy antagonism *and* the express goal of agonistic pluralism. My contention is that one cannot. If you believe that what motivates people is the articulation of populist antagonism, you cannot publicly proclaim that this construction is only a means for agonistic pluralism. The end that Mouffe seeks is frustrated by its public proclamation. She cannot reveal her end to the people who are to realize it, because according to her own argument they are motivated by something else, namely populist antagonism.

While populism works by articulating antagonism, its aim is to create a new consensus. The combination of antagonism and consensus in populism might sound paradoxical, but as I argued in Chapter 5, this combination can be explained by the fact that "the people" in populism never refers to the whole population but always only to a part. Populism aims for the voice of the real people to prevail, and insofar as the real people are the only ones who count, this amounts to a form of consensus. It is true, as Mouffe stresses, that populist politics will often break the existing consensus, but this does not mean that the aim of populism is the creation of "an agonistic struggle between different projects of society."[52] The aim and logic of populism is to eradicate divisions and disagreements, not to give people as a diverse body of citizens a range of choices to choose between. Populists may use conflict as a temporary means, but the goal is always a new consensus – a new hegemony, in the Gramscian vocabulary used by Mouffe and Laclau.[53] If this is right, Mouffe cannot make her argument for the democratizing effect of populism public, because the public appeal of populism (a new consensus, where disagreeing others have been excluded) stands in opposition to the end posited by Mouffe (agonistic pluralism with real choice for citizens).

As mentioned above, the publicity condition entails that the principles or set of ideas that one professes should be the same principles or set of

[51] Schmitt, *Concept of the Political*. On Laclau's Schmittian moments, see Arato, "Political Theology and Populism."
[52] Mouffe, *For a Left Populism*, 17.
[53] Stavrakakis, "Populism and Hegemony."

ideas that one uses to evaluate their effects. Thus, if one promotes populism, which is constituted by a set of ideas (including antagonism and the creation of a new consensus), then one should evaluate the effects with the same set of ideas. It violates the publicity condition if one evaluates the effects of populism with non-populist standards such as agonistic pluralism and free choice between different projects for society. When Mouffe advocates populism, she does so with a set of ideas that cannot be shared with the people who are to realize the promise of her argument or maxim. For on her own account, the people are motivated by the public appeal of populist ideas, and not by her version of democracy. In this way, her argument is esoteric. It can achieve its aim only by hiding it.

From the perspective of the publicity condition and the ideal of democratic respect that it expresses, the fundamental problem with Mouffe's argument for the democratizing effects of populism is that she does not take seriously the reasons people have for supporting populism. Mouffe never really engages with the validity of populism's claims, its understanding of how to relate to disagreeing others, or which conception of democracy populism promotes. She considers only the external effects of populism. In this way, she takes an observer attitude, which entails seeing populism as a form of treatment and external control of people. By taking this observer attitude to populism, Mouffe creates a sharp division between her own defense of populism and the reasons that motivate supporters of populism. Consequently, the latter cannot see themselves in the praise of populism that we find in Mouffe's argument.

It is by creating divergence between the ideas that are proclaimed by populists (for example, that the people is a unity and morally right) and her reason for promoting populism (agonistic pluralism) that Mouffe's democratic argument in favor of populism fails the publicity condition. The question raised by the publicity condition is whether the reasons for promoting a set of ideas can be accepted not by an external observer, but by people who take a participant attitude. That is, theorists who promote populism for its ability to correct or deepen democracy must be able to do so in a way that can be publicly recognized and accepted by followers of populism. When we adopt the participant attitude, we respect followers of populism as persons who believe in the rightness of populist ideas and principles. Thus, when I engage with a populist as a participant, I take her at her word as someone who believes that society is divided into two antagonistic camps and that the people is a unity whose will should be expressed immediately and directly in political decisions. When the ideas and claims that define populism are reduced to mere means, then the people who believe in those ideas are also treated as mere means. Failing the publicity condition, and adopting an observer attitude, Mouffe's argument for the democratic effects of populism treats followers of populism as mere means for the realization of ends that they do not share. The radical position fails the publicity condition not just in relation to the persons populism excludes, but also in relation to the people for whom populism claims to speak.

Before proceeding, we should consider the fact that there are many examples of government action that cannot be made public but which nevertheless seem just, and hence the objection that the publicity condition is too stringent a condition for political action. For example, a government cannot publicly announce a plan to make an anti-Mafia operation on a certain date without this undermining the operation, but this does not show the operation to be unjust.[54] Regarding this type of example, remember that for Kant, it is not the action but its maxim that must be compatible with publicity. That is, it is the principle explaining the action that must be capable of being communicated to the public. A government can publicly justify that it is fighting crime and that its timing and tactics will be kept secret, as long as its methods are within the limits of the law (which must be public). The reasons for keeping some government actions secret can be made public.

Admittedly, it is possible to come up with harder cases, and I do not pretend to be able to respond to them all. However, for our purposes the issue is not whether the maxim of this or that government action can withstand publicity, but rather whether the publicity condition is too stringent a standard for the assessment of the proposition that we should promote populism to further non-populist ends. My suggestion is that political positions that promote ideas that concern and fundamentally affect our view of society, human motivations, and basic norms for political interaction ought to be able to withstand publicity. As such a set of ideas, populism potentially transforms our understanding of democracy, and thus arguments that promote it have to be put to a stringent test. Thus, my application of the publicity condition in this chapter is not about the justice of specific policies, nor does it exclude all forms of secrecy in the strategies of political parties.

6.3 Conflict, Politicization, and Polarization

I would like to go into some more depth with the argument that populism can correct or deepen democracy *by introducing conflict*. The idea is that there is an interplay between the populist creation of conflict, the politicization of issues that have been suppressed, the provision of new

---

[54] Gosseries and Parr, "Publicity."

alternatives to the electorate, the mobilization of otherwise excluded or apathetic groups, challenges to the status quo, and prospects for necessary change.[55] As Mansbridge and Macedo put it, "in moments when the political system has become so rigid or elite-centered that it fails to acknowledge popular demands, populism is a *democratic way* to shake up the status quo."[56] I agree that conflict can be good for democracy, but I shall argue that it depends on the type of conflict. Even if shaking up the status quo is sometimes essential to make democracy live up to its promise, not all ways of doing so are equally democratic.

Defenders of populism argue that criticism of the conflicts created by populism is really just an attempt to protect existing privileges and avoid political change.[57] They are right that this may be the case, but it does not have to be the case. It is essential that our criticism of populism does not turn into a delegitimization of dissent or a conservative protection of the status quo. To avoid the latter, it is important to make clear that the problem with populism is not that it presents radical alternatives, expresses dissent from existing policies, or brings in new voices. The problem with populism is that it promotes a form of conflict *that itself delegitimizes dissent and disagreement.*

The question is not whether democracy should include conflict or not, but rather what kind of conflict is conducive to democracy. In relation to our discussion,[58] I want to stress that a conflict is democratic if and only if it (1) provides a multiplicity of ideological or policy alternatives, (2) presents them as alternatives that people can legitimately choose between as free and equal persons, and (3) enables public scrutiny and the subjection to trial by discussion of the alternatives over which there is conflict. If a conflict counteracts these three requirements rather than promoting them, it is not a democratic conflict. Let us consider how populism relates to each of the three requirements in turn.

First, then, for a conflict to be democratic, it must provide the electorate with a multiplicity of ideological and policy alternatives.[59] However, the type of conflict introduced by populism rather presents the electorate with a dual choice of "us" or "them." Moreover, populists

[55] Canovan, "Taking Politics to the People"; Laclau, *On Populist Reason*; Mouffe, *For a Left Populism*; Stavrakakis, "Populism in Power."
[56] Mansbridge and Macedo, "Populism and Democratic Theory," 73, emphasis added.
[57] Laclau, *On Populist Reason*, 266; Mouffe, *For a Left Populism*, 17–18; Stavrakakis, "Populism in Power."
[58] I write "in relation to our discussion," because the following requirements of a democratic conflict do not constitute an exhaustive list but are those requirements that are most relevant for my current purposes.
[59] The following draws on Rostbøll, "Populism and Two Kinds."

do not primarily present the latter choice as an *ideological* one. While it would be wrong to deny that populist parties sometimes present alternatives to existing policies, these are rarely clearly defined policies, much less based on a clear ideological position.[60] Populism rather polarizes in terms of identity. "Us" and "them" are different identity groups more than they are different ideological positions.[61] Most importantly for our purposes, populists seldom speak about how they *disagree* with the positions of their opponents. They rather speak about the opponent as self-serving, corrupt, and unconcerned with the views of "the people." Populist conflict is rooted in the claim that "the people" and "the elite" are different types of identity, and that they have different characters, rather than being a matter of making *disagreement* visible. This is also clear in Laclau's suggestion that "the people" is an empty signifier, which means that populism must reduce to a minimum any programmatic content.[62]

Second, in order for a conflict over alternatives to be democratically valuable, the alternatives must be presented as alternatives that citizens can legitimately choose between as free and equal persons. While in opposition, populists present themselves as an alternative to mainstream parties and politics as usual, but populism is not truly committed to the idea that the people can legitimately choose between different options. As mentioned before, populist parties do not present themselves as one possible option among others that citizens as participants can choose between, but as the *only legitimate option*. We see this in the fact that populists only praise the possibility of alternative choices while in opposition; when they attain governmental power, they suppress and delegitimize opposition and dissent.[63] And this is not a contingent matter but follows logically from the populist view of the people and popular sovereignty. So, even if populism shatters the existing consensus, this does not mean that populists are committed to establishing a new political landscape with clear ideological alternatives between which citizens can freely choose. When populists attain governmental power, they continue to polarize by speaking of some elite they are up against (the "deep state" and the like[64]), but they do not show in word or deed that they are committed to respecting

[60] Rosanvallon, *Le siècle du populisme*, 72–4.
[61] Urbinati, *Me the People*, 26, 37.
[62] Laclau, "Populism," 157.
[63] Levitsky and Loxton, "Populism and Competitive Authoritarianism"; Rovira Kaltwasser, "Ambivalence of Populism," 196–9; Weyland, "Populism and Authoritarianism."
[64] Donald Trump often referred to "the deep state" as an elite he was fighting. See Horwitz, "Trump and the 'Deep State.'"

ideological disagreements or participation as involving a choice between alternatives. Thus, if the aim is to promote free choice among different political projects, populist politics is not the road to take, because such free choice is not the type of conflict that characterizes populist polarization, and nor is it a norm to which populism is committed.

Third, in order for conflict over different projects of society to be democratically valuable, it must be possible for citizens to learn about the alternatives and subject them to trial by discussion.[65] This is required in order for citizens to make an enlightened choice.[66] Does populist polarization and conflict satisfy this requirement? Scholars who argue that populism can correct democracy highlight that it brings in new voices and concerns. However, populist politics prevents society from having a productive discussion of the issues it brings up. The reason for this is that populists do not bring issues to the political agenda as substantive issues about which there can be reasonable disagreement. They bring them forward as the concerns of the people, which for them excludes the need for policy argument and justification.[67] The problem is a fundamental one, namely that populism promotes an understanding of politics not as about debating differences of opinion, but as about antagonism between different identity groups. If you disagree with populist demands, you cannot respond by way of policy argument, for the political logic introduced by populism – "populist polarization" – has transformed the conflict into something different. The conflict now concerns whether or not you are for or against the people, or which group you belong to, the people or the elite.[68] In the polarizing logic of populism, those who disagree with populist demands are simply told that the latter express the will of the people. The fact is that populism is not committed to the contestability and public justification of its own claims, which means that populist polarization does not allow different political projects to be scrutinized, compared, and subjected to trial by discussion.[69]

Conflict is conducive to democracy only if the parties express their differences as substantive disagreements, and if they do so as part of a

---

[65] For the idea of "trial by discussion," see Manin, *Principles of Representative Government*, 183–92; Rosenblum, *On the Side*, 148–56; White and Ypi, *Meaning of Partisanship*, 76–7.

[66] According to Dahl (*Democracy and Its Critics*, 111–12), enlightened understanding is one of the core criteria of a democratic process, because before the people can get what it wants or considers best, it must first know what it wants or considers best.

[67] Weale, *Will of the People*, 114.

[68] As de la Torre ("Resurgence of Radical Populism," 388) puts it, in populism "the political field is reduced to a camp where citizens can choose either to acclaim the leader or to be condemned to ostracism as enemies of the leader and hence of the people and of the nation."

[69] White and Ypi, *Meaning of Partisanship*, 22n55, 55, 64, 76–7.

process that they acknowledge they share with their adversaries. These are exactly the conditions of publicity and the participant attitude. Publicity and the participant attitude do not discourage dissent, but they require that it be expressed as a form of disagreement within a shared enterprise. As John Dewey writes, democracy depends on "faith in the possibility of conducting disputes, controversies and conflicts as cooperative undertakings in which both parties learn by giving the other a chance to express itself, instead of having one party conquer by forceful suppression of the other."[70]

As previously mentioned, some writers defend populist conflict creation and politicization as a necessary means to create political change. While it is true that existing democracies are often too rigid and resistant to necessary change, it should also be clear that not all change is for the better. The citizenry needs to be able to discuss which changes are improvements and which are not. If what I have said above is right, populist politics does not promote conditions that are conducive to common deliberation on substantive matters of ideology or policy, and thus it does not contribute to the people's ability to make a reasoned choice about which direction their society should take. This shortcoming is not made good by theoretical defenses of populism such as those of Mouffe and Laclau, which also fail to explain which conditions and procedures are required for people's ability to distinguish between better and worse projects of society.[71] In short, left populism tells the people *what* to choose, not *how* to choose. It leaves us with nothing but the decisionism of an arbitrary choice.

In fact, Mouffe's own distinction between antagonism and agonism entails an acknowledgment that not all forms of conflict are conducive to democracy. She argues that the aim of democratic politics is to transform antagonistic relations between enemies into agonistic pluralism, which requires that one treat one's opponent as a legitimate adversary rather than an enemy. This position depends on consensus about the liberal democratic values of freedom, equality, and mutual toleration.[72] What I do not see is how this defense of agonistic pluralism as opposed to antagonistic politics is compatible with Mouffe's promotion of populism. Mouffe takes seriously neither what actual populists say nor what they do.[73] Populist politics does not transform antagonism into agonism, but lives and breathes the former.

---

[70] Dewey, "Creative Democracy," 243.
[71] Arato, "Political Theology and Populism," 165–6; Ochoa Espejo, "Power to Whom," 73–4; Urbinati, *Me the People*, 144; Valdivielso, "Outraged People," 304, 307.
[72] Mouffe, *Democratic Paradox*, 101–5; Mouffe, *For a Left Populism*, 90–3.
[73] Cohen, "What's Wrong."

Mouffe might defend herself with her anti-essentialism and insist that one can invoke "the people" as a strategy without really thinking the people exist and thus without this discourse having any of the anti-pluralist consequences often associated with populism.[74] But can the populist politician publicly proclaim that the people does not exist but is a social construction? Moreover, if one really is a social constructivist, one should be aware of the power of one's own constructions. Highly pertinent here is Judith Butler's anti-essentialist and social constructivist argument against feminists who use the category of "women" for purely strategic purposes:

> The suggestion that feminism can seek wider representation for a subject that it itself constructs has the ironic consequence that feminist goals risk failure by refusing to take account of the constitutive powers of their own representational claims. This problem is not ameliorated through an appeal to the category of women for merely "strategic" purposes, for strategies always have meanings that exceed the purposes for which they are intended. In this case, exclusion itself might qualify as such an unintended yet consequential meaning.[75]

Similarly, I think that Mouffe fails to take account of the constitutive powers and exclusionary consequences of the populist claim to representation of the people. No matter the purpose, and regardless of underlying theoretical stances such as anti-essentialism, when "the people" is invoked in public discourse in the way populists invoke it, it will shape common meanings and practices of democracy.

Populists and their apologists complain that their opponents – anti-populists and "the elite" – do not listen to their concerns. Yet by failing to adhere to the publicity condition and norms of democratic respect, they deny their adversaries the opportunity to do so. Indeed, that might be exactly their strategy. On the one hand, populists and their theoretical defenders demand respect for the concerns of "the people," and on the other hand, they do so in a way that undercuts the common standpoint from which alone citizens can engage in mutually respectful interaction. This might be a strategically clever move if their aim is to win a battle, but it fails to express and create the kind of democratic process that the theoretical defenders would regard as realizing their end of correcting and deepening democracy.

6.4   A Bad School of Democracy

In this section, I argue that the idea that populism can correct democracy is shortsighted and fails to consider its effects on the common political culture from which citizens learn about politics. As we saw in the

---

[74] Mouffe, *For a Left Populism*, 41–2, 62.
[75] Butler, *Gender Trouble*, 6.

presentation of the publicity condition earlier in this chapter, part of its rationale is the contention that the ideas promoted in public shape a society's political culture, and that citizens learn about their roles, rights, and obligations from this culture. If you cannot want other citizens to be educated by the set of ideas you promote – populism, for example – then you have failed to adhere to the publicity condition. Arguments for the promotion of populism for the sake of non-populist ends, which we are considering in this chapter, do not take sufficient account of the transformative and educative effects of populism. These arguments seem to assume that we all know what democracy means and requires, and that populism can help to correct some shortcomings in the functioning of contemporary democracies without affecting our very understanding of democracy. But we cannot treat our understanding of democracy as a constant that is unaffected by the ideas we, or political leaders, promote and disseminate. Moreover, as I stressed earlier in this book, the rise of populism and our current democratic malaise remind us how important the political culture of a society is for the good functioning of its democratic institutions.

Over the course of this book, we have seen that populism has its own understanding and interpretation of key democratic ideas such as popular sovereignty, representation, and majority rule. Crucially, and as we have just discussed, populism has its own idea of how to engage in political conflict and how one ought to treat political opponents. These interpretations and the set of claims mentioned in the Introduction threaten to permeate our common political culture if populism spreads and is not countered with better interpretations, ideas, and reasons. If the populist understanding of democracy comes to constitute our public political culture, it will be *this* understanding of democracy that educates citizens about what it means to live in a democracy, what they owe and do not owe to political opponents, how and to what extent they should and should not cooperate with others, and so on. Theorists who defend populism as a way to correct democracy fail to consider the risk of promoting a political culture that will teach the people populist ideas about what democracy is. If these theorists do not want a populist regime or a populist transformation of democracy, they should reconsider their public endorsement of populism. And, as I argued above, they cannot publicly proclaim that their end is not populism but something else (agonistic democracy, for example) without this undermining what they seek to achieve by promoting populism.

The argument in this section assumes that the quality, shape, and even survival of democracy depend on informal norms and citizens' understandings of their roles, rights, and obligations. The idea goes back at least to Alexis de Tocqueville's great work *Democracy in America*. Based on his observations during his visit to the United States in 1831, Tocqueville argues that "the maintenance of the democratic republic in the United States" depends on "mores," that is, on "the different notions possessed by men, the various opinions current among them, and the sum of ideas that shape mental habits" – in short, "the whole moral and intellectual state of a people."[76] Contemporary political scientists such as Steven Levitsky and Daniel Ziblatt agree with Tocqueville that informal norms are crucial for the survival of democracy. Moreover, they agree that these norms are not just a matter of "personal dispositions ... but rather shared codes of conduct that become common knowledge within a particular community or society – accepted, respected, and enforced by its members."[77] It is exactly the "ideas that shape mental habits," the "moral and intellectual state of a people," the shared norms that are "enforced by its members" that are at play in the rise populism.

My contention is not only that common knowledge about and enforcement of informal democratic norms are crucial for the quality and survival of democracy, but that these are fragile achievements in need of constant reaffirmation in word and deed. Respect for disagreement and political opponents, the spirit of compromise, the willingness to listen to and learn from fellow citizens are all great public goods that citizens learn from one another and the public political culture of society. They are not virtues that we can take for granted. As Rawls argues, they belong to a society's "political capital," and like all forms of capital, they are "built up slowly over time [.... They] can depreciate ... and must be constantly renewed by being reaffirmed and acted on in the present."[78] The argument for the corrective value of populism for democracy seems to assume that we can take common knowledge of democratic norms for granted, and that populism will bring us closer to those norms. But populism, as we have seen, does not reaffirm or act on the virtues of what I call democratic respect, and my worry is that it will destroy the political culture – the norms, ideas, and mental habits – that sustains democratic citizenship. Indeed, in some countries it has already done so.[79]

A society's normative order and political culture are not only affected by changes in our ideas and understandings. Social and economic changes also affect how people see their own place, role, and status in

[76] Tocqueville, *Democracy in America*, 287.
[77] Levitsky and Ziblatt, *How Democracies Die*, 101. See also Dahl's reference to Tocqueville in *Democracy and Its Critics*, 89.
[78] Rawls, *Justice as Fairness*, 118.
[79] Levitsky and Ziblatt, *How Democracies Die*, 97–117.

society. In Chapter 2, I argued that this fact calls for a form of solidarity where we actively include everyone and show that they have a legitimate place in society. Solidarity as active inclusion has both an expressive and a material dimension, and in many places it requires a profound restructuring of social and economic institutions.[80] So, upholding the political capital of democratic respect is not just a matter of keeping on doing the same thing. The normative order of mutual respect and equality is fragile and should not simply be blindly reproduced; it must be rethought and rearticulated in light of new circumstances. Thus, my aim is by no means to defend the status quo, but rather to show that populist politics is not the way to go if we want to deepen democracy and promote democratic respect. As Nadia Urbinati pointedly puts it: "Populism is a bad school of political participation."[81]

The argument in this section is more instrumental and consequentialist than most of the arguments made in this book. I have argued that the publicity condition is also about the political, social, and psychological consequences of making or not making one's position public. Of course, this consequentialism makes my argument vulnerable to empirical falsification. For example, some might argue and demonstrate that promoting populism in public or using populist strategies does not have the detrimental consequences for the political culture and citizens' habits that I suggest. However, I would point out that comparative political scientists have shown that earlier and current waves of populism have influenced the political culture and informal norms of countries around the world.[82] Moreover, I should stress that it is not my argument that the use of populist strategies can never correct or improve democracy. Clearly, there are cases where populist parties have had a positive effect on democracy, at least along some dimensions. However, these cases all seem to be limited to populists in opposition, whereas populists who attain governmental power over the long run will threaten democracy, at least if other parts of society do not stand up against and limit their power.[83] Thus, my reason for applying the publicity condition is that it is crucial that populism should not become the publicly accepted way of doing politics, and that it should not come to shape our mental habits, because this will not correct democracy understood in non-populist terms, but rather will undermine it.

---

[80] Exactly which changes are needed depends on the context. Unfortunately, it is beyond the scope of the present study to consider this issue.

[81] Urbinati, *Me the People*, 197.

[82] Levitsky and Ziblatt, *How Democracies Die*, 97–117.

[83] Houle and Kenny, "Political and Economic Consequences"; Mudde and Rovira Kaltwasser, "Populism: Corrective *and* Threat."

My fundamental objection to the radical position, which suggests that one can use populist politics as a means to revitalize and deepen democracy, is that it legitimizes populism and makes it part of our public political culture. If proponents of this position such as Mouffe defended populist ideas and wanted to promote a populist understanding of democracy, then we could discuss that. However, Mouffe's own standard for a good democracy is not populistic. That is, she relies on the non-populist, indeed anti-populist, idea of agonistic pluralism. If our aim is to legitimize not populist politics and a populist regime but rather a form of politics where opponents are respected as legitimate adversaries, I would suggest that we look for other means that do not include all the dangers of populism. This is partly an empirical argument about how promoting populist politics will undermine democratic habits and commitments, but it is not only that. The very idea of promoting one set of ideas (populism) for the sake of another set of ideas (agonistic democracy within a liberal framework) is deeply disrespectful of the very people who are to realize the aims we are seeking.

Populism includes a number of substantive ideas about the circumstances and nature of politics and democracy. It promotes and spreads distinctive claims about how democracy should recognize the people. If this is right, we cannot treat it as a neutral tactic or strategy that can be used equally for many different ends. Moreover, to treat populism as a mere strategy is to use as means those people who actually believe in and accept populist ideas. We can only see populism as a strategy for non-populist ends if we adopt an observer attitude through which we regard the people who are to realize those ends as objects of control, treatment, and manipulation. To use populism as a means for correcting democracy understood in non-populist terms is not to respect the people, but to deny them the standing of co-rulers who can participate equally with everyone else in shaping their community according to their own ideas.

Bibliography

Abizadeh, Arash. "Does Collective Identity Presuppose an Other? On the Alleged Incoherence of Global Solidarity." *American Political Science Review* 99.1 (2005): 45–60.

Abts, Koen, and Stefan Rummens. "Populism versus Democracy." *Political Studies* 55.2 (2007): 405–24.

Akkerman, Agnes, Cas Mudde, and Andrej Zaslove. "How Populist Are the People? Measuring Populist Attitudes in Voters." *Comparative Political Studies* 47.9 (2014): 1324–53.

Anderson, Carol. *White Rage*. London: Bloomsbury, 2020.

Anderson, Elizabeth. "Democracy: Instrumental vs. Non-Instrumental Value." In *Contemporary Debates in Political Philosophy*, ed. Thomas Christiano and John Christman. Chichester: Wiley-Blackwell, 2009, 213–27.

Anderson, Elizabeth. *The Imperative of Integration*. Princeton: Princeton University Press, 2010.

Anderson, Elizabeth S. "What Is the Point of Equality?" *Ethics* 109.2 (1999): 287–337.

Appiah, Kwame Anthony. *The Ethics of Identity*. Princeton: Princeton University Press, 2005.

Appiah, Kwame Anthony. *The Honor Code: How Moral Revolutions Happen*. New York: W. W. Norton, 2010.

Applebaum, Anne. *Twilight of Democracy: The Failure of Politics and the Parting of Friends*. London: Penguin, 2020.

Arato, Andrew. "Political Theology and Populism." *Social Research* 80.1 (2013): 143–72.

Arato, Andrew, and Jean L. Cohen. "Civil Society, Populism, and Religion." *Constellations* 24.3 (2017): 283–95.

Arato, Andrew, and Jean L. Cohen. *Populism and Civil Society: The Challenge to Constitutional Democracy*. Oxford: Oxford University Press, 2022.

Ash, Timothy Garton. "Only Respect for the 'Left Behind' Can Turn the Populist Tide." *The Guardian*, September 28, 2017. www.theguardian .com/commentisfree/2017/sep/28/far-right-rightwing-nationalism-populist [accessed February 4, 2021].

Barry, Brian. *Culture and Equality: An Egalitarian Critique of Multiculturalism*. Cambridge, MA: Harvard University Press, 2002.

Beerbohm, Eric. "The Problem of Clean Hands: Negotiated Compromise in Lawmaking." In *Compromise: Nomos LIX*, ed. Jack Knight. New York: New York University Press, 2018, 1–52.

Bejan, Teresa M. *Mere Civility: Disagreement and the Limits of Toleration.* Cambridge, MA: Harvard University Press, 2017.

Bellamy, Richard. "Democracy, Compromise and the Representation Paradox: Coalition Government and Political Integrity." *Government and Opposition* 47.3 (2012); 441–65.

Benhabib, Seyla. *The Claims of Culture.* Princeton: Princeton University Press, 2002.

Benjamin, Martin. *Splitting the Difference: Compromise and Integrity in Ethics and Politics.* Lawrence: University Press of Kansas, 1990.

Berlin, Isaiah. "Two Concepts of Liberty." In *Four Essays on Liberty.* Oxford: Oxford University Press, 1969, 118–72.

Berman, Sheri. "The Causes of Populism in the West." *Annual Review of Political Science* 24 (2021): 71–88.

Berman, Sheri. "Populism Is a Symptom Rather than a Cause: Democratic Disconnect, the Decline of the Center-Left, and the Rise of Populism in Western Europe." *Polity* 51.4 (2019): 654–67.

Bhambra, Gurminder K. "Brexit, Trump, and 'Methodological Whiteness': On the Misrecognition of Race and Class." *British Journal of Sociology* 68.S1 (2017): 214–32.

Bickerton, Christopher, and Carlo Invernizzi Accetti. "Populism and Technocracy: Opposites or Complements?" *Critical Review of International Social and Political Philosophy* 20.2 (2017): 186–206.

Bird, Colin. "Status, Identity, and Respect." *Political Theory* 32.2 (2004): 207–32.

Bohman, James. "Deliberative Democracy and Effective Social Freedom: Capabilities, Resources, and Opportunities." In *Deliberative Democracy: Essays on Reason and Politics*, ed. James Bohman and William Rehg. Cambridge, MA: MIT Press, 1997, 321–48.

Bohman, James. *Public Deliberation: Pluralism, Complexity, and Democracy.* Cambridge, MA: MIT Press, 1996.

Bonikowski, Bart. "Ethno-Nationalist Populism and the Mobilization of Collective Resentment." *British Journal of Sociology* 68.S1 (2017): 181–213.

Brighouse, Harry. "Egalitarianism and Equal Availability of Political Influence." *Journal of Political Philosophy* 4.2 (1996): 118–41.

Broockman, David E., and Christopher Skovron. "Bias in Perceptions of Public Opinion among Political Elites." *American Political Science Review* 112.3 (2018): 542–63.

Brubaker, Rogers. "Why Populism?" *Theory and Society* 46.5 (2017): 357–85.

Brunkhorst, Hauke. *Solidarity: From Civic Friendship to a Global Legal Community.* Cambridge, MA: MIT Press, 2005.

Buchanan, Allen. "Democracy and Secession." In *National Self-Determination and Secession*, ed. Margaret Moore. Oxford: Oxford Scholarship Online, 2003, 14–33. https://doi.org/10.1093/0198293844.001.0001.

Buss, Sarah. "Respect for Persons." *Canadian Journal of Philosophy* 29.4 (1999): 517–50.

Butler, Judith. *Gender Trouble: Feminism and the Subversion of Identity.* New York: Routledge, 2006.

Canovan, Margaret. *The People.* Cambridge: Polity, 2005.

Canovan, Margaret. "Taking Politics to the People: Populism as the Ideology of Democracy." In *Democracies and the Populist Challenge*, ed. Yves Mény and Yves Surel. New York: Palgrave, 2002, 25–44.

Canovan, Margaret. "Trust the People! Populism and the Two Faces of Democracy." *Political Studies* 45.1 (1999): 2–16.

Caramani, Daniele. "Will vs. Reason: The Populist and Technocratic Forms of Political Representation and Their Critique to Party Government." *American Political Science Review* 111.1 (2017): 54–67.

Chambers, Simone. "Democracy and Constitutional Reform: Deliberative versus Populist Constitutionalism." *Philosophy & Social Criticism* 45.9–10 (2019): 1116–31.

Chambers, Simone. "Democracy, Popular Sovereignty, and Constitutional Legitimacy." *Constellations* 11.2 (2004): 153–73.

Chambers, Simone. "How Can the People Rule?" Unpublished manuscript.

Christiano, Thomas. *The Constitution of Equality: Democratic Authority and Its Limits*. Oxford: Oxford University Press, 2008.

Christiano, Thomas. "Political Equality." In *Majorities and Minorities: Nomos XXXII*, ed. John. W. Chapman and Alan Wertheimer. New York: New York University Press, 1990, 151–83.

Christiano, Thomas. *The Rule of the Many: Fundamental Issues in Democratic Theory*. Boulder, CO: Westview Press, 1996.

Cohen, Jean L. "Populism and the Politics of Resentment." *Jus Cogens* 1.1 (2019): 5–39.

Cohen, Jean L. "What's Wrong with the Normative Theory (and the Actual Practice) of Left Populism." *Constellations* 26.3 (2019): 391–407.

Cohen, Jean L., and Andrew Arato. *Civil Society and Political Theory*. Cambridge, MA: MIT Press, 1992.

Cohen, Joshua. "Deliberation and Democratic Legitimacy." In *Deliberative Democracy: Essays on Reason and Politics*, ed. James Bohman and William Rehg. Cambridge, MA: MIT Press, 1997, 67–92.

Cohen, Joshua. "Democracy and Liberty." In *Deliberative Democracy*, ed. Jon Elster. Cambridge: Cambridge University Press, 1998, 185–231.

Cohen, Joshua. "Procedure and Substance in Deliberative Democracy." In *Deliberative Democracy: Essays on Reason and Politics*, ed. James Bohman and William Rehg. Cambridge, MA: MIT Press, 1997, 407–37.

Craiutu, Aurelian. *Faces of Moderation: The Art of Balance in an Age of Extremes*. Philadelphia: University of Pennsylvania Press, 2017.

Cramer, Katherine J. *The Politics of Resentment: Rural Consciousness in Wisconsin and the Rise of Scott Walker*. Chicago: University of Chicago Press, 2016.

Crick, Bernard. "Populism, Politics and Democracy." *Democratization* 12.5 (2005): 625–32.

Cruft, Rowan. "On the Non-Instrumental Value of Basic Rights." *Journal of Moral Philosophy* 7.4 (2010): 441–61.

Dahl, Robert A. *Democracy and Its Critics*. New Haven: Yale University Press, 1989.

Darwall, Stephen. "Respect as Honor and as Accountability." In *Honor, History, and Relationship: Essays in Second-Personal Ethics II*. Oxford: Oxford University Press, 2013, 11–29.

Darwall, Stephen. *The Second-Person Standpoint: Morality, Respect, and Accountability*. Cambridge, MA: Harvard University Press, 2006.

Darwall, Stephen L. "Two Kinds of Respect." *Ethics* 88.1 (1977): 36–49.

De la Torre, Carlos. "The Resurgence of Radical Populism in Latin America." *Constellations* 14.3 (2007): 384–97.

Dewey, John. "Creative Democracy: The Task before Us." In *The Political Writings*, ed. Debra Morris and Ian Shapiro. Indianapolis: Hackett, 1993, 240–5.

Dewey, John. *The Public and Its Problems*. Athens, OH: Swallow Press, 1954.

Dworkin, Ronald. "Liberalism." In *Public and Private Morality*, ed. Stuart Hampshire. Cambridge: Cambridge University Press, 1978, 113–43.

Eatwell, Roger. "Populism and Fascism." In *The Oxford Handbook of Populism*, ed. Cristóbal Rovira Kaltwasser, Paul Taggart, Paulina Ochoa Espejo, and Pierre Ostiguy. Oxford: Oxford University Press, 2017, 363–83.

Ellis, Elisabeth. *Kant's Politics: Provisional Theory for an Uncertain World*. New Haven: Yale University Press, 2005.

Elster, Jon. "Some Notes on 'Populism.'" *Philosophy & Social Criticism* 46.5 (2020): 591–600.

Eribon, Didier. *Returning to Reims*. London: Penguin, 2019.

Estlund, David. "Beyond Fairness and Deliberation: The Epistemic Dimension of Democratic Authority." In *Deliberative Democracy: Essays on Reason and Politics*, ed. James Bohman and William Rehg. Cambridge, MA: MIT Press, 1997, 173–204.

Estlund, David M. *Democratic Authority: A Philosophical Framework*. Princeton: Princeton University Press, 2008.

Feinberg, Joel. "The Nature and Value of Rights." *Journal of Value Inquiry* 4.4 (1970): 243–57.

Finchelstein, Federico. *From Fascism to Populism in History*. Oakland: University of California Press, 2019.

Forst, Rainer. "The Limits of Toleration." *Constellations* 11.3 (2004): 312–25.

Forst, Rainer. *The Right to Justification*. New York: Columbia University Press, 2012.

Forst, Rainer. "'To Tolerate Means to Insult': Toleration, Recognition, and Emancipation." In *Recognition and Power: Axel Honneth and the Tradition of Critical Social Theory*, ed. Bert van den Brink and David Owen. Cambridge: Cambridge University Press, 2007, 215–37.

Forst, Rainer. "Two Pictures of Justice." In *Justification and Critique: Towards a Critical Theory of Politics*. Oxford: Polity, 2014.

Fourie, Carina. "To Praise and to Scorn: The Problem of Inequalities of Esteem for Social Egalitarianism." In *Social Equality: On What It Means to be Equals*, ed. Carina Fourie, Fabian Schuppert, and Ivo Wallimann-Helmer. Oxford: Oxford University Press, 2015, 87–106.

Fraser, Nancy, and Axel Honneth, ed. *Redistribution or Recognition? A Political-Philosophical Exchange*. London: Verso, 2003.

Freeman, Samuel. "The Burdens of Public Justification: Constructivism, Contractualism, and Publicity." *Politics, Philosophy & Economics* 6.1 (2007): 5–43.

Fukuyama, Francis. *Identity: The Demand for Dignity and the Politics of Resentment*. New York: Farrar, Straus, and Giroux, 2018.

Galeotti, Anna Elisabetta. "Rescuing Toleration." *Critical Review of International Social and Political Philosophy* 24.1 (2021): 87–107.

Galston, William A. *Anti-Pluralism: The Populist Threat to Liberal Democracy.* New Haven: Yale University Press, 2018.

Gest, Justin, Tyler Reny, and Jeremy Mayer. "Roots of the Radical Right: Nostalgic Deprivation in the United States and Britain." *Comparative Political Studies* 51.13 (2018): 1694–1719.

Gidron, Noam, and Peter A. Hall. "Populism as a Problem of Social Integration." *Comparative Political Studies* 53.7 (2020): 1027–59.

Gilens, Martin. *Affluence and Influence: Economic Inequality and Political Power in America.* Princeton: Princeton University Press, 2012.

Gosseries, Axel, and Tom Parr. "Publicity." *Stanford Encyclopedia of Philosophy,* ed. Edward N. Zalta, 2018. https://plato.stanford.edu/archives/win2018/entries/publicity/ [accessed April 29, 2019].

Green, Leslie. "Two Worries about Respect for Persons." *Ethics* 120.2 (2010): 212–31.

Gutmann, Amy, and Dennis Thompson. "The Mindsets of Political Compromise." *Perspectives on Politics* 8.4 (2010): 1125–43.

Gutmann, Amy, and Dennis Thompson. *The Spirit of Compromise: Why Governing Demands It and Campaigning Undermines It.* Princeton: Princeton University Press, 2012.

Gutmann, Amy, and Dennis Thompson. *Why Deliberative Democracy?* Princeton: Princeton University Press, 2004.

Habermas, Jürgen. *Between Facts and Norms.* Cambridge: Polity, 1996.

Habermas, Jürgen. "Discourse Ethics." In *Moral Consciousness and Communicative Action.* Cambridge: Polity, 1990, 43–115.

Habermas, Jürgen. "Popular Sovereignty as Procedure." In *Between Facts and Norms.* Cambridge: Polity, 1996, 463–90.

Habermas, Jürgen. "Reply to Symposium Participants, Benjamin N. Cardozo School of Law." In *Habermas on Law and Democracy: Critical Exchanges,* ed. Michael Rosenfeld and Andrew Arato. Berkeley: University of California Press, 1998, 381–452.

Habermas, Jürgen. *The Structural Transformation of the Public Sphere.* Cambridge, MA: MIT Press, 1989.

Habermas, Jürgen. "Struggles for Recognition in the Democratic Constitutional State." In *Multiculturalism,* ed. Amy Gutmann. Princeton: Princeton University Press, 1994, 107–48.

Habermas, Jürgen. *The Theory of Communicative Action: Volume One.* Cambridge: Polity, 1984.

Hansen, Mogens Herman. *The Athenian Democracy in the Age of Demosthenes: Structure, Principles, and Ideology.* Norman: University of Oklahoma Press, 1999.

Harris, Cheryl I. "Whiteness as Property." *Harvard Law Review* 106.8 (1993): 1707–91.

Hieronymi, Pamela. *Freedom, Resentment, and the Metaphysics of Morals.* Princeton: Princeton University Press, 2020.

Hill, Thomas E., Jnr. *Respect, Pluralism, and Justice: Kantian Perspectives.* Oxford: Oxford University Press, 2000.

Hirvonen, Onni, and Joonas Pennanen. "Populism as a Pathological Form of Politics of Recognition." *European Journal of Social Theory* 22.1 (2019): 27–44.

Hochschild, Arlie Russell. *Strangers in Their Own Land: Anger and Mourning on the American Right*. New York: New Press, 2018.

Holmes, Stephen. *Passions and Constraint: On the Theory of Liberal Democracy*. Chicago: University of Chicago Press, 1995.

Honneth, Axel. "Redistribution as Recognition: A Response to Nancy Fraser." In *Redistribution or Recognition? A Political-Philosophical Exchange*, ed. Nancy Fraser and Axel Honneth. London: Verso, 2003, 110–97.

Honneth, Axel. *The Struggle for Recognition: The Moral Grammar of Social Conflicts*. Cambridge, MA: MIT Press, 1996.

Houle, Christian, and Paul D. Kenny. "The Political and Economic Consequences of Populist Rule in Latin America." *Government and Opposition* 53.2 (2018): 256–87.

Horwitz, Robert B. "Trump and the 'Deep State.'" *Policy Studies* 42.5–6 (2021): 473–90.

Hussain, Waheed. "Pitting People against Each Other." *Philosophy & Public Affairs* 48.1 (2020): 79–113.

Inglehart, Ronald. *The Silent Revolution*. Princeton: Princeton University Press, 1977.

Inglehart, Ronald, and Pippa Norris. "Trump and the Populist Authoritarian Parties: The Silent Revolution in Reverse." *Perspectives on Politics* 15.2 (2017): 443–54.

Iyengar, Shanto, Yphtach Lelkes, Matthew Levendusky, Neil Malhotra, and Sean J. Westwood. "The Origins and Consequences of Affective Polarization in the United States." *Annual Review of Political Science* 22 (2019): 129–46.

Iyengar, Shanto, Gaurav Sood, and Yphtach Lelkes. "Affect, Not Ideology: A Social Identity Perspective on Polarization." *Public Opinion Quarterly* 76.3 (2012): 405–31.

Jones, Peter. "Equality, Recognition and Difference." *Critical Review of International Social and Political Philosophy* 9.1 (2006): 23–46.

Jones, Peter. "Respecting Beliefs and Rebuking Rushdie." *British Journal of Political Science* 20.4 (October 1990): 415–37.

Jones, Peter. *Rights*. Basingstoke: Macmillan, 1994.

Jones, Peter, and Ian O'Flynn. "Can a Compromise Be Fair?" *Politics, Philosophy & Economics* 12.2 (2013): 115–35.

Kant, Immanuel. "An Answer to the Question: What Is Enlightenment?." In *Practical Philosophy*, ed. Mary J. Gregor. Cambridge: Cambridge University Press, 1996, 15–22.

Kant, Immanuel. "Groundwork of the Metaphysics of Morals." In *Practical Philosophy*, ed. Mary J. Gregor. Cambridge: Cambridge University Press, 1996, 37–108.

Kant, Immanuel. "The Metaphysics of Morals." In *Practical Philosophy*, ed. Mary J. Gregor. Cambridge: Cambridge University Press, 1996, 353–603.

Kant, Immanuel. "Toward Perpetual Peace." In *Practical Philosophy*, ed. Mary J. Gregor. Cambridge: Cambridge University Press, 1996, 311–52.

Kazin, Michael. *The Populist Persuasion: An American History*, rev. edn. Ithaca: Cornell University Press, 2017.

Kelsen, Hans. *The Essence and Value of Democracy.* Lanham: Rowman & Littlefield, 2013.

Knight, Jack, and James Johnson. "What Sort of Equality Does Deliberative Democracy Require?" In *Deliberative Democracy: Essays on Reason and Politics,* ed. James Bohman and William Rehg. Cambridge, MA: MIT Press, 1997, 279–319.

Kolers, Avery. *A Moral Theory of Solidarity.* New York: Oxford University Press, 2016.

Kolodny, Niko. "Rule Over None I: What Justifies Democracy?" *Philosophy & Public Affairs* 42.3 (2014): 195–229.

Korsgaard, Christine M. *Creating the Kingdom of Ends.* Cambridge: Cambridge University Press, 1996.

Krastev, Ivan. "Majoritarian Futures." In *The Great Regression,* ed. Heinrich Geiselberger. Cambridge: Polity, 2017, 65–77.

Krause, Sharon R. *Liberalism with Honor.* Cambridge, MA: Harvard University Press, 2002.

Kuflik, Arthur. "Morality and Compromise." In *Compromise in Ethics, Law, and Politics: Nomos XXI,* ed. James R. Pennock and John W. Chapman. New York: New York University Press, 1979, 38–65.

Kymlicka, Will. *Contemporary Political Philosophy,* 2nd edn. Oxford: Oxford University Press, 2002.

Laclau, Ernesto. "An Interview with Ernesto Laclau: Questions from David Howarth." In *Ernesto Laclau: Post-Marxism, Populism and Critique,* ed. David Howarth. London: Routledge, 2015, 257–71.

Laclau, Ernesto. *On Populist Reason.* London: Verso, 2005.

Laclau, Ernesto. "Populism: What Is in a Name?" In *Ernesto Laclau: Post-Marxism, Populism and Critique,* ed. David Howarth. London: Routledge, 2015, 152–64.

Laclau, Ernesto, and Chantal Mouffe. *Hegemony and Socialist Strategy: Towards a Radical Democratic Politics.* London: Verso, 1985.

Lafont, Cristina. *Democracy without Shortcuts: A Participatory Conception of Deliberative Democracy.* Oxford: Oxford University Press, 2020.

Laitinen, Arto. "From Recognition to Solidarity: Universal Respect, Mutual Support, and Social Unity." In *Solidarity: Theory and Practice,* ed. Arto Laitinen and Anne Birgitta Pessi. Lanham: Lexington Books, 2014, 126–54.

Laitinen, Arto, and Anne Birgitta Pessi. "Solidarity: Theory and Practice – an Introduction." In *Solidarity: Theory and Practice,* ed. Arto Laitinen and Anne Birgitta Pessi. Lanham: Lexington Books, 2014, 1–29.

Lefort, Claude. "Human Rights and the Welfare State." In *Democracy and Political Theory.* Minneapolis: University of Minnesota Press, 1988, 21–44.

Levitsky, Steven, and James Loxton. "Populism and Competitive Authoritarianism in Latin America." In *Routledge Handbook of Global Populism,* ed. Carlos de la Torre. London: Routledge, 2018, 334–50.

Levitsky, Steven, and Daniel Ziblatt. *How Democracies Die: What History Reveals about Our Future.* New York: Viking, 2018.

Lijphart, Arend. *Democracies: Patterns of Majoritarian and Consensus Democracy in Twenty-One Countries.* New Haven: Yale University Press, 1984.

Lister, Andrew. "Public Reason and Moral Compromise." *Canadian Journal of Philosophy* 37.1 (2007): 1–34.

Luban, David. "The Publicity Principle." In *The Theory of Institutional Design*, ed. Robert E. Goodin. Cambridge: Cambridge University Press, 1996, 154–98.

Mair, Peter. "Populist Democracy vs Party Democracy." In *Democracies and the Populist Challenge*, ed. Yves Mény and Yves Surel. New York. Palgrave, 2002, 81–98.

Manin, Bernard. "On Legitimacy and Political Deliberation." *Political Theory* 15.3 (1987): 338–68.

Manin, Bernard. *The Principles of Representative Government*. Cambridge: Cambridge University Press, 1997.

Mansbridge, Jane, and Stephen Macedo. "Populism and Democratic Theory." *Annual Review of Law and Social Science* 15 (2019): 59–77.

Mansbridge, Jane, James Bohman, Simone Chambers, David Estlund, Andreas Føllesdal, Archon Fung, Cristina Lafont, Bernard Manin, and José Luis Martí. "The Place of Self-Interest and the Role of Power in Deliberative Democracy." *Journal of Political Philosophy* 18.1 (2010): 64–100.

Margalit, Avishai. *On Compromise and Rotten Compromises*. Princeton: Princeton University Press, 2010.

Markell, Patchen. *Bound by Recognition*. Princeton: Princeton University Press, 2003.

Marx, Karl. "On the Jewish Question." In *The Marx-Engels Reader*, ed. Richard Tuck, 2nd edn. New York: W. W. Norton, 1978, 26–52.

Mason, Andrew. *Community, Solidarity and Belonging*. Cambridge: Cambridge University Press, 2000.

Mason, Lilliana. *Uncivil Agreement: How Politics Became Our Identity*. Chicago: University of Chicago Press, 2018.

May, Kenneth O. "A Set of Independent Necessary and Sufficient Conditions for Simple Majority Decision." *Econometrica: Journal of the Econometric Society* 20.4 (1952): 680–4.

May, Simon Căbulea. "Moral Compromise, Civic Friendship, and Political Reconciliation." *Critical Review of International Social and Political Philosophy* 14.5 (2011): 581–602.

May, Simon Căbulea. "No Compromise on Racial Equality." In *Compromise and Disagreement in Contemporary Political Theory*, ed. Christian F. Rostbøll and Theresa Scavenius. New York: Routledge, 2018, 34–49.

May, Simon Căbulea. "Principled Compromise and the Abortion Controversy." *Philosophy & Public Affairs* 33.4 (2005): 317–48.

McBride, Cillian. *Recognition*. Cambridge: Polity, 2013.

McCarty, Nolan. *Polarization: What Everyone Needs to Know*. Oxford: Oxford University Press, 2019.

McCormick, John P. *Machiavellian Democracy*. Cambridge: Cambridge University Press, 2011.

McCormick, John P. "Machiavellian Democracy: Controlling Elites with Ferocious Populism." *American Political Science Review* 95.2 (2001): 297–313.

McCormick, John P. "The New Ochlophobia? Populism, Majority Rule, and Prospects for Democratic Republicanism." In *Republicanism and the Future of Democracy*, ed. Yiftah Elazar and Geneviève Rousselière. Cambridge: Cambridge University Press, 2019, 130–51.

McCoy, Jennifer, Tahmina Rahman, and Murat Somer. "Polarization and the Global Crisis of Democracy." *American Behavioral Scientist* 62.2 (2018): 16–42.

McKean, Benjamin L. "Toward an Inclusive Populism? On the Role of Race and Difference in Laclau's Politics." *Political Theory* 44.6 (2016): 797–820.

Mény, Yves, and Yves Surel. "The Constitutive Ambiguity of Populism." In *Democracies and the Populist Challenge*, ed. Yves Mény and Yves Surel. New York: Palgrave, 2002, 1–21.

Mény, Yves, and Yves Surel. *Par le people, pour le people: Le populisme et les démocraties*. Paris: Fayard, 2000.

Michelman, Frank. "Justification (and Justifiability) of Law in a Contradictory World." *Justification: Nomos XXVIII*, ed. J. Ronald Pennock and John W. Chapman. New York: New York University Press, 1986, 71–99.

Mill, John Stuart. *Considerations on Representative Government*. In *On Liberty and Other Essays*, ed. John Gray. Oxford: Oxford University Press, 1998, 203–467.

Mill, John Stuart. *On Liberty*. In *On Liberty and Other Writings*. Edited by Stefan Collini. Cambridge: Cambridge University Press, 1989, 1–115.

Miller, David. *On Nationality*. Oxford: Clarendon Press, 1995.

Moffitt, Benjamin. *The Global Rise of Populism: Performance, Political Style, and Representation*. Stanford: Stanford University Press, 2016.

Montesquieu, Charles-Louis de Secondat. *The Spirit of the Laws*. Cambridge: Cambridge University Press, 1989.

Moody-Adams, Michelle M. "Democratic Conflict and the Political Morality of Compromise." In *Compromise: NOMOS LIX*, ed. Jack Knight. New York: New York University Press, 2018, 186–219.

Moore, Barrington. *Injustice: The Social Bases of Obedience and Revolt*. White Plains, NY: M. E. Sharpe, 1978.

Mouffe, Chantal. *The Democratic Paradox*. London: Verso, 2009.

Mouffe, Chantal. *For a Left Populism*. London: Verso, 2018.

Mounk, Yascha. *The People vs. Democracy: Why Our Freedom Is in Danger and How to Save It*. Cambridge, MA: Harvard University Press, 2018.

Mudde, Cas. *The Far Right Today*. Cambridge: Polity, 2019.

Mudde, Cas. "Populism: An Ideational Approach." In *The Oxford Handbook of Populism*, ed. Cristóbal Rovira Kaltwasser, Paul Taggart, Paulina Ochoa Espejo, and Pierre Ostiguy. Oxford: Oxford University Press, 2017, 27–47.

Mudde, Cas. *Populist Radical Rights Parties in Europe*. Cambridge: Cambridge University Press, 2007.

Mudde, Cas. "The Populist Zeitgeist." *Government and Opposition* 39.4 (2004): 541–63.

Mudde, Cas. "Three Decades of Populist Radical Right Parties in Western Europe: So What?" *European Journal of Political Research* 52.1 (2013): 1–19.

Mudde, Cas, and Cristóbal Rovira Kaltwasser. "Populism." In *The Oxford Handbook of Political Ideologies*, ed. Michael Freeden, Lyman Tower Sargent, and Marc Stears. Oxford: Oxford University Press, 2013, 493–512.

Mudde, Cas, and Cristóbal Rovira Kaltwasser. *Populism: A Very Short Introduction*. Oxford: Oxford University Press, 2017.

Mudde, Cas, and Cristóbal Rovira Kaltwasser. "Populism: Corrective *and* Threat to Democracy." In *Populism in Europe and Americas: Threat or Corrective for Democracy?*, ed. Cas Mudde and Cristóbal Rovira Kaltwasser. Cambridge: Cambridge University Press, 2012, 205–22.

Muirhead, Russell. *The Promise of Party in a Polarized Age*. Cambridge MA: Harvard University Press, 2014.

Muirhead, Russell, and Nancy L. Rosenblum. "Political Liberalism vs. 'The Great Game of Politics': The Politics of Political Liberalism." *Perspectives on Politics* 4.1 (2006): 99–108.

Müller, Jan-Werner. "Capitalism in One Family." *London Review of Books* 38.23 (2016): 10–14. www.lrb.co.uk/the-paper/v38/n23/jan-werner-mueller/capitalism-in-one-family [accessed September 30, 2020].

Müller, Jan-Werner. *Democracy Rules*. London: Allen Lane, 2021.

Müller, Jan-Werner. "The People Must Be Extracted from within the People: Reflections on Populism." *Constellations* 21.4 (2014): 483–93.

Müller, Jan-Werner. "Populism and Constitutionalism." In *The Oxford Handbook of Populism*, ed. Cristóbal Rovira Kaltwasser, Paul Taggart, Paulina Ochoa Espejo, and Pierre Ostiguy. Oxford: Oxford University Press, 2017, 590–606.

Müller, Jan-Werner. *What Is Populism?* Philadelphia: University of Pennsylvania Press, 2016.

Mutz, Diana C. "Status Threat, Not Economic Hardship, Explains the 2016 Presidential Vote." *Proceedings of the National Academy of Sciences* 115.19 (2018): E4330–9.

Nagel, Thomas. "Agent-Relativity and Deontology." In *Deontology*, ed. Stephen Darwall. Malden: Blackwell, 2003, 90–111.

Näsström, Sofia. *The Spirit of Democracy: Corruption, Disintegration, Renewal*. Oxford: Oxford University Press, 2021.

Ochoa Espejo, Paulina. "Power to Whom? The People between Procedure and Populism." In *The Promise and Perils of Populism*, ed. Carlos de la Torre. Lexington: University Press of Kentucky, 2015, 59–90.

Offe, Claus. "'Homogeneity' and Constitutional Democracy: Coping with Identity Through Group Rights." *Journal of Philosophy* 6.2 (1998): 113–41.

Olson, Joel. "Whiteness and the Polarization of American Politics." *Political Research Quarterly* 61.4 (2008): 704–18.

O'Neill, Martin. "Philosophy and Public Policy after Piketty." *Journal of Political Philosophy* 25.3 (2017): 343–75.

O'Neill, Onora. "Abstraction, Idealization and Ideology in Ethics." In *Moral Philosophy and Contemporary Problems*, ed. J. D. G. Evans. Cambridge: Cambridge University Press, 1987, 55–69.

O'Neill, Onora. *Acting on Principle: An Essay on Kantian Ethics*, 2nd edn. Cambridge: Cambridge University Press, 2013.

O'Neill, Onora. *Constructions of Reason: Explorations of Kant's Practical Philosophy*. Cambridge: Cambridge University Press, 1989.

O'Neill, Onora. "Enlightenment as Autonomy: Kant's Vindication of Reason." In *The Enlightenment and Its Shadows*, ed. Peter Hulme and Ludmilla J. Jordanova. London: Routledge, 1990, 184–99.

Pappas, Takis S. *Populism and Liberal Democracy: A Comparative and Theoretical Analysis*. Oxford: Oxford University Press, 2019.

Patten, Alan. "Populist Multiculturalism: Are There Majority Cultural Rights?" *Philosophy & Social Criticism* 46.5 (2020): 539–52.

Pettit, Philip. *On the People's Terms: A Republican Theory and Model of Democracy.* Cambridge: Cambridge University Press, 2012.

Pettit, Philip. *Republicanism: A Theory of Freedom and Government.* Oxford: Oxford University Press, 1997.

Pitkin, Hanna. *The Concept of Representation.* Berkeley: University of California Press, 1967.

Przeworski, Adam. *Crises of Democracy.* Cambridge: Cambridge University Press, 2019.

Rawls, John. *Justice as Fairness: A Restatement.* Cambridge, MA: Harvard University Press, 2001.

Rawls, John. *Lectures on the History of Moral Philosophy.* Cambridge, MA: Harvard University Press, 2000.

Rawls, John. *Political Liberalism.* New York: Columbia University Press, 1996.

Rawls, John. *A Theory of Justice*, rev. edn. Cambridge, MA: Belknap, 1999.

Richardson, Henry S. *Democratic Autonomy: Public Reasoning about the Ends of Policy.* Oxford: Oxford University Press, 2002.

Richardson, Henry S. "Noncognitivist Trumpism: Partisanship and Political Reasoning." *Journal of Social Philosophy* 50.4 (2019): 642–63.

Riker, William. *Liberalism against Populism.* Prospect Heights: Waveland Press, 1982.

Roberts, Kenneth M. "Populism and Democracy in Venezuela under Hugo Chavez." In *Populism in Europe and Americas: Threat or Corrective for Democracy?*, ed. Cas Mudde and Cristóbal Rovira Kaltwasser. Cambridge: Cambridge University Press, 2012, 136–59.

Roberts, Kenneth M. "Populism and Polarization in Comparative Perspective: Constitutive, Spatial and Institutional Dimensions." *Government and Opposition* (2021): 1–23. https://doi.org/10.1017/gov.2021.14.

Rosanvallon, Pierre. *Democratic Legitimacy: Impartiality, Reflexivity, Proximity.* Princeton: Princeton University Press, 2011.

Rosanvallon, Pierre. *Le siècle du populisme: Histoire, théorie, critique.* Paris: Seuil, 2020.

Rosenblum, Nancy L. *On the Side of the Angels: An Appreciation of Parties and Partisanship.* Princeton: Princeton University Press, 2008.

Rossi, Enzo. "Consensus, Compromise, Justice, and Legitimacy." *Critical Review of International Social and Political Philosophy* 16.4 (2013): 557–72.

Rostbøll, Christian F. "Autonomy, Respect, and Arrogance in the Danish Cartoon Controversy." *Political Theory* 37.5 (2009): 623–48.

Rostbøll, Christian F. "Compromise and Toleration: Responding to Disagreement." In *Compromise and Disagreement in Contemporary Political Theory*, ed. Christian F. Rostbøll and Theresa Scavenius. New York: Routledge, 2018, 17–33.

Rostbøll, Christian F. *Deliberative Freedom: Deliberative Democracy as Critical Theory.* Albany: State University of New York Press, 2008.

Rostbøll, Christian F. "Democracy as Good in Itself: Three Kinds of Non-Instrumental Justification." In *Constitutionalism Justified: Rainer Forst in Discourse*, ed. Ester Herlin-Karnell and Matthias Klatt. Oxford: Oxford University Press, 2020, 235–63.

Rostbøll, Christian F. "Democratic Respect and Compromise." *Critical Review of International Social and Political Philosophy* 20.5 (2017): 619–35.

Rostbøll, Christian F. "Dissent, Criticism, and Transformative Political Action in Deliberative Democracy." *Critical Review of International Social and Political Philosophy* 12.1 (2009): 19–36.

Rostbøll, Christian F. "Freedom of Expression, Deliberation, Autonomy, and Respect." *European Journal of Political Theory* 10.1 (2011): 5–21.

Rostbøll, Christian F. *Immanuel Kant.* Copenhagen: Jurist- og Økonomforbundets Forlag, 2015.

Rostbøll, Christian F. "Impartiality, Deliberation, and Multiculturalism." Paper presented at "What's the Culture in Multiculturalism? What's the Difference of Identities?" (conference), University of Aarhus, Denmark, May 22–4, 2003.

Rostbøll, Christian F. *Jürgen Habermas.* Copenhagen: Jurist- og Økonomforbundets Forlag, 2011.

Rostbøll, Christian F. "Kant and the Critique of the Ethics-First Approach to Politics," *Critical Review of International Social and Political Philosophy* 22.1 (2019): 55–70.

Rostbøll, Christian F. "Kant, Freedom as Independence, and Democracy." *Journal of Politics* 78.3 (2016): 792–805.

Rostbøll, Christian F. "Kantian Autonomy and Political Liberalism." *Social Theory and Practice* 37.3 (2011): 341–64.

Rostbøll, Christian F. "Non-Domination and Democratic Legitimacy." *Critical Review of International Social and Political Philosophy* 18.4 (2015): 424–39.

Rostbøll, Christian F. "The Non-Instrumental Value of Democracy: The Freedom Argument." *Constellations* 22.2 (2015): 267–78.

Rostbøll, Christian F. "Populism and Two Kinds of Polarization." Unpublished manuscript.

Rostbøll, Christian F. "Populism, Democracy, and the Publicity Requirement." *Constellations* (2022): 1–14. https://doi.org/10.1111/1467-8675.12625.

Rostbøll, Christian F. "Second-Order Political Thinking: Compromise versus Populism." *Political Studies* 69.3 (2021): 559–76.

Rostbøll, Christian F. "The Use and Abuse of 'Universal Values' in the Danish Cartoon Controversy." *European Political Science Review* 2.3 (2010): 401–22.

Rostbøll, Christian F., and Theresa Scavenius. "Introduction." In *Compromise and Disagreement in Contemporary Political Theory*, ed. Christian F. Rostbøll and Theresa Scavenius. New York: Routledge, 2018, 1–14.

Rousseau, Jean-Jacques. *On the Social Contract.* In *The Basic Political Writings.* Translated and edited by Donald A. Cress. Indianapolis: Hackett, 1987, 141–227.

Rovira Kaltwasser, Cristóbal. "The Ambivalence of Populism: Threat and Corrective for Democracy." *Democratization* 19.2 (2012): 184–208.

Rozenberg, Joshua. *Enemies of the People? How Judges Shape Society.* Bristol: Bristol University Press, 2020.

Rummens, Stefan. "Populism as a Threat to Liberal Democracy." In *The Oxford Handbook of Populism*, ed. Cristóbal Rovira Kaltwasser, Paul Taggart, Paulina Ochoa Espejo, and Pierre Ostiguy. Oxford: Oxford University Press, 2017, 554–70.

Rummens, Stefan. "Staging Deliberation: The Role of Representative Institutions in the Deliberative Democratic Process." *Journal of Political Philosophy* 20.1 (2012): 23–44.

Runciman, Walter Garrison. "'Social' Equality." *Philosophical Quarterly* 17.68 (1967): 221–30.

Ruser, Alexander, and Amanda Machin. *Against Political Compromise: Sustaining Democratic Debate*. London: Routledge, 2017.

Sabl, Andrew. "The Two Cultures of Democratic Theory: Responsiveness, Democratic Quality, and the Empirical-Normative Divide." *Perspectives on Politics* 13.2 (2015): 345–65.

Sandel, Michael. *The Tyranny of Merit: What's Become of the Common Good?* New York: Farrar, Straus, and Giroux, 2020.

Sangiovanni, Andrea. "Solidarity as Joint Action." *Journal of Applied Philosophy* 32.4 (2015): 340–59.

Sartori, Giovanni. *Parties and Party Systems: A Framework for Analysis*. Colchester: ECPR Press, 2005.

Scanlon, T. M. "The Difficulty of Tolerance." In *The Difficulty of Tolerance*. Cambridge: Cambridge University Press, 2003, 187–201.

Scanlon, T. M. *What We Owe to Each Other*. Cambridge, MA: Harvard University Press, 1998.

Schedler, Andreas. "Democratic Reciprocity." *Journal of Political Philosophy* 29.2 (2021): 252–78.

Schmitt, Carl. *The Concept of the Political*. Chicago: University of Chicago Press, 1996.

Schmitt, Carl. *The Crises of Parliamentary Democracy*. Cambridge, MA: MIT Press, 1985.

Schmitter, Philippe C., and Terry Lynn Karl. "What Democracy Is ... and Is Not." *Journal of Democracy* 2.3 (1991): 75–88.

Schneewind, J. B. "Autonomy, Obligation, and Virtue: An Overview of Kant's Moral Philosophy." In *The Cambridge Companion to Kant*, ed. Paul Guyer. Cambridge: Cambridge University Press, 1992, 309–41.

Schwartzberg, Melissa. *Counting the Many: The Origins and Limits of Supermajority Rule*. Cambridge: Cambridge University Press, 2013.

Schwarze, Michelle. *Recognizing Resentment*. Cambridge: Cambridge University Press, 2020.

Sennett, Richard. "Even If Donald Trump Loses the Election, the US Isn't Going to Heal Anytime Soon." *The Guardian*, November 2, 2020. www.theguardian.com/commentisfree/2020/nov/02/donald-trump-us-election-base-extreme [accessed November 19, 2020].

Sennett, Richard. *Respect in a World of Inequality*. New York: W. W. Norton, 2003.

Sennett, Richard, and Jonathan Cobb. *The Hidden Injuries of Class*. Cambridge: Cambridge University Press, 1972.

Shapiro, Ian. *Politics against Domination*. Cambridge, MA: Harvard University Press, 2016.

Shapiro, Ian. *The State of Democratic Theory*. Princeton: Princeton University Press, 2003.

Sindberg, Mathias. "Kendt sociolog: Black Lives Matter-demonstrationerne kan give Trump fire år mere i Det Hvide Hus." *Information*, June 25, 2020. www.information.dk/udland/2020/06/kendt-sociolog-black-lives-matter-demonstrationerne-kan-give-trump-fire-aar mere-hvide-hus [accessed June 26, 2020].

Smith, Rogers M., and Desmond King. "White Protectionism in America." *Perspectives on Politics* 19.2 (2021): 460–78.

Spruyt, Bram, Gil Keppens, and Filip Van Droogenbroeck. "Who Supports Populism and What Attracts People to It?" *Political Research Quarterly* 69.2 (2016): 335–46.

Stavrakakis, Yannis. "Populism and Hegemony." In *The Oxford Handbook of Populism*, ed. Cristóbal Rovira Kaltwasser, Paul Taggart, Paulina Ochoa Espejo, and Pierre Ostiguy. Oxford: Oxford University Press, 2017, 535–53.

Stavrakakis, Yannis. "Populism in Power: Syriza's Challenge to Europe." *Juncture* 21.4 (2015): 273–80

Strawson, Peter F. "Freedom and Resentment." In *Free Will*, ed. Gary Watson. Oxford: Oxford University Press, 1982, 59–80.

Taggart, Paul. "Populism and the Pathology of Representative Politics." In *Democracies and the Populist Challenge*, ed. Yves Mény and Yves Surel. New York: Palgrave, 2002, 62–80.

Taylor, Charles. "The Politics of Recognition." In *Multiculturalism*, ed. Amy Gutmann. Princeton: Princeton University Press, 1994, 25–74.

Thompson, Edward P. *The Making of the English Working Class*. London: Gollancz, 1963.

Thucydides. *History of the Peloponnesian War*. London: Penguin, 1972.

Tocqueville, Alexis de. *Democracy in America*. New York: Harper Perennial, 1988.

Urbinati, Nadia. *Democracy Disfigured*. Cambridge, MA: Harvard University Press, 2014.

Urbinati, Nadia. *Me the People: How Populism Transforms Democracy*. Cambridge, MA: Harvard University Press, 2019.

Urbinati, Nadia. "Political Theory of Populism." *Annual Review of Political Science* 22 (2019): 111–27.

Urbinati, Nadia. "Populism and the Principle of Majority." In *The Oxford Handbook of Populism*, ed. Cristóbal Rovira Kaltwasser, Paul Taggart, Paulina Ochoa Espejo, and Pierre Ostiguy. Oxford: Oxford University Press, 2017, 571–89.

Valdivielso, Joaquín. "The Outraged People: Laclau, Mouffe and the Podemos Hypothesis." *Constellations* 24.3 (2017): 296–309.

Valentini, Laura. "Justice, Disagreement and Democracy." *British Journal of Political Science* 43.1 (2013): 177–99.

Vlastos, Gregory. "Justice and Equality." In *Theories of Rights*, ed. Jeremy Waldron. Oxford: Oxford University Press, 1984, 41–76.

Waldron, Jeremy. "Cultural Identity and Civic Responsibility." In *Citizenship in Diverse Societies*, ed. Will Kymlicka and Wayne Norman. Oxford: Oxford University Press, 2000, 155–74.

Waldron, Jeremy. "Dignity and Rank." In *Dignity, Rank, and Rights*, ed. Meir Dan-Cohen. Oxford: Oxford University Press, 2012, 13–46.

Waldron, Jeremy. *The Dignity of Legislation*. Cambridge: Cambridge University Press, 1999.

Waldron, Jeremy. *Law and Disagreement*. Oxford: Oxford University Press, 1999.

Waldron, Jeremy. "Law, Dignity, and Self-Control." In *Dignity, Rank, and Rights* ed. Meir Dan-Cohen. Oxford: Oxford University Press, 2012, 47–70.

Waldron, Jeremy. "A Right to Do Wrong." *Ethics* 92.1 (1981): 21–39.

Wall, Steven. "Rooted Reciprocity." *Journal of Moral Philosophy* 16.4 (2019): 463–85.

Watson, Gary. "Responsibility and the Limits of Evil: Variations on a Strawsonian Theme." In *Free Will and Reactive Attitudes: Perspectives on P. F. Strawson's "Freedom and Resentment,"* ed. Michael McKenaa and Paul Russell. London: Routledge, 2008, 115–41.

Weale, Albert. *The Will of the People: A Modern Myth*. Cambridge: Polity, 2018.

Weinstock, Daniel M. "Compromise, Pluralism, and Deliberation." *Critical Review of International Social and Political Philosophy* 20.5 (2017): 636–55.

Weinstock, Daniel M. "The Ethics of Compromise." In *Compromise and Disagreement in Contemporary Political Theory*, ed. Christian F. Rostbøll and Theresa Scavenius. New York: Routledge, 2018, 65–78.

Weinstock, Daniel M. "On the Possibility of Principled Moral Compromise." *Critical Review of International Social and Political Philosophy* 16.4 (2013): 537–56.

Wenar, Leif. "Rights." Stanford Encyclopedia of Philosophy, ed. Edward N. Zalta, 2021. https://plato.stanford.edu/archives/spr2021/entries/rights/ [accessed March 30, 2021].

Wendt, Fabian. *Compromise, Peace and Public Justification: Political Morality Beyond Justice*. London: Palgrave Macmillan, 2016.

Weyland, Kurt. "Populism: A Political-Strategic Approach." In *The Oxford Handbook of Populism*, ed. Cristóbal Rovira Kaltwasser, Paul Taggart, Paulina Ochoa Espejo, and Pierre Ostiguy. Oxford: Oxford University Press, 2017, 48–72.

Weyland, Kurt. "Populism and Authoritarianism." In *Routledge Handbook of Global Populism*, ed. Carlos de la Torre. London: Routledge, 2018, 319–33.

Weyland, Kurt. "Populism as a Political Strategy: An Approach's Enduring – and Increasing – Advantages." *Political Studies* 69.2 (2021): 185–9.

White, Jonathan, and Lea Ypi. *The Meaning of Partisanship*. Oxford: Oxford University Press, 2016.

Wikipedia contributors. "Enemies of the People (Headline)." *Wikipedia*, February 17, 2022. https://en.wikipedia.org/wiki/Enemies_of_the_People_ (headline) [accessed March 7, 2022].

Williams, Bernard. "Persons, Character and Morality." In *Moral Luck*. Cambridge: Cambridge University Press, 1981, 1–19.

Williams, Zoe. "Nigel Farage's Victory Speech Was a Triumph of Poor Taste and Ugliness." *The Guardian*, June 24, 2016. www.theguardian.com/commentisfree/2016/jun/24/nigel-farage-ugliness-bullet-fired [accessed April 30, 2020].

Wind, Marlene. *The Tribalization of Europe: A Defence of Our Liberal Values*. Cambridge: Polity, 2020.

Wolkenstein, Fabio. "What Can We Hold against Populism?" *Philosophy & Social Criticism* 41.2 (2015): 111–29.

Wuthnow, Robert. *The Left Behind.* Princeton: Princeton University Press, 2019.

Young, Iris Marion. *Inclusion and Democracy.* Oxford: Oxford University Press, 2000.

Young, Iris Marion. *Justice and the Politics of Difference.* Princeton: Princeton University Press, 1990.

Zakaria, Fareed. *The Future of Freedom: Illiberal Democracy at Home and Abroad.* New York: W. W. Norton, 2003.

Žižek, Slavoj. "Against the Populist Temptation." *Critical Inquiry* 32.3 (2006): 551–74.

Zurn, Christopher F. "Populism, Polarization, and Misrecognition." In *The Theory and Practice of Recognition*, ed. Onni Hirvonen and Heikki J. Koskinen. London: Routledge, 2022, 131–49.

Zylberman, Ariel. "Why Human Rights? Because of You." *Journal of Political Philosophy* 24.3 (2016): 321–43.

Index